FUNDAMENTAL PROBLEMS
OF LABOUR RELATIONS
IN THE LAW OF THE EUROPEAN
SOCIALIST COUNTRIES

FUNDAMENTAL PROBLEMS OF LABOUR RELATIONS IN THE LAW OF THE EUROPEAN SOCIALIST COUNTRIES

BY

LÁSZLÓ TRÓCSÁNYI

AKADÉMIAI KIADÓ, BUDAPEST 1986

The original

A MUNKAJOGVISZONY ALAPKÉRDÉSEI
AZ EURÓPAI SZOCIALISTA ORSZÁGOK JOGÁBAN

Közgazdasági és Jogi Könyvkiadó, Budapest

Translated by

MIKLÓS ZEHERY

ISBN 963 05 3652 8

PREFACE

The aim of the present work is to seek the common elements existing in the law of the European socialist countries in the present phase of development of the law in respect of the main problems of labour relations, first and foremost the establishment, modification, and termination of these relations. Obviously, common elements of this kind are characteristic of other fields of the law as well; however, as regards labour relations in particular, they are worthy of interest considering the special importance of these relations on account of their character and frequency; and their significance greatly increased with regard to the continuously intensifying socialist inter-State cooperation. The success or failure of the elaboration of the common elements is thus not at all irrelevant for the relationships existing among the socialist States themselves.

Of course, the basic trend of legal similarity in the appearance of labour relations does not mean the disappearance of differences in the formation of legal systems of the various socialist States, which, in view of the historical antecedents and the varying solutions related to the different economic mechanisms of the countries, is fairly obvious. Admittedly, it would be a mistake to contest or not to recognize the specific features, just as to deny the existence of common necessities and endeavours to solve the problems of labour relations in the law of the European socialist countries. The aspects of comparative law are in the foreground of the present work, with a view to obtaining a scientific synthesis and presenting a summary of the main issues. The analysis has been concentrated on the predominant points, but a number of contingent problems have also been considered.

First of all, the investigations are based on the positive rules of the law of the individual countries. Furthermore, comments interpretative in nature as expressed in their jurisprudence of labour law are also taken into account and, where necessary, due attention is given to the legal practice of the countries concerned.

The Author

CONTENTS

1. INTRODUCTION

1.1 Social and economic order as determining factors in establishing the framework for the performance of work

The productive activities of society have always manifested themselves in different ways in the different periods of history. A general feature is that individual legal arrangements have always been adjusted to the respective social and economic conditions which served as their basis. When the bourgeoisie was confronted with the feudal system, the starting point of the legal regulation was the concept of the so-called free labour contract, and this was regarded as the natural and most suitable foundation for establishing labour relations. The concept of the free labour contract was of great importance for the bourgeoisie with its aim of obtaining increasingly stronger positions, as it met the requirements of free competition in the best way, and it allowed employers to place at their maximum disposal a labour force, which was anyhow almost completely at their mercy. Moreover, the formal framework for acquiring the surplus value for individual purposes was thus constituted.[1] The first dispositions bearing upon labour contracts (contracts governing wages, and service contracts) appeared in the bourgeois formulated civil codes.[2] In spite of the circumstance that the dispositions of the civil codes regulating labour contracts were based upon the principles of the freedom and equality of the parties, it was obvious that the autonomy of the contracting parties was

[1] Taking the Hungarian legal literature of the earlier periods, this process of development is demonstrated fairly well in KOVRIG (1936, p. 31). To quote the author: "Freedom gave the workers independence, at the same time, however, released the bonds through which, partly by applying the principle of mutual assistance, the existence of the workers was assured in an established way in cases of economic or personal crisis. Thus, agricultural workers ceased to live in rural communities of their own or within the confines of landlords' estates, meaning organic ties that gave them traditional protection against uncertainty of existence. While becoming independent and free, they became isolated and deprived of companions, exposed to the arbitrariness of their counterparts with a stronger economic background." For later Hungarian literature, see LŐRINCZ (1974, pp. 21 et seq.). To quote: "According to the legal regulation, employees are free and equal to employers. In fact, the economic necessity is so strong, however, that workers can sell their labour only under unfavourable conditions. As a consequence of this, it is agreeable for capitalists to conclude 'free' contracts with workers deprived of the means of production, i.e. without any legal restrictions, because they may set conditions under the pretext of 'free bargaining' on account of their economic position, which ensures profit for them...". The author then refers to the circumstance that the labour movement is not strong enough in this first phase of the capitalist-formulated regulation of labour relations to compel legislation to accept and enact legal rules of actual importance ensuring labour protection.
[2] Articles 1781 and 1982 of the *Code Civil* inspired by Napoleon; Articles 1151 et seq. of the Austrian Civil Code; Articles 611 et seq. of the German Civil Code; Articles 1550 et seq. of the Hungarian Draft Civil Code.

nothing but a formality. For this reason, and with a view to ending the most striking abuses, the intervention of public power became unavoidable.[3] To achieve this purpose, on the one hand, and mainly due to fears stemming from the strengthening of the organizational frames and the increasing weight of the workers' movement, on the other, legal rules bearing upon the permissible duration of working time, paid leave, and the creation of safer conditions of work were issued in several countries.[4]

The collective agreement appeared, in particular, as an important means in the struggle fought by the working class for improving working conditions. Among the capitalist conditions, the main purpose was first to ensure the fixing of minimum wages and then more favourable working conditions, the latter to be observed by the employers by having concluded individual labour contracts. Usually, the conditions of work concerned were outside the scope of regulation of the so-called labour safety legislation.[5]

The image outlined above remained unchanged up to the present time in so far that labour regulations appear in the early-capitalist States in the form of acts and collective agreements. Working conditions and other related problems are regulated in different ways for the various categories of employees, such as manual and white-collar workers, civil servants, etc. so that a uniform regulation of labour law failed to come to existence.[6] Accordingly, neither could a uniform concept of labour relations take shape under the conditions prevailing in early-capitalist society.[7]

[3] "It is easy to foresee that, as regards the legal regulation of work, public law will gain more ground than before, at the expense of civil law, as the events taking place in our age give a good testimony of this. In the rules of recent legislation on service contracts the number of compulsory statutes considerably increases; collective agreements should be understood as belonging in this category, provided that they accept only under specific conditions as valid the contracts regulating producing work." — TRÓCSÁNYI, József (Sárospatak), 1910/9, p. 2.

[4] VINCENTI (1942), p. 27.

[5] The sphere of regulation of the collective agreements includes, in some countries, e.g. in the USA and partly also in Japan, fundamental problems whose regulation is reserved elsewhere to labour law legislation.

[6] Nevertheless, reference should be made to the circumstance that, as regards some points of regulation, a sort of levelling-up took place—after the Second World War in particular. Thus, protection in case of notice has been enforced in general also for employees working in the private sector, although this was characteristic earlier only of the labour relations of employees working in the civil service. Previous differences in respect of working time were pushed into the background as well. With service offences, disciplinary measures are imposed on civil servants; for the private sector, the fines, penalties imposed in the workshop are the counterparts of disciplinary measures. All this does not mean that a uniform concept cf law of the two sectors would be at hand. Among other points, the main differences between civil service and the private sector lie in the fact that, for the civil service, in several capitalist countries, a collective agreement cannot be concluded; the settlement of labour disputes is outside the competence of the courts of justice: and the right to strike is inadmissible or limited by legal rules.

[7] Regarding the recent legal literature in the Western world, some authors consider the concept of labour relations as those of the exchange of commodities as outmoded; notwithstanding, there are not insignificant differences in respect of the content and terminological denomination of the various concepts. For recent non-socialist legal literature see MAYER-MALY (1970), pp. 59 et seq.; HUECK–NIPPERDAY (1970), pp. 46 et seq.; REHBINDER

The situation is completely different under the conditions of the socialist social and economic order in which the overwhelming part of the means of production is collective property: the management of the economy as a whole is the task of the State administration. Furthermore, the said arrangement obviously involves nation-wide co-operation based on the coordinated work of all the members of society; within this cooperative framework the division of work-force and the means of production in the required proportions and the material interests of the individual members of society in the work performed for society are to be ensured. Additionally, the working conditions enabling the work targets to be complied with, are to be ensured as well.[8]

Nevertheless, the socialist State is not in a position to realize directly all the various concrete phases of work, i.e. they can be achieved only by means of special partial cooperation, making use, first and foremost, of State-owned enterprises. In view of this, the work to be performed by the individual members of socialist society may be realized only by means of the partial cooperations mentioned above, within the nation-wide cooperation of society. In other words, the realization of society's concrete labour relations requires the existence of special forms of organization. Individual citizens join then in the process of work of society through the organizational forms mentioned above, i.e. the various labour organizations.

Bearing in mind what has been said the conclusion may be drawn saying that, under conditions of socialism, the labour relations of society come into existence between the individual citizens as employees, on the one hand, and the economic, administrative, and social organizations, on the other. The mentioned labour relations within society ensure that the required work-force for the organizations concerned will be provided; as regards workers and employees, the labour relations ensure their right to work, their share in the national income, i.e. the right to share in the socialist distribution of goods, as well as the right to participate in the organization, administration, and supervision of the activities of the enterprises within the framework of the principle of workshop democracy.[9] Labour relations are understood to mean the way of organizing the participation of the citizens in the work of society through the intermediary of the employers.

The Yugoslav concept is a special case, shows some differences to the above scheme of socialist social order. Under its terms, labour relations should be

---

(1973), pp. 24 et seq. Thus, it is well worth mentioning that the term *'louage de service'*, i.e. leasing of service, was used in Article 1780 of the French *Code Civil,* and the term *'contract de travail',* i.e. labour contract, started to be used only as late as about the end of the 19th century. It may be read in the relevant legal literature that—beyond terminological problems—the usage of a new term, labour contract, revealed the decline of the 'leasing of service' as such; it was considered to be a patrimonial exchange contract anyway, which 'on account of its purely materialist concept, disregarded the personality of the workers'. Cf. CAMERLYNCK–LYON-CAEN (1970), p. 108.

8 The commodity character of work-force in capitalism and the termination of this concept in socialism is dealt with in detail by WELTNER (1965), pp. 5 et seq. — It seems to be sufficient just to draw attention to this problem here.

9 WELTNER–NAGY (1974), p. 105.

understood as mutual relations between working men and women as human elements, or participants of the associated work, realizing their right to work in the basic organizations of the associated work, and entering into mutual labour and a self-managing relationship with each other by utilizing the means of production which are a collective property.[10] The meaning of the term 'mutual relations' has not been precisely delimited in the relevant Yugoslav legal literature and has not acquired an unequivocal interpretation.[11] Even so it may be taken for granted that it means a concept relating to the form of organization of the participation of citizens in the work of society, only making use of a different theoretical construction and equally different modes of solution, in practice.

1.2 Labour relation as a basic legal institution serving the performance of work

Under the conditions of the socialist social and economic order, labour relations tend to appear in the form of relations governed by labour law, this latter representing a separate branch of socialist law. The fact that labour law is a separate branch in socialist law serves to emphasize the concept of socialist law, making clear the separation of labour relations from commodity relations. The emergence of conditions that made necessary the establishment of specific fundamental principles and methods of solution bearing upon labour relations, accordingly, the qualification of this complex of legal rules as a separate branch of law results from a social and economic necessity which, in fact, is then reflected and expressed in it. This statement is also valid, in general, with regard to the Yugoslav model, with the difference, however, that in it a revised comprehensive concept of legal rules bearing upon associated work comprises, apart from the rules of labour law, rules from the fields of administrative law, financial law, farmers' cooperative law, civil law, etc.

Regarding the performance of work within the framework of socialist labour relations, it usually takes place in the form of employment by the socialist enterprises, organizations, and institutions. Employment is realized in the form of a hierarchic structure the most characteristic constituent element of which on the employer's side is the right of instruction, and on the employee's side the duty of complying with the instructions. This arrangement is needed in order to achieve that the appropriate utilization of the work-force is ensured within an economic or administrative organization. True, the hierarchic structure expresses, substantially, only an organizational legal subordination, nevertheless, it appears to be a very important criterion for the qualification of the particular relationship established for carrying on work as labour relationship with all its legal consequences or for its delimitation from some other relationships also established for the performance of work based, however, not on the

---

[10] Article 161 of the 1976 Act on associated work.
[11] ABRAHAMSBERG–AMUŠIĆ (1975/1-3), pp. 16 et seq.

12

hierarchic structure but some other arrangement. If unequivocal decisions are to be brought in respect of problems related to an actual labour relationship, the regular character of performing the work, and its being carried on within the community of the workers as well as the use of the equipment of the company concerned may furnish further guidance.[12]

It would seem to be appropriate here to make some additional remarks on the foregoing. The relations of subordination and superordination, thus the right to give orders and the duty to comply with these orders are enforced only in respect of the performance of work: as regards, however, the establishment, modification, and termination of labour relations governed by the law (to be dealt with in the following sections in detail), coordination is predominant in this field, though unilateral constitutive acts are also admitted, regarding in particular the modification of labour relations on the part of the enterprise (employer). Furthermore, both the enterprise (employer) and the employee are allowed to terminate a labour relationship unilaterally.

As for the fundamental problems affecting labour relations, all socialist countries have unified regulations. On the basis of labour relations governed by the law, the essential point here is that workers and employees have the right and duty to work; the rights and duties of the employers involve: the giving of employment, the remuneration of the workers and employees for their work, and the rendering of other services for them, resulting from their labour relations. Nevertheless, some kind of differentiation may be observed within the unified regulations necessitated, among other points, by the differences in the forms and modes in which the citizens participate in the work of society, as well as by the differing nature of the various conditions of work and of the work performed, varying according to the individual sectors of the national economy and to the individual trades and professions. Having this in view, distinction may be made according to labour relations existing with economic State organizations; economic organizations belonging in the budgetary system; and within these, classification may be continued according to labour relations with the organs of State power and State administration, courts of justice, prosecutor's offices, public institutions, departments responsible for postal and telecommunication services, social organizations, agricultural and industrial cooperatives, with individual employers; and finally, atypical labour relations, e.g. that of outworkers, also make a category. Let us emphasize here, that differentiation does not go beyond the scope of unified labour regulations covering the various types of labour relations.

The starting point for our analyses to be presented here was the basic type,

---

[12] WELTNER had pointed out that for determining the concept of labour relations governed by the law, and delimiting it, it was of primary importance that employees were bound to comply with their tasks within their sphere of activities according to the instructions of the director of the enterprise. This is the legal criterion with the highest importance among the elements of the legal content and concept of labour relations. This criterion demonstrates the most specific feature of labour relations which may best delimit labour relations governed by the law from civil law relations bearing upon the performance of work. See WELTNER (1962), p. 131.

i.e. the general regulation with an all-embracing binding force. It produced the framework that was able to serve as a basis for drawing conclusions, permitting one to make general statements. As regards particular regulations, placed within the said framework, they are not without interest when the main features of development are set out, but details are beyond the scope of the present work.

1.3 Delimitation of the examined subject

We are concerned here with labour relations governed by the law. This means that only those legal relations are dealt with in the following discussion which are regarded to be labour relations by the legal system of the particular State, irrespective of the circumstance that the rules of labour law may also comprise other relations connected with the performance of work as well. We wish to analyse first and foremost the socialist views relating to the economic, social and judicial elements of labour relations governed by the law. Then we turn to the presentation of such modes that serve to promote the establishing of labour relations.

Particular attention is paid to the subject of the labour relation in view of the circumstance that the formation of labour relations may be attributed principally to the legal acts of the same. In this respect the participation of third parties in the constitutive activities concerned with labour relations will also be considered.

The fundamental investigations of the present work are concerned with the establishment, modification, and termination of labour relations. Within this area, the problems are envisaged, first and foremost, that may give rise to principal interest from the point of view of the constitutive activities concerned with labour relations. In this respect, the primary aim is to reveal the common necessities of the legal development of the socialist countries; at the same time, the specific features that are in an interplay with the common necessities of the legal development of the individual socialist countries are also demonstrated. The investigations presented in this work have their main support from the application of the method of legal comparison; in line with this, references to the most important historical antecedents proved to be necessary as well.

Special consideration will be given in the closing part of the work to the role of trade unions concerned with the functioning of labour relations. By dealing with this point in a separate chapter, emphasis will be given to the function assigned to the trade unions, which are to be realized in the form of constitutive activities concerned with the labour relations.

So far as the Soviet literature is concerned particular attention is drawn to MIRONOV;[13] as regards Soviet national law GINTZBURG is of fundamental importance.[14] Turning to the legal literature of the various socialist countries,

[13] MIRONOV (1975), p. 144.
[14] GHINTZBURG (1977), p. 310.

the following publications are worthy of mention: For Czechoslovakia PUDIK-BENEŠ;[15] BERNARD-PAVLÁTOVÁ[16]. For the German Democratic Republic KAISER-KIRSCHNER-SCHULTZ[17], KIRSCHNER-MICHAS,[18] MICHAS[19]. For Romania BELIGRĂDEANU[20]. Apart from MIRONOV (1975) the authors of all the other papers referred to had in mind only to present their national legal system. In this respect they provide a reliable source of information.[21]

Regarding the Hungarian literature of labour law, a comparative legal analysis of labour relations is given in SZÁSZY's work.[22] Furthermore, material based on a broad-scale legal comparison is to be found in the works of WELTNER, who had always taken care of complementing his studies by analysing and presenting the relevant material of the foreign legal systems.[23]

Works making use of legal comparison have a particular significance in the field of the distinct branches of law, as they make it possible not only to present an extensive demonstration of the examined legal institutions but they also facilitate the elaboration of theoretical problems of legal comparison and the carrying out of summing-up work in order to obtain syntheses of principles at a general level. A part field of labour law, i.e. the labour relation regarded as such by the particular legal system, is set out in the present volume by making use of legal comparison with regard to the law of European socialist countries, because to arrive at syntheses of principles was also among the aims set by the author for himself.[24]

---

[15] PUDIK-BENEŠ (1974), p. 248.

[16] BERNARD-PAVLÁTOVÁ (1979), p. 368.

[17] KAISER-KIRSCHNER-SCHULZ (1974), p. 343.

[18] KIRSCHNER-MICHAS (1978).

[19] MICHAS (1974), p. 80.

[20] BELIGRĂDEANU (1978), p. 240.

[21] Largely for practical purposes, FREUND (1980), p. 136, is well worth mentioning in this field. As indicated in the Preface of FREUND's study, the part dealing with the termination of labour relations is due to be published in a separate volume.

[22] SZÁSZY (1969), pp. 263–497.

[23] Regarding this point of view, of particular interest is his work of 1965.

[24] It should be mentioned here only as a preliminary remark that, when making reference to the Hungarian Labour Code, Act No. II of 1967 amended by Law-decree No. 29 of 1979 is concerned. Its rule of implementation is Decree No. 48/1979 (XII. 1) of the Council of Ministers. (The relevant data bearing upon the legal rules of other countries are given at the appropriate places.)

2. ESSENTIAL ECONOMIC, SOCIAL, AND JURIDICAL CHARACTERISTICS OF LABOUR RELATIONS

Within the socialist legal system, socialist jurisprudence has paid attention almost continuously to the problem of labour relations, and this has been particularly true since the beginning of the 1950s. The dispute in the Soviet Union between MOSKALENKO, on the one hand, and ALEKSANDROV and PASHERSTNIK, on the other, regarding, the problem of differences between labour relations under socialist and capitalist conditions or, in other words, the possible existence of common elements between capitalist and socialist-based labour relations, has been kept well in mind. Since the 1950s the view may be regarded as established that common features between capitalist and socialist labour relations can be traced but, in fact, only in the technical and in the formal sense. Thus, it is a common feature that, by dint of their labour, workers and employees regularly perform work according to the instructions of their employer.[1]

The specific features of socialist labour relations may be found clearly in the various formulations of concepts set out in the literature of socialist labour law. Here only recent statements will be commented on.

With regard to the Soviet legal literature, the socialist labour relationship governed by the law is to be understood (as given in the 1972 edition of ALEKSANDROV's textbook) as a comradely cooperation of men and women, liberated from exploitation, in which one of the parties, i.e. the workers and employees, accept the duty to perform some kind of work in accordance with a given service function (special field or training), entering the community of a given socialist enterprise (institution or organization), and to subject themselves to the internal statutes (rules of work) of their employer; at the same time, the workers and employees are entitled to participate in matters relating to the management of the employer's enterprise, together with other members of the workers' and employees' community; as regards the other party, i.e. the employing enterprise, institution or organization, it undertakes: to remunerate its workers and employees in relation to the quantity and quality of their work; to ensure that the conditions of work are safe for the employees' health, and are such as permit the achievement of a high rate of efficiency of the rendered work; also, the employing enterprise is bound to provide for the material and cultural demands of its employees.[2]

We can see also from the work edited by ANDREYEV[3] that the idea of

[1] For the evaluation of the dispute see WELTNER (1962), pp. 70–71.
[2] ALEKSANDROV, ed. (1972), p. 154.
[3] ANDREYEV, ed. (1971), pp. 53–54.

16

labour relations means a comradely cooperation of men and women liberated from exploitation in which one side of the parties, i.e. the workers and employees, performs given tasks of work, carries on work in the specified way, and observes the prescribed rules of work; the other side of the parties, i.e. the enterprises, institutions, etc. is required to create labour possibilities and conditions representing no danger to health and ensuring a high rate of efficiency of work; furthermore, the employees are remunerated in relation to the quantity and quality of the work performed by them, and care is taken to meet the material and cultural demands of the workers.

As could be inferred, the two above-mentioned definitions have several common elements, such as determining labour relations as a relationship based on cooperation between men and women liberated from exploitation; performance of specified tasks of work, giving essentially the definition of the scope of activity; the requirement to observe the internal statutes (rules of work) of the employing body; the remuneration of work in relation to its quantity and quality; the establishment of conditions ensuring the labour safety required for the protection of the employees, and for a high rate of efficiency of the work; provision to meet the material and cultural demands of the workers and employees. Furthermore, ALEKSANDROV (1972) emphasizes, on the part of the employees, the necessity of entering the community of fellow-workers and the right to participate in matters bearing upon the management of the enterprise; in turn, ANDREYEV (1971) mentioned the accomplishment of work in the prescribed way as a criterion of a labour relationship.

GHINTZBURG started from the statement that a socialist labour relationship was nothing other than the legal expression of the relations of a socialist cooperation of work. According to his view the relations existing between the participants of socialist cooperation of work have a three-dimensional construction, that is, they are of organization-technical and economic, as well as labour law character. Emphasis is laid here on the volitional character of labour relations, with a simultaneous hint, however, to the circumstance that the organization-technical and the economic relations do have volitional elements as well. Besides, the authoritative character of labour relations is emphasized. The main feature of direction is the organization of the collective work of the participants in a working process, depending on the level of technical development and the content and character of the guided work, with the essential point, however, that the employee considers the decision taken by the organizer of the work as binding for him and this is observed in his actual activity. The severity of this binding element may vary, i.e. it may be the communication of a direct instruction, advice, or recommendation. At the same time, the 'guiding authority' of the leader in the working process is combined with another principle, i.e. the participation of the employees (workers) in the management of their employing body (enterprise). This participation may appear in different forms.[4]

As regards the legal literature in Bulgaria, the concept of labour relations

[4] GHINTZBURG (1977), pp. 38 et seq.

has been dealt with in detail by RADOILSKI.[5] In his view, the socialist labour relationship represents individual labour relations regulated by law, expressing comradely co-operation of men and women free from exploitation. Within this relationship, one of the parties, i.e. the worker or employee, places his/her labour at the disposal of the other party, i.e. an enterprise, institution or organization, within the frame of a profession or function, in order to perform a specified kind of work within a fixed working time, subjecting himself to the established disciplinary rules of work. The other party, i.e. an enterprise, institution or organization undertakes the obligation to pay salary or wages, in relation to the quantity and quality of the performed work, and to ensure safe conditions of work in order to protect the health of the workers and employees; that is, conditions which are favourable for a high rate of efficiency of the work; in addition, care is taken to meet the material and cultural demands of the workers and employees. The fundamental necessities of socialist society, and the principle of the distribution by rendered work, are clearly reflected in the labour relationship, therefore, the realization of several principles of the socialist organization of labour is ensured. The said necessities and principles are realized within labour relations first and foremost by means of the undertaking of obligations by the enterprise, institution or organization at whose disposal the labour has been put.

Looking at the Czechoslovak literature of labour law, the work of WITZ should be mentioned. We see from this author that the rights and duties of the subjects of a labour relationship are directed: from the side of the workers and employees to the performance of the work in compliance with the instructions of the particular socialist organization concerned; from the side of the socialist organization (employer), the main points concern the payment of wages (salary) for the work as rendered, the assurance of the conditions of work and the realization of taking care of the workers and employees.[6] In BERNARD–PAVLÁTOVÁ reference is made to the condition that a socialist labour relationship has two fundamental, inseparable elements. The first concerns the individual performance of work, through which the workers and employees participate in the fulfilment of the targets of the organization, within the community of workers and in compliance with the instructions of the enterprise; in return for his work, the employee is paid and enjoys other remunerations and allowances connected with the existence of the labour relationship. The other element of a labour relationship concerns the participation of the workers and employees in the promotion, direction, and inspection of the activity of the organization employing them, equally within the community of the workers. The participation of the workers and employees in the promotion, direction, and inspection of the activity of the employing organization is realized, first and foremost, through the trade unions, i.e. their competent local organs.[7]

As for the literature of the German Democratic Republic, BREDERNITZ–

[5] RADOILSKI (1957), pp. 170–173.
[6] WITZ (1971), I, p. 70.
[7] BERNARD–PAVLÁTOVÁ (1979), p. 7.

KUNZ have attempted to extend the concept of labour relations. In their view, all approaches linked with the problem of labour relations are static, accordingly they fail to reflect the dynamics of the course of development of the community and the individual workers. It can be seen that these views claim for a multiple construction of the conditions of work. Essentially, they would comprise the following social relations:

– relations between the enterprise and its leading organs on the one hand, and the individual employees on the other;

– relations between the structural units and the leading organs of the enterprise on the one hand, and between the individual employees, on the other;

– relations between the enterprise or the leading organs of its structural units, respectively, on the one hand, and the communities of the employees of the enterprise or the bodies of the workers and employees authorized to participation in the management on the other;

– relations between the bodies of the workers and employees authorized to participation in the management on the one hand, and the workers and employees on the other.[8]

The views outlined here may be summed up by saying that the characteristics of labour relations are not regarded as legal relations of individual character, established between enterprises and employees; instead, these relations represent the socialist collective work of production communities organized and directed by the State in conformity with the principle of democratic centralism. The work performed by the individual workers and the communities of workers within these relations appears directly as social collective work. Nevertheless, the fundamental act of the establishment of a labour relationship is the labour contract through which the right to work of the workers and employees is enforced.

The mentioned concept of labour relations failed, however, to gain ground on a broader scale in the German Democratic Republic. In this respect, MICHAS put his view that the right to work of the workers and employees is enforced by the labour relationship, since this is the means through which the workers and employees join in the social process of work, in conformity with the requirements of the national economy and the enterprise on the one hand, and their professional training on the other;[9] the multiple construction of labour relations is not dealt with in his work.

Also in the course of the disputes concerning the GDR Draft Labour Code, enacted in 1977, the point was emphasized according to which the putting forth of the personality in the most important field of human life, i.e. the social process of work, is made possible by the socialist State by ensuring the right to work. Accordingly, the dispositions bearing upon the conclusion, modification, and cancellation of labour contracts represent important legal means for integrating the labour of the workers into the working process, in

[8] BREDERNITZ–KUNZ (1969/2), pp. 197–198.
[9] MICHAS (1970), pp. 143–144.

conformity with the professional training of the individual workers and the social requirements. Thus, the workers and employees, and the enterprise, have to reach agreement with each other in respect of the establishment of labour relations.[10]

The concept of labour relations was comprehensively dealt with by WELT-NER in the Hungarian literature.[11] He pointed out that labour relations, as regards their legal form, represent a relationship of individual character also under the conditions of socialism. Thus, a labour contract is concluded by a worker as an individual and a socialist economic or administrative organ having an independent capacity of an employer to act as subject at law. This legal relationship of individual character must not be confused with the individual character of capitalist labour relations, in connection with which it is to be mentioned even if only as one example that individual (personal) property is not identical with private property.[12]

The purpose of a labour relationship is nothing else but the carrying on of labour, or the utilization of this latter, for direct participation in the work of society or for a share from the national income.[13]

From the viewpoint of the socialist economic (administrative, social, etc.) organization—functioning by making use of the means of production in State or collective property—this relationship is established in order to ensure the work-force required for the fulfilment of its plan targets, while the workers and employees enter this relationship with a view to realizing their right to work by performing regular work, ensuring thus their participation in the national income, in conformity with the principles of socialist distribution.[14]

As regards the enforcement of the principle of equivalence in labour relations, the employees do not get directly, in the form of wages and other remunerations and allowances granted within the frames of labour relations, the value produced by the utilization of their labour. The share of each employee from the national income may only be in relation to the quantity and quality of the work as actually performed. Moreover, the effect of the lack of equivalence is perceivable in several respects. So, an employee does not take the risk of the work performed by him if the inefficiency of the work cannot be attributed to him. The responsibility for risks is limited, however, even in the case of imputability, for—as is laid down in the regulations concerning payment in the case of rejects—responsibility has to be adjusted to a particular wage. In the case of damages caused by negligence, the responsibility of the workers and employees is limited, i.e. indemnity may only be related to a specified part of their wages and it cannot be imposed, in general, for lost profits.[15]

Nevertheless, if the relations between individual employees and society are

10 MICHAS (1977/5), pp. 131–132.
11 WELTNER (1962), p. 410.
12 WELTNER (1962), p. 68.
13 WELTNER (1962), p. 75.
14 WELTNER (1962), p. 182.
15 WELTNER–NAGY (1974), p. 112.

considered not only within the frame of labour relations but in their global scope, it will be clear, as set forth by WELTNER, that the law of equivalence comes into display well within the relationship, for the full amount of the national income is utilized in the interests of the workers and employees and through labour relations and other social relations. Socialist labour relations express a relationship between individual workers and employees, and the entire society, represented by the socialist State. This relationship is characterized by the feature that the totality of the production realized by society is distributed in accordance with the interests of the workers and employees.[16]

The view according to which the individual legal relations existing between the workers and employees, and the enterprise, should be replaced by some sort of a multilateral legal relation has not gained ground in the Polish legal literature either. As was pointed out by SZUBERT, the said views are based on the beyond doubt correct statement according to which there exist actual social and legal bonds within an enterprise uniting the workers and employees in the community as a whole; nevertheless, to relate all these to a single legal formula would only lead to an extremely complicated construction of legal relation.[17]

In SWIECICKI's view, a labour relationship is to be understood as a legal relation whose subject matter is the performance of work against remuneration and in a subordinated way, i.e. not independently but under the employer's instruction. However, this author adds to the definition mentioned above that it is coupled to the abstractly considered fact of the performance of subordinated work against remuneration, without saying anything of the scope and quality of the content of the legal relationship in question, in a given social and economic system, and a given phase of development of the State and of social development. Legal relations, in fact, also reflect some specific criteria beyond those characteristic of all consensual relations. These specific features increase, furthermore, in relation to the appreciation of human work in the given society, and to the legal status of those performing it.[18] Thus, the characteristic features of the content of socialist legal relations comprise, among other points, the organizing and protecting function of labour relations, appearing in organizing the working process and ensuring the protection of the workers and employees; the taking over of the production and economic risks by the employer; the habitual conformity of the duties of the parties with the classic principle of *facio ut des,* completed with other duties that express the principle of equivalence.[19]

As for the relevant legal literature published in Romania, the nature of labour relations is analysed by MILLER who points out that a complex legal relationship is established between employees and employers as a result of

[16] WELTNER (1962), pp. 143–144.
[17] SZUBERT (1972), pp. 96–97.
[18] SWIECICKI (1974/4), p. 319.
[19] SWIECICKI (1969), pp. 140–141.

the conclusion of a labour contract, containing several rights and duties. The fundamental characteristic features of labour relations mean—in MILLER's view—that the subject of a labour relationship is 'live work' and that the employees are subordinated to a given enterprise, and they enjoy protection within the frames of labour relations.—The said statement according to which the subject of a labour relationship is 'live work' means particularly that the workers and employees place their labour at the employer's disposal, i.e. their physical power and mental gifts as well as the time they use in carrying on their work. The duties undertaken by the employees mean the performance of work, i.e. their availability offered to the enterprise in order to perform work. On the basis of the performed work the other party is then obliged to provide compensation. This compensation, i.e. the wage, is due to the workers and employees in return for their labour made available to the other party. In the socialist social order there is a strict relationship between work and its remuneration. The socialist distribution of wealth is effected in relation to the quantity, quality, and social importance of work, and the social value of work is determined by the said three components. It is the purpose of the system of wages to establish a close relationship between the performance of work and its remuneration, in this way creating the necessary conditions for the broad-scale application of the principle of the equivalence of services in the field of labour relations.[20]

As regards Romanian jurisprudence, the definition given by BELIGRĂ-DEANU is worth mentioning.[21] In his wording, labour relations are to be understood as social relations regulated by the law and established between a person, on the one hand, and in the overwhelming majority of the cases, a State organ, a unit of a cooperative or some other social organization on the other, through which the right to work and the duty of working of the person concerned is realized, i.e. he is able to perform work subject to the organization whose community of labour he joined.

The main difference between the Yugoslav concept and the views outlined above appears by considering that, for the former, a labour relationship is not regarded as an individual legal relation between the enterprise and the employees but as a relationship existing between the workers and employees themselves; this come into being by the entering into work of workers and employees in a labour organization, resulting from their intention to realize their right to work; by entering into work, workers and employees become members of the labour community concerned. According to BALTIĆ, this means the appearance of two elements in the situation of the worker and employee, viz (i) their joining in a labour organization and (ii) their subsequent incorporation into the labour community. As a result of this, relations between free and equal workers and employees come into being within the labour community.[22] The said relations have, first of all, a social and economic character; regarding, however, some of their aspects, they rep-

---

[20] MILLER (1969/2), pp. 212, 214–215, 218–219.
[21] BELIGRĂDEANU (1978), p. 12.
[22] BALTIĆ (1967/1), p. 177.

resent legal relations as well, stemming from specific rights and duties, constituting the responsibility of the members of this labour community, and all these points result from acts, statutes, and other dispositions of a general nature of the organization of associated work.[23] This concept is in conformity with the fundamental Yugoslav idea according to which inter-enterprise relations represent, in fact, relations between the workers and employees themselves, being both the producers, and the participants in the management of the enterprise.[24]

Essentially, the major part of the views referred to and outlined above may be summed up so as to say that, as regards the socialist social order, the fundamental purpose of labour relations is the assurance of the workforce needed for the enterprise to fulfil its targets, on the one hand, and the enforcement of the rights of workers and employees, on the other. As for the content of labour relations, it is clear that numerous rights and duties exist on the side of both the enterprise and the workers and employees. Taking the enterprise first, one of the most important rights is that of giving instructions, the corresponding duty being, on the part of the employees, the performance of work in compliance with the instructions; or, more precisely, the state of being available to perform the required work. The employees are entitled to remuneration for the performed work, or, again more precisely, for placing their labour at the disposal of the employers; the corresponding duty of the employer is to pay wages and render other services and allowances as specified. Summing up, labour relations mean, primarily, participation in the work of society, i.e. the realization of the right to work.

Workers and employees receive the counter-value of the work they have performed partly directly and partly indirectly, and this arrangement results from the circumstance that part of the national income flows directly back to the workers and employees in order to meet their personal demands; the remaining part of the national income is utilized, in fact, in accordance with the interests of the workers and employees, in the form of indirect services and allowances, partly within the frames of labour relations, such as services in the field of social welfare, cultural needs, national insurance, professional training, etc., and partly outside those frames, at all-society level (e.g. various social funds, public health services, national defence, public order, etc.).[25] This arrangement of participation in the national income is realized in conformity with the law of socialist distribution, i.e. the rate of this participation in the national income depends on the resources of society and the quantity of the available consumer goods.

[23] According to Article 161 of the 1976 Yugoslav Act on associated work, the labour relations of the workers and employees united in associated work are to be understood as meaning the interrelations of the workers and employees in the basic organization of associated work, or community of work, created by the workers and employees for realizing their right to work and also to utilize the means of production of society, by dint of common work performed with the use of the means of production of society. See VELIMIROVIĆ (1977/1), pp. 78–97.

[24] PECZE–TRÓCSÁNYI (1978).

[25] WELTNER (1962), p. 143.

The right of participation in the management of the enterprise within the frames of workshop democracy is also ensured in the field of labour relations. Considering this fact, it seems to be evident to the partisans of almost all views mentioned above that labour relations represent means through which an individual employee becomes a member of the working community, participating thereby in the planning, organization, administration, and supervision of the activities of the enterprise employing him.

With respect to the principle of equivalence, some contradictions seem to exist. In the views of SWIECICKI and MILLER, one of the characteristic features of socialist labour relations is a close connection between the performance of work and the remuneration for work, reflecting the principle of equivalence. WELTNER was of the opinion, at the same time, that the principle of equivalence was not enforced within the frames of socialist labour relations, for the employees did not receive directly the value produced in providing their labour, taking into account the remunerations given within the frames of their actual labour relations.

The above-outlined contradiction is only apparent. As SWIECICKI put it, historical progress has been advancing toward the more and more complete and real liberation of working men and women from exploitation. Labour contracts ensure a formal compensation of the legal statuses of employees and employers. In fact, the tendency of future development means to continue to reduce the existing inequality and, with its ultimate elimination, granting rights to the employees so as to serve as a counter-balance against the economic dominance of the employer. Progress leads to socialization of the means of production and to workers' and employees' participation in the management of the enterprise.[26]

Emphasizing the enforcement of the principle of equivalence under the conditions of socialism and within the frames of labour relations, the starting point is essentially, for the authors mentioned above, that labour relations represent a relationship between the individual workers and employees and society as a whole, represented by the socialist State, therefore, the law of equivalence is being enforced in the relationship connecting the employees with society.

WELTNER's opinion is that so far as it concerns labour organization, equivalence is being realized on a social scale.[27] The point here is not the enforcement of the principle of the equivalence of performance under the law of obligations. This is reflected not only by the fact that the employees do not receive the full value of their performance directly, within the framework of their labour relations, but also by that if an employee is not able to perform work, in concrete cases specified in the respective legal rules (e.g., compliance with social obligations, off-time, illness, etc.), his right to wages or other services continues to exist.[28]

---

[26] SWIECICKI (1974/4), p. 311.
[27] WELTNER–NAGY (1974), p. 112.
[28] SWIECICKI (1974/4), p. 320.

Taking the present phase of social development, with the continuous advance of socialist economic integration, the intensification of existing cooperation between the socialist States and the birth of new forms of cooperation, it seems that the scope of indirect remuneration, due to the employees as the counter-value of the work performed by them, assumes broader bases. Under these circumstances, the values produced by the workers increase actually not only the national income of the country concerned but, through the medium of the working cooperations, the economic and scientific–technical basis of the other countries participating in the respective cooperation as well, which goes together with the advantage that a larger scale of goods will be produced and so also distributed and not only within a single country but all the countries participating in the cooperation by receiving their share from the increased national income.

As a result of the afore-mentioned, the horizon of the law of socialist distribution will also be extended, i.e. it will be realized not only within the boundaries of a single State but in respect of all States cooperating within the framework of socialist economic integration. Thus the utilization of the national income for the workers outside the frames of labour relations will gain new aspects.[29]

---

[29] Recently JONCZYK (1984) dealt with the fundamental problems of labour relations, in detail, in Poland.

3. ARRANGEMENTS PROMOTING THE ESTABLISHMENT OF LABOUR RELATIONS

As has already been mentioned, labour relations are established, on the part of the employees, to make use of their right to work; on the part of the enterprises, the point is to fulfil their targets. As a rule, the operations needed for the accomplishment of these aims are effected without the participation of State bodies. Notwithstanding, special situations may occur implying controversies between the realization of the right to work on the scale of society as a whole and the actual enforcement of the right to work of individual citizens (workers and employees).[1] Thus, specific branches of the national economy should be promoted more intensively than others: the workforce becomes free for employment elsewhere in some enterprises as a result of the scientific–technical revolution while other enterprises have to suffer from a shortage in work-force; development of technologies requires new types of professional training at a higher level, which is a constantly recurring problem; the first entering into work of young specialists also tends to raise problems, e.g. most of them prefer to settle down in the capital or the major urban centres thereby causing—at the same time—an insufficiency of specialists in the remaining areas.[2]

The bodies concerned with labour placement give some help overcoming these difficulties. Several variants are applicable in this field, such as professional retraining, professional counselling, study scholarship contracts, labour placement, the obligation of giving preference. All these channels have the ultimate function of promoting the establishment of labour relationships. As the porpuose here in view may best be achieved by means of labour placement, attention should first be paid to this institution.

3.1 Labour placement

The purpose of workers' and employees' placement is, first of all, to inform people of work vacancies or to give them advice concerning employment opportunities, or more exactly to establish contact between applicants and prospective employers. Consultation with job agencies is left to the employee's

[1] WELTNER–NAGY (1974), p. 125.

[2] Therefore there are about 2000 inhabitants to one dentist in Budapest, while the ratio is about 1 to 10 000 in the countryside. (Statement made by the dean of the Faculty of Dentology of the Semmelweis University for Medicine, Budapest, at the graduation ceremony in 1977. No substantial changes have occurred since then.)

choice, though there may be specific cases when both the enterprise and the workers and employees are required to have consultations with agencies of placement.

Analysing the history of the institution in question, it may be stated that while a compulsory system of the placement of workers and employees was functioning as perhaps the most important mechanism of the employment of workers in almost all socialist States until the mid-fifties, a trend of its being pushed into the background could be observed in the 1960s. Placement obtained again a higher importance in some countries, e.g. in Poland[3] and Hungary[4], in the mid 1970s, and since then the modes of reintroducing compulsory placement have been regulated on a broader scale than earlier.

For the enterprises concerned, compulsory labour placement means that labour relations can be established by the enterprise only through the channel of labour agencies, apart from the exceptions laid down in the respective labour rules. Compulsory placement of workers and employees of some enterprises proved to be a suitable way of promoting the meeting of the work-force demand of these enterprises of major importance to the national economy, of offering increased preferences in employment to women, young people, and those needing more assistance in view of their social conditions. In brief, considerations of work-force economy can make it necessary to introduce compulsory labour placement in respect of some enterprises.

As for recent developments in Hungary, the facultative character of workers' and employees' placement came more and more into the foreground. This development meant that the employment of citizens seeking work and the meeting of work-force demands of enterprises should be facilitated by having recourse to the institution of administrative labour placement and manpower recruitment. To this end, the agencies of labour placement are charged with giving information and with recommending vacant situations for applicants, on the one hand, and with providing available manpower for the employers, on the other, and, moreover, with taking the steps needed to establish contact and formulate the labour contracts in the case of mutually suitable conditions for the parties.

Meanwhile, compulsory labour placement continued to be valid for exceptional cases, e.g. the head of the county (metropolitan) council is authorized to order that labour relations may be established only through the agencies, administration of labour placement in specified fields of work, e.g. those suitable for persons whose capability of doing work has been altered. With

[3] The procedure applicable to the employment of persons directed to work by the competent body of State administration or applying for employment in possession of a permit issued by the competent regional organ of the State administration is laid down in Resolution No. 185 of the Council of Ministers, taken on 20 August, 1976 (*Monitor Polski*, 1976, No. 36). For the relevant literature, see GRZYMKOWSKI (1975), p. 216. (Review in *Nowe Prawo* 3/1976, p. 487.)

[4] Decree No. 7/1976 (IV. 10) Min. of Lab. on labour placement, organized employment and recruitment, furthermore statute No. 5/1976 of the Municipal Council of Budapest on the regulation of labour placement and recruitment (*Fővárosi Közlöny*, No. 9–10/1976).

rules of this kind, labour contracts concluded without the services of the agencies, administration of labour placement, have no validity.[5]

According to another principle of general character, an employer is not obliged to employ a person sent to him by these agencies of labour placement. In turn, an applicant for a work situation cannot be compelled to accept the job offered by the employment office.[6]

Furthermore, there is an intermediate arrangement between facultative and compulsory labour placement, i.e. when the employer is authorized to refuse the employment of a person sent to him by the employment office only in cases specified in the relevant legal rule. Accordingly, if the labour placement authority refuses to agree with the arguments of the employer, it is entitled to order the employer to effect the employment in question.[6/a]

The employment of young specialists starting their professional career represents a specific form of labour placement. The purpose of the regulation is to help graduates to obtain practical training, and to provide assurance to the enterprises that their manpower demands will continuously be met. According to the legal rules in some countries, the employment of young specialists starting their professional career is realized in the form of the so-called compulsory professional practice system. Essentially, this means that newly graduated specialists are directed by a special advisory board of placement to an enterprise, organization or institution, with a field of activity conforming to their professional qualification usually for a specified period (generally three years); in the vast majority of cases, the young specialists then enter into a labour relationship with the said enterprise, organization or institution by concluding a labour contract.

With regard to the Soviet Union, young people graduating from a high school or a specialized public school, are directed to enterprises, organizations, or institutions in which they then have to work for a minimum period of three years. The direction to work and the relevant administrative aspects are carried out by special placement boards set up in some of the high schools; such boards have representatives of ministries and other administrative bodies to which the employers in question (enterprises, organizations, or institutions) are subordinated. Employers are not allowed to engage the said young people without a disposition taken within the mentioned placement system.

Placing the employee in work is effected by means of the said disposition, containing the denomination of the place of work and the kind of work as well as the amount of the salary.[7]

---

[5] Articles 2 and 6 of Decree No. 29/1980 (XII. 29) Min. of Lab.

[6] Subsection 3, Article 4 of Decree No. 29/1980 (XII. 29) Min. of Lab.

[6/a] This is the fact in Czechoslovak law. Cf. PAVLÁTOVA–WIESNEROVÁ (1979).

[7] Decree of 18 March, 1968, on the employment of students graduated in high schools and specialized secondary schools. *Sbornik sakhonodatyelnikh aktov o trude* (Collection of the rules of labour law). Isd. Yur. Lit., Moscow 1974, pp. 247–256.

28

Virtually the same regulation is in force in Romania, Poland and the German Democratic Republic.[8]

The course of development in Czechoslovakia took the same way at the beginning, i.e. students graduating from high schools were directed to an enterprise or organization to establish a labour relationship, by means of a disposition taken by the ministry of education, and they had then to work there for a minimum period of three years.[9] This arrangement was replaced later by the so-called recommendations for engagement, issued by the school in question to the enterprise or organization concerned, which was then obliged to establish a labour relationship with the young graduate recommended by the school.[10] Accordingly, the enterprises and/or organizations were obliged to conclude a labour contract; similarly, the graduates were obliged in terms of their having been given employment. This regulation was modified again later; under a new rule, the central organs or the district councils or other authorized bodies were bound to determine the enterprises or organizations obliged to employ an appropriately set number of young graduates. It was thus the task of the school to take care of the employment of its graduates in close cooperation with the enterprises concerned.[11] This regulation was, in turn, modified, prescribing for the enterprises and organizations concerned the conclusion of a labour contract with graduates prior to the termination of their studies.[12] According to the latest regulation, the students in question are now free to choose in applying for employment, on the basis of lists sent to the schools. Also, they are allowed without restriction to approach potential employers directly.[13]

The reason why Czechoslovakia changed from previous restrictions more and more to the system of the free employment of young graduates was the shortage in manpower; with this in view, applicants for work were practically in a position to enter into a labour relationship freely, in spite of existing restrictions of legal rules, if they were reluctant to accept the place of work designated to them.[14] According to the summing-up investigations carried out in this field, the overwhelming majority of high schools graduates, i.e. 78 per cent in the years from 1973 to 1975, found employment without having made recourse to the administrative labour placement channels of the national committees or the schools.[15]

[8] Law-decree No. 158/1970 on the direction to productive work of students graduated in the regular courses of the institutions of higher education. (Republished in *Buletinul Oficial*, No. 84/1974); Act No. 48/1964 of 25 February, 1964, on the employment of graduate students of high schools. *(Dziennik Ustaw,* No. 8/1964); Decree No. 25/1968 of 13 January, 1968, on the employment of graduate students of the universities of medicine *(Monitor Polski,* No. 4/1968); Decree of 3 December, 1971, on the employment of graduate students *(Gbl.* II, p. 297).

[9] Government Decrees No. 20/1952 Sb. and 56/1953. Sb.

[10] Government Decree No. 24/1959 Sb.

[11] Government Decree No. 16/1963 Sb.

[12] Government Decree No. 74/1965 Sb.

[13] Government Decree No. 38/1967 Sb.

[14] JÁGERSKY, G., Personal consultation in Bratislava, 1 September 1976.

[15] BELINA (1977/1), p. 80.

The initial period of the corresponding legal development in Hungary was of the same nature. The institution of compulsory professional practice appeared already in the 1951 Labour Code; the issue was newly regulated in 1953. According to the dispositions of the said rules, those who graduated from a university (college), specialized school or special professional course were obliged, in order to obtain more professional practice, or to complete their present knowledge, to enter into the employment of the enterprise designated to this end by the particular school and the competent minister, and to work there for the period prescribed for compulsory professional practice. The system of compulsory professional practice was maintained in Hungary for the longest time in respect of the graduated students of schools providing specialized training for the health service.[16]

In respect of the entering into employment of the graduate students of regular courses of colleges, it was ruled in 1961 that the various ministers should designate the enterprises or first-instance organs and institutions in which young specialists would have the opportunity to obtain professional practice. The enterprises, organs or institutions so designated were then bound to issue announcements concerning vacant posts in the relevant colleges, through the channel of the ministry that exercised supervision over them. The dispositions of the Labour Code were applicable to the labour relations of young specialists. Nevertheless, if the labour relationship was terminated before the end of the period of professional practice as provided, on account of a cause due either to the young specialist or the enterprise, the specialist in question could be employed only by the designated enterprise until the accomplishment of the prescribed period.[17]

A new system concerning the first employment of young specialists was set up in 1977, which was rather restrictive, for the only permissible way of entering into labour relations was the application for employment by means of compulsory competition; the said young specialists could not change their employment for a period of three years, unless they entered a newer compulsory competition. This system was modified with effect from 1 January, 1981, in so far as employment upon application through competition continued to be the main rule, but a young specialist was allowed to enter into the first labour relationship even without application through competition if he failed to obtain employment by the prescribed way within a three-month-period reckoned from the granting of his diploma. Besides, the ministers of health,

[16] Article 132 of Law-decree No. 7 of 1951 (Labour Code); Article 132 of Law-decree No. 25 of 1953 (Amendment and Supplement of the Labour Code); Law-decree No. 46 of 1957 concerning the repeal of the dispositions bearing upon compulsory professional practice; and its amendment: Law-decree No. 31 of 1958. Under the terms of the preceding rule, students graduating in a specialized health school were obliged to serve a professional practice time in a health institute or body designated to this end. This Law-decree was invalidated by Article 68 of the Act II of 1967 (Labour Code).

[17] Decree No. 21/1961 (V. 25) Govt. bearing upon the employment of graduate students of high schools; invalidated by Article 130 of Decree No. 34/1967 (X. 8) Govt. on the implementation of the Labour Code.

justice, and culture were authorized to regulate employment through application by competition in the field of medical, legal, and education services with some differences from the general rule, in compliance with the specific demands in the said scopes of working activity, including also the changes of employment of those already working under a labour contract.

Under the terms of the said new regulation, lawyers graduating after the introduction of the previous system, with more restrictions, i.e. 1st January, 1977, and working within the framework of a labour relationship, are now permitted to change employment without applying for it through competition.[18]

Concerning the form of compulsory professional practice in which a recently graduated young specialist enters into a labour relationship through the intermediary of administrative organs, the problem of the legal status of the specialists concerned appears as a point to be clarified. According to the prevailing view expressed in the Soviet legal literature, two kinds of social relation are established in these cases: first, a relationship governed by law of public administration between the young high-school graduates and the administrative organ carrying out their distribution within the available places of work, and second, a labour relationship between the specialist on the one hand, and the organization for which the specialist starts to work, on the other. The administrative act constitutes a condition for the establishment of labour relations; on its basis the young graduate and the designated organization conclude a labour contract. The designation of the place of employment of the young graduate, even if effected by means of an authoritative act, is not independent of the intention of the person concerned, for he was requested at the time of admission to the respective school to declare his consent to accept employment in the place of work to be designated after having finished his studies.[19]

A different view may be met also occasionally according to which two separate administrative acts should be distinguished in cases of compulsory labour placement, i.e. the authoritative direction to take up work, and the entry of the employee concerned into the community of the workers. The administrative character of the latter act would not exclude, however, conclusion of a labour contract by the parties, as the direction to enter into work takes place in compliance with the intention of the interested person in the majority of cases.[20]

After all, it can be stated that labour placement by administrative means, the first entry into work of young graduates included, serves in all its variants to give employment to applicants for work, on the one hand, and to

---

[18] Resolution of the Council of Ministers No. 1951/1980 (XII. 12), invalidating the Resolution of the Council of Ministers No. 1023/1976 (VII. 15) relating to the subject matter concerned. For detailed rules, see Decree of the Minister of Labour No. 21/1980 (XII. 12) and other related ministerial decrees.

[19] KARPUSHIN (1958), pp. 115–166. Essentially the same point of view may be read in the Romanian legal literature. See STANOIU (1974/5), p. 4.

[20] GHEIHMAN (1973/5), p. 111.

meet the manpower demand of the enterprises, on the other. This activity is thus utilizable to influence the plan-conform employment of the work-force, in accordance with national and local interests.[21]

3.2 Vocational counselling, professional training, and scholarship contracts

These institutions have a function promoting the establishment of labour relations. Of course, there are differences in the law of the various countries in respect of their realization but the fundamental tendency has been the same, i.e. the competent State organs are obliged to assist citizens in choosing their employment, to be in accordance with the needs of society and their individual interests, in acquiring the knowledge necessary for practising the chosen employment, and in ensuring the conditions for the execution of the employment corresponding to the previously obtained professional training.[22]

1. The rules of labour law ensure that young people are able to work in accordance with their knowledge and abilities, to obtain professional practice and further training, in conformity with the available possibilities of society, as well as to participate in the planning and management activities of the enterprises.[23] In order that young employees may develop their abilities and talent in the very field which suits them most, it is necessary, however, to help them to recognize their own abilities and talent and to choose their appropriate profession, in accordance with the mentioned factors. This is the functional purpose of vocational counselling, i.e. to make it possible for young people to choose the profession most suited to their abilities and, in possession of the obtained information, to continue their studies accordingly.[24] More precisely, vocational counselling facilitates the choice of the appropriate course of training for those who wish to continue studying, on the one hand, and gives advice on choosing the appropriate place of work for those who prefer to enter into a labour relationship, on the other.[25]

[21] This view is expressed in Article 3 of the Romanian Labour Code of 1972 as follows: "The division and full and reasonable utilization of manpower reserves are realized in conformity with the targets of the national plan of economic and social development, the requirements of the continuous increase of the economic and social efficiency of work, and the necessity of the harmonic and balanced development of each county of the State."

[22] With the emphasis laid on the requirement to ensure employment corresponding to professional qualification, the last aspect of these demands, is accentuated in Para. 3 of Article 10 of the 1974 Labour Code of Poland.

[23] This is explicitly emphasized in Article 4 of the 1977 Labour Code of the German Democratic Republic.

[24] Para 1 Article 21 of Hungarian Labour Code: a joint resolution of the Government (No. 1004, 1982, II. 10) and of the Cultural Minister (No. 3/1982, II. 10) on vocational counselling. As regards Czechoslovakia, vocational counselling is realized there, with a general character, within the field of application of the legal rules bearing upon the tasks of the enterprises and national committees with respect to providing for the necessary conditions of work (Act No. 70/1958 Sb. Govt. Decree No. 92/1958 Sb.).

[25] NAGY, L. (1978), pp. 275–291.

This activity is particularly important if it is considered that teenagers, i.e. boys and girls of 14, having finished their studies in the primary school, still have no definite ideas of how to shape their future in numerous cases; accordingly, the guidance of the counsel may be of vital importance in deciding their future. The competent organs are in a position to draw the attention of young people to professions which are not in the focus of interest, either because they seem to offer no prospects—possibly on account of erroneous expectations—or because they are simply unknown to the young people concerned. In addition to the above-said, the attention of interested persons may be drawn, within the activity of the vocational counselling administration, to the casual overemployment in this or that branch of profession that would probably raise problems in case of a choice in favour of a profession within this field.

In that it is on the basis of the national economic plan, vocational counselling should be carried out with due consideration to the need of specialists of the various branches and regional units of the economy.

2. The purpose of professional training in the socialist society is primarily to meet the demands of the national economy for an increasing number of available specialists with an equally increasing level of professional knowledge. On the other hand, it is also destined to provide citizens with the professional knowledge needed for practising their chosen activity.

The relation between specialized secondary schools and enterprises participating in professional training in practice has come more and more into the foreground within the field of vocational training. Thus, the specialized secondary schools perform their educating and training work, aimed at grantig a trade qualification, in co-operation with the enterprises, cooperatives, state organs, institutions, and institutes, functioning in the field of the training at issue such as industry, agriculture, food supply, trade, catering, transports, telecommunication or other services. The tasks of training in practice are performed in a training course organized by the respective school or enterprise. The educating work is organized by the specialized secondary school, in co-operation with the interested enterprises and it is the duty of the school to take care of the direction and inspection of the educating and training courses. Also, these courses may be realized through the co-operation of a single secondary school and several enterprises or, in turn, one enterprise and several specialized secondary schools. The co-operation of the school and the enterprise is established in the form of an agreement.[26]

The specialized secondary schools designated for the said courses (in the field of industry, building and construction, agriculture, food industry, and forestry) are obliged to organize vocational instruction and training so that they can grant the qualification required for skilled workers in the respective profession, including a higher theoretical basis, on the one hand, and to pre-

[26] Resolution of the Council of Ministers No. 1019/1976 (VI. 24) on the cooperation of specialized secondary schools and enterprises participating in professional training in practice and on the various problems of the vocational training of skilled workers in specialized secondary schools.

pare for continued studies at a higher level, corresponding to the field of education of the secondary school concerned, on the other.[27]

The recent development of the system of professional training is more and more characterized by an extensive connection between theory and practice, in due consideration of the scientific–technical development and the indispensable professional knowledge related to it. The purpose of this institution is to offer ways and means to prepare for the training of skilled workers-to-be and to offer specialized extension studies at a higher level, and to ensure that the professional practice of the graduates meets the required standard set for young skilled workers.

3. Study scholarship contracts serve to meet the demand for specialists of the enterprises, first and foremost in respect of persons with a higher professional graduation. Under the terms of a scholarship contract, the enterprise undertakes to provide grants for the students for the period of the specified studies, and the other party undertakes to carry on the studies as provided in the contract, and to work for the enterprise concerned for a definite period, after having finished his/her studies.[28] With regard to students attending a regular course, the organizing enterprise is obliged to declare that it will employ the students at the end of the course and in a sphere of activity corresponding to their training. In respect of students not attending a regular course, the obligation of employment is only binding for the enterprise if it agreed to this in this sense. Enterprises are free to conclude a scholarship contract with their own employees, with persons not being in a labour relationship or even with employees of another enterprise.

As a matter of fact, the conclusion of a scholarship contract releases applicants to a post which can be filled otherwise only by means of application by compulsory competition, through participation in the competition.

Regarding the legal rules of the different countries various types of scholarship contracts present themselves. Thus, the institution of the so-called qualification contract *(Qualifizierungsvertrag)* is known in the law of the German Democratic Republic.[29] The rights and duties stipulated in a qualification contract become content elements of the relevant labour contract for the training period. Qualification contracts are concluded on the basis of the qualification plans of the individual enterprises. According to the Czechoslovak law, the enterprise may conclude an agreement with an employee in which the former obliges itself to make it possible for the employee to obtain a professional qualification or to extend the existing one; the charges of the employee include the obligation to continue to work for the enterprise in question for a specified period of time following the acquisition of the qualification or, failing to do so, to compensate the enterprise for the charges incurred in connection with the acquisition or extension of professional qualification. This rule is similar to that of the Hungarian law, with the difference that, according to the disposi-

[27] Joint Decree No. 14/1976 (XII. 1), Min. of Lab. and of Educ., on the vocational training of skilled workers in specialized secondary schools.
[28] Para 2 Article 21 of the Hungarian Labour Code.
[29] Article 153 of the Labour Code of the German Democratic Republic.

tions of the Czechoslovak Labour Code, the possibility of concluding agreements of the mentioned kind is open only to employees of the enterprise in question.[30]

As for Poland, the Labour Code contains a hint that the enterprises facilitate for their employees to complete their knowledge based on school graduation and to increase the level of their professional qualification, in a scope to be fixed by the Council of Ministers, in concert with the Central Council of Trade Unions.[31] The details are set out in special legal rules.

By instituting scholarship contracts and similar agreements, the legislator's purpose was to make possible for the enterprises the regular supply of specialists to meet their demands, together with an appropriate replacement of cadres; these institutions rank among those serving to promote the establishment of labour relations.

3.3 Obligation to give preference

It is a consequence of the principle of granting special protection to pregnant and nursing mothers and women in charge of children below a specified age that it is impermissible to refuse to employ women on account of their pregnancy or nursing tasks. The said principle is explicitly laid down in the Labour Code of the Russian Soviet Federated Socialist Republics.[32] This follows also the rule of more general character according to which women should have the guarantee that they may be employed in any post or place of work, in conformity with their qualification and abilities. To this end, the necessary conditions of work have to be secured.[33] As a rule, it is the responsibility of the enterprises to ensure appropriate employment possibilities for women; the council organs have to give them assistance in case of need.

Regarding the Hungarian regulation, it goes beyond the rules mentioned in the preceding in so far as an obligation is stipulated to give preference in employment to pregnant women and mothers with young children, i.e. supposing equal conditions the enterprises are obliged to give preference in employment to female workers of the said categories.[34] The mentioned rule confirms, essentially, the prohibition of discriminating against women.

[30] Article 143 of the Labour Code of Czechoslovakia. For comments on this legal disposition see MIKYSKA (1977/9).

[31] Para 1, Article 103 of the Labour Code of Poland.

[32] Article 170. See NETCHAYEVA (1979/9), pp. 137 et seq.

[33] Explicit rules are provided in this respect in Article 149 of the Labour Code of Czechoslovakia; subsection 1, Article 151 of the Labour Code of Romania; and Article 240 of the Labour Code of the German Democratic Republic.

[34] Para 2, Article 19 of the Labour Code. According to Position 97 taken up by the Labour Law Department of the Supreme Court (see *Munkaügyi Közlöny*, 1978/2) for the application of the disposition of Para 2, Article 19 of the Labour Code, a mother nursing a young child or young children is understood to be a female employee nursing or taking care of a child (or children) younger than six years of age. It should be just noted that, as regards the practice, no aversion can be experienced in respect of the employment of pregnant women and mothers nursing young children. The practice complying with the disposition of the legal rule in question may be attributed, last but not least, to shortage in manpower.

According to Hungarian law, persons having done their regular military service have to be preferred at the establishment of a labour relationship, supposing otherwise equal conditions. Nevertheless, this disposition is only applicable within a period of two years reckoned from the completion of the regular military service of the person concerned.[35]

With regard to the care to be taken for persons with a decreased capacity to work, a great variety of rules is provided for this purpose in the law of the various countries. The basic aim of the legal policy has been to promote the employment of persons with a decreased capacity to work in appropriate places of work, making it possible for them to engage in the working process in conformity with their capacities. According to Hungarian law, enterprises shall be under the obligation to re-employ persons who have recovered their working ability, if they became disabled in the enterprise previously through an industrial accident or occupational disease, and their employment was then terminated by granting them a disability pension.[36]

However, in our view, it would be convenient to move forward further, in order to ensure the right to work for the persons with a decreased capacity to work. This proposal results from the circumstance that the Hungarian legal dispositions bearing upon the regulation of the situation of persons with a decreased capacity to work concern, as a rule, the persons, who as a consequence of the deterioration of the state of health, became unable to perform a full-value job in their place of work, suffered from an industrial accident or occupational disease during their labour relations, or must not be employed in their previous field of activity in their place of work on account of the prohibitive disposition of a legal rule.[37] The assistance of the council organs to those with a decreased capacity to work concerning their employment will affect, principally, the persons whose existing employment cannot be continued adequately, and the rules relating to the employment of persons with a decreased capacity to work are not applicable, as a rule, to persons being disabled by birth or who became disabled as a consequence of the deterioration in their state of health which may have occurred irrespective of their actual work. Care should be taken of them, in principle, through the channels of social welfare administration. We are of the opinion that appropriate facilities ought to be granted to these persons also within the scope of the rules of labour law; in particular, their employment ought to be facilitated; e.g. the places of work reserved by the individual enterprises for persons with a decreased capacity to work should be filled, in the absence of persons with a decreased capacity to work among their own employees, by other persons with a decreased capacity to work, not employed by the respective enterprise, and irrespective of the cause of their disabled condition. This would mean the stipulation of a general obligation of the individual enterprises to give preference to persons with a decreased capacity to work in respect of the relevant places of work.

35 Article 49 Act No. IV of 1960 on national defence.
36 Para 1, Article 19 of the Labour Code.
37 Joint Decree No. 1/1967 (XI. 22) of Min. of Lab., of Health, and of Finance, on the regulation of the situation of employees with a decreased capacity to work.

According to the Czechoslovak law, an enterprise is not allowed to refuse to establish a labour relationship with a person with decreased capacity to work making reference to his state of health if his employment was recommended by the competent national committee in a place of work figuring in the list of places of work reserved to citizens falling into this category. The recommendation of the national committee has a compulsory character for the enterprises.[38]

Clearly, the aim of the legal policy has been here to promote the easiest possible employment of persons with a decreased capacity to work, in conformity with their state of health, abilities, and professional qualifications. In line with this, the respective legal rules have to ensure here the necessary bases, to make it possible for the competent State organs to take the decisions needed for the best solution of the problem, with a due co-ordination of social and individual interests.

The realization of the mentioned principle may offer an important field of activity also for the administrative organs of labour placement. As is expressed in the legal literature of the German Democratic Republic, the activity of the said organs is not limited to give assistance concerning employment at appropriate places of work, but they have increasing influence in respect of the obligation of the enterprises, laid down in the Labour Code, to establish places of work that are suitable for employing women, juveniles, workers of older age, and persons with a decreased capacity to work. This obligation includes the establishment of places of work and workshops of sheltered character, set up for workers to be rehabilitated.[39] In our view, this field is bound to have an increasingly high importance for labour placement.[40]

[38] As regards the practical efficiency of the disposition in question, doubts were expressed in the Czechoslovak legal literature, for it is not excluded by the rule in question for an enterprise to refuse to conclude a labour relationship with reference to another cause, although the refusal was based actually on the state of health of the applicant. As concerns applicants with a decreased capacity to work, it is only the protection of general character that may be applied to them, i.e. enterprises are not allowed to refuse the establishment of a labour relationship with applicants recommended by the executive organs of the national committee provided that the conditions required for filling vacant posts of work are met, on the one hand, and unless a serious prohibitive reason exists, on the other. The points the existence of which gives the right to an enterprise to refuse the establishment of a labour relationship are enumerated exhaustively in the legal rule concerned. If the respective national committee disagreed with the cause of refusal, the rules of the respective administrative procedure authorize the committee to take a decision binding the enterprise to employ the applicant in question. See BELINA (1977), p. 81.

[39] BEYREUTHER (1981/1), p. 7.

[40] SCHLEGEL (1980/4), pp. 177–178.

4. THE CAPACITY TO ACT AS SUBJECT AT LAW WITH RESPECT TO LABOUR LAW; THE FORMATION OF EMPLOYMENT RELATIONS

4.1 General considerations

Labour relations are established, modified or terminated, and the parties to them, i.e. employees and the employers, act in specific ways having effect on the conditions of labour. The parties to a labour relationship are subject at labour law and they are the holders of rights and duties deriving from the labour law relation.[1]

The possibility of being an employee or employer, involving specific rights and obligations, has always depended on a given social and economic order. The employee's or employer's capacity to act as subject at law has always been determined by the given legal order.

Considering the mentioned problem from the employee's side, reference should be made here only to the point that the possibility of developing the employee's capacity to act as subject at law emerged as late as in the capitalist society, as this possibility was not afforded in slave-holding societies and in feudalism. In these phases of human history workers' and employees' capacity to carry on productive work was coupled with the means of production not by their deliberate intention. The necessity and possibility of developing the employees' capacity to act as subject at law emerged only with the birth of capitalism, as the employees became then free, from juridical point of view, to dispose of their capacity to work. This possibility was put into form by the concluding of sale and purchase contracts, under the terms of which the employee's capacity to work was coupled with the means of production not without their deliberate intention. By selling his habour the employee gave up, at the same time, his claim for the product or surplus value produced by using his capacity to work. The employee's claim of this kind could not be laid because the means of production were not in collective property but were owned by individuals, persons or companies, so that the employees were not entitled to a partial share of ownership.

Socialist societies have a completely different arrangement. The employee's capacity to act as subject at law means here that the employee, as a result of his partial ownership, has a real possibility to enter into a labour relationship; on the basis of this relationship the workers and employees are entitled to participate directly in the productive activities of society within the community of a given enterprise, and through the agency of the latter; they have a share in the national income, and take part in the management, organization, and

---

[1] For the elements, and the subjects, of socialist legal relations, see in details SZABÓ (1963), p. 359.

supervision of the activities of the enterprise. The right to work means thus in socialism the essential content of an employee's capacity to act as subject at law, and this right receives also appropriate enforcement.[2]

Considering the employers' side, the same course of development may be observed. Only a short reference should be made here to the point that while in capitalism the interests of production require from everybody who is in possession of the means of production that, in view of the fundamental purpose to cause the means of production to function, he or she must have the employer's capacity to act as subject at law, irrespective of the circumstance whether the means of production are owned by a physical person or a legal entity, under the conditions of the socialist social and economic order the employer's capacity to act as subject at law is excluded or severely limited, as will be dealt with in detail in the following paragraph, concerning the areas in which the labour relationship may lead to the individual expropriation of the surplus value.

Concerning the employee's capacity to act as subject at law reference should be made here to the legal capacity and the capacity of disposal under the terms of labour law.

The legal capacity—meaning the parties' capacity to act as subject at law, i.e. that they are holders of rights and duties—constitutes a fundamental point in every branch of law. Besides, it is a concept varying with the course of historical development, i.e. it has always depended on the given stage of development. That the legal capacity of what persons and authorities, and to what extent is recognized by the State.

As a result of newer developments, the possibility of being subject of positive legal relations is recognized and ensured for each citizen, by all legal systems, mostly in the constitution of the State. The detailed regulation of the establishment and termination of the legal capacity is formulated in the norms of the different branches of law; as a matter of fact, the formulation differs according to the character of the social conditions to be regulated, and by considerations the concrete requirements receive. For example, the legal capacity is recognized already for the unborn child *(nasciturus)* under the terms of civil law thereby giving the most extensive regulation of capacity to act as subject at law, in comparison with the other branches of law.[3]

Regarding the capacity to dispose as subject at law, i.e. the capacity of the citizens to acquire rights and undertake obligations for their own name, by their own will, and by means of their own acts, it is also regulated in detail by the legal norms of the distinct branches of law. In fact, the circumstances that matter concerning when a full capacity to dispose can be granted in the various branches of law may differ from each other most substantially. When taking a decision on the capacity of disposal, considering the juridical possibilities coupled with the capacity to dispose, sometimes involving various degrees of risks—the requirements should well differ from the ones which are

[2] WELTNER (1965), p. 75 et seq.
[3] RYBKOVÁ (1970/6), p. 351.

decisive for the regulation of the legal capacity. To take an example, reference may be made again to the rules of civil law which, though recognizing the legal capacity on a broad scale grants the full capacity of disposal only to adults.

The varying contents and extents of the employees' legal capacity and their capacity to dispose are laid down in the respective legal norms of labour law. More precisely, these legal norms contain stipulations as regards: (a) the holders of the legal capacity, from the aspects of labour law, together with the extent thereof, to be understood as persons' capacity, recognized by law, to become subject of labour relationships in order to realize their right to work; (b) the holders of capacity to dispose under the rules of labour law, i.e. the possibility of acquiring rights and undertaking obligations under the rules of labour law, for the own name, by the own will, and through the own act of the authorized person.

After having surveyed the set of problems related to the employee's capacity to act as subject at law attention should be paid to the problem of the employer's capacity to act as subject at law. Several problems present themselves also in this field. First of all whether the associations of enterprises, on the one hand, and the units of organization within an enterprise, on the other, may dispose of an employer's capacity to act as subject at law. It is also a point well worth of interest to set out the sphere within which private employers are allowed to carry on activities in the socialist countries or, in other words, to set out the development of the capacity to act as subject at law in the private sector, from the aspects of labour law. Moreover, however brief, some attention will be paid to the modes of the participation of third parties in the formation of a labour relationship. Admittedly, this problem links more to the question of establishing the labour relationship since, however, within the present chapter we essentially deal with the co-operation among the subjects of labour relationships, the issue dealing with the role of third parties should come also here.

4.2 Legal capacity and capacity to dispose as elements of the employee's capacity to act as subject at law

1. The employee's capacity to act as subject at law raises the question whether the employees' legal capacity involves their capacity to dispose *ipso iure,* or a difference should be made at all between legal capacity and capacity to dispose within the concept of the capacity to act as subject at law, also in the field of labour law, i.e., whether capacity to dispose and legal capacity coincide or not in the field of labour law, in other words, whether the employees' capacity to act as subject at law implies that they are authorized, in any case, to conclude a labour contract for themselves with full legal force.

The main rule is, indeed, that one having the capacity to act as subject at law under the terms of labour law, i.e. allowed to be the subject of a labour relationship, is authorized to conclude a labour contract for himself. This is the consequence of the circumstance that everybody is free to dispose of his own capacity to carry on work. Accordingly, it is not necessary in the field of labour law in general to separate the legal capacity and the capacity to dispose.[4]

Nevertheless, some exceptions have been made from the said principal rule in the legislation of the individual countries, first of all in the interests of juveniles, arising mainly from the consideration that it is a decisive influencing factor for the entire career of a young man whether he enters into a labour relationship having finished his studies in the primary school or continues studying. Accordingly, the different regulations have a protective character, aimed to prevent young men to take decisive steps without due consideration.[5] The different regulation is motivated, at the same time, also by the circumstance that, from the point of view of a given work in prospect, the physical and intellectual abilities of a young man are best known by his parent or legal guardian. On the other hand, some differences of the regulation result from the institution of compulsory school attendance. These two aspects give primarily the basis of our analysis with regard to the relevant regulation of the individual countries. The employee's legal capacity and capacity to dispose may also be separated from each other in some cases of guardianship. (A short reference will be made to this point as well.)

The legal rules of the individual countries do not show conformity in determining the age of years from the completion of which a juvenile is entitled to establish a labour relationship for himself, with no need of consent, on the one hand, or which involve some restrictions, on the other.

Concerning Hungary, the legal capacity to act as employee is now laid down by the 1979 amendment to the Labour Code, replacing the previous provision of fourteen years, by constituting fifteen years of age, saying that employment can be entered into by any person, who shall have completed the fifteenth year of his life, unless an exception is provided in a legal rule, and provided that he completed the attendance of primary school successfully or has been exempted from regular school attendance; between terms, employment can be entered into without fulfilling the two conditions referred to above. Nevertheless, a juvenile not having completed his sixteenth year of age needs the consent of his parent or legal guardian when first entering into employment.[6]

---

4 In conformity with the mentioned rule, it has been expressed in the Soviet legal literature that, as regards the fields of labour law the legal capacity and the capacity to dispose appear simultaneously. They represent in labour law the complex capacity of a physical person to be the subject of a labour relationship, to establish a labour relationship by his own will, and to dispose of his earnings. — Cf. ALEKSANDROV, ed. (1966), p. 150.

5 WELTNER–NAGY (1974), p. 121.

6 Article 18, Para 2 of the Labour Code; Article 5 of the Law-decree on the Enforcement of the Labour Code. The formal requirements of the consent of the legal guardian are not laid down in the respective legal rules. Considering that, unless a disposition to the contrary exists, declarations in connection with labour relations may be made without specific normative requirements (Article 3 of the Labour Code), a verbal consent has a full legal effect as well. In this case it is convenient, however, for the enterprise to make a record, in order to avoid possible subsequent disputes.

The dispositions referred to above mean that, although the legal capacity and the capacity to dispose are granted—from the point of view of labour law, in general—by the relevant rules of Hungarian law with the completion of the fifteenth year of life, the capacity to dispose is not granted in labour law in respect of the first entering into employment of juveniles who have not completed their sixteenth year of life; a person with a limited capacity to dispose is otherwise entitled to enter into a labour relationship even without the consent of his parent or legal guardian. In the absence of the consent of the parent or the legal guardian, the contractual act of will of a juvenile will not be valid, i.e. it will be considered as void; this can be corrected, however by the parent's or legal guardian's subsequent approval of the conclusion of the labour contract concerned.[7]

The position taken by the law of the German Democratic Republic seems to be stricter. Similarly as in the disposition of the previous Hungarian law, the legal capacity in the GDR labour law is granted for the citizens with the completion of their fourteenth year of age; nevertheless, a labour contract can be concluded with a juvenile person before the completion of his eighteenth year of age only upon the preliminary consent in writing of the person in charge of his education.[8] This rule results from the different character of the capacity to dispose in the GDR labour law from that of the legal capacity as is expounded by MICHAS.[9] Thus, juveniles not having completed their eighteenth year of age have a limited capacity to dispose in GDR labour law. Juveniles are allowed to conclude a labour contract which then can be modified or terminated, these acts need, however, the approval of the person in charge of their education.[10] Beyond doubt this is a major restriction in com-

7 Para 2, Article 18 of the Labour Code.

8 Para 3, Article 41 of the 1977 Labour Code of the German Democratic Republic. As is laid down in Article 39 of the Code, a labour relationship may be established with a juvenile by means of a labour contract if the juvenile person has completed his sixteenth year of age by the beginning of the work in question, and complied with the compulsory attendance of the ten-year polytechnical school. It is equally permissible to establish a labour relationship with a juvenile who completed his fourteenth year of age and, for whatever reason but with the approval of the director of the respective school, abandoned the attendance of the ten-year polytechnical school. Nevertheless, the consent of the person authorized to take charge of the education is always required for the establishment of a labour relationship with a juvenile not having completed his eighteenth year of age. The requirement of the attendance of the ten-year polytechnical school prescribed in the Labour Code is a new disposition, in conformity with the actual situation, i.e. the overwhelming majority of the juveniles in question prefers to attend the said ten-year course prior to entering into a labour relationship. Cf. MICHAS (1977/5), p. 132.

9 MICHAS (1970), p. 148 (... to be understood as the capacity to establish, modify or terminate a labour relationship by the own act of the person concerned). — The view was expressed in the legal literature also later that a future employee has to be actually in the position of complying with the responsibility coupled to the conclusion of a labour contract, and this condition can be only met with full age, i.e. completed eighteen years. KIRSCHNER–MICHAS (1978), pp. 13–14.

10 Para (1), Article 49; and Para (1), Article 54 of the GDR Labour Code. NEUMANN (1973/12), p. 369. The person in charge of the education of the juvenile concerned is entitled to lodge a complaint against a notice or dismissal, also by his own will, i.e. without

parison with that provided by the Hungarian law. According to the disposition of a separate GDR rule, the establishment of the first labour relationship of a juvenile not having completed his eighteenth year of age needs, in addition to the afore-mentioned, the approval of the department for professional training and counselling of the district council being competent according to the place of residence of the juvenile.[11] This rule was not invalidated by the Act concerning the coming into force of the 1977 Labour Code.

The arrangement given in the Romanian law has an intermediate place between the regulations as provided by the laws of Hungary and the German Democratic Republic. Here, too, the starting point is the completion of the fourteenth year of age. From this date on, the legal capacity is granted to juveniles. As to details, juveniles with completed fourteen years of age are admitted to temporary work; they may be employed by industrial plants with completed fifteen years of age, with the approval of their parent or guardian. Nevertheless, the work to be performed has to be in conformity with their physical fitness and their knowledge. With the completion of their sixteenth year of age, juveniles are free to conclude a labour contract, without the consent of a third party. Having completed the age mentioned above, each citizen capable of working is then obliged to perform work, qualified as useful for society, until reaching the age specified for retirement by the law, exception made for those who are attending a school.[12] The approval of the parent or guardian, required of those being between their fourteenth to sixteenth year of age, is a condition of their capacity to dispose.[13] Accordingly, the juveniles of the said age have only a restricted capacity to dispose of their own ability to work under labour law.[14]

Similarly as in the stipulation of the law of the German Democratic Republic, the completion of the eighteenth year of age has a significance in the Czechoslovak law as well for, in case of the establishment of a labour relationship by a person younger than eighteen years, the employer is obliged to require an approving declaration of the parent or guardian of the juvenile concerned.[15] Nevertheless, the mentioned declaration is not a document by which the juvenile's capacity to dispose is restricted, since the labour contract—even if concluded by a juvenile against the will of his parent or guardian—will be valid.

---

the consent of the juvenile concerned. DITTRICH (1973/18), p. 567. Nevertheless, the consent of the person authorized to take care of the education of the juvenile is not required to the dismissal. TRÄGER (1974/11), p. 338. On the other hand, the approval of the district council is required. Cf. Para 1 (c), Article 59 the GDR Labour Code.

[11] See Para 6 of the Instruction of August 31, 1966, bearing upon the entering into employment of juveniles having completed their ten-year primary school studies. (*Gbl.* II, p. 624). KAISER–KIRSCHNER–SCHULZ (1974), p. 38.

[12] Article 7 of the 1972 Romanian Labour Code.

[13] FLORESCU (1969/1), pp. 81–95.

[14] For this subject see also GHIMPU (1969/1), pp. 37–38; STANOIU (1967/2), pp. 177–180; BELIGRĂDEANU (1978), p. 39.

[15] Article 164 of the Czechoslovak Labour Code, published in a unified construction in 1975.

Here the intention expressed in the Labour Code is rather to make it possible for the parent or guardian concerned to obtain information of the conclusion of a labour contract by the juvenile under his responsibility in due time, on the one hand, and to ensure the possibility of influencing the declaration of the juvenile by means of a stipulation of the law, on the other.[16] Another provision of the Czechoslovak law, also well worth of interest, prescribes that an employee is allowed to conclude a contract (agreement) involving his financial liability only after having completed his eighteenth year of age. With this rule a connection has been established in the Czechoslovak law between the responsibility for inventories and the capacity to act as subject at law in the field of labour law.[17] As the Hungarian law does not contain a restricting rule of this kind, employees not having completed their eighteenth year of age are allowed e.g. to be employed as shop cashiers. According to WITZ's opinion, the requirement to set up stricter conditions for granting capacity to dispose in labour law in respect of the employee's age limits has been justified in view of the circumstance that the fulfilment of the obligations resulting from a contract (agreement) of this kind needs inevitably the existence of major personal and professional experiences, and young men and women not having completed their eighteenth year of age do not dispose, generally, of these experiences as yet. The rule thus provides equally for the protection of juvenile employees and of collective property.[18] It seems to be convenient to remark in respect of the afore-said that, in our view, the regulation referred to above consitutes a problem more for the legal capacity than for the capacity to dispose in the field of labour law; what matters here is namely that only a person with completed eighteen years of age is allowed to be the subject of a contract (agreement) and, according to the explicit disposition of the relevant legal rule, even his parent or guardian is not entitled to conclude a contract (agreement) for him in which financial liability is concerned.

Apparently the situation is just the opposite in cases in which the employee's legal capacity and the capacity to dispose are granted at a relatively higher age, with the possibility of an escalation towards a lower age. Under the terms of the Soviet law, the employee's legal capacity and the capacity to dispose are granted, e.g., upon the completion of the sixteenth year of age; nevertheless, the employment of persons of fifteen to sixteen years of age is also admitted with the consent of the local trade union committee.[19] (A similar disposition is provided in the Bulgarian legal rule.[20]) According to the concept expressed in the Soviet legal literature, the legal capacity to dispose is admitted in labour law at the age set as an age limit for also the ability to carry on work from both physiological and psychological aspects, and this age is fixed

[16] BERNARD–PAVLÁTOVÁ (1979), p. 47.
[17] Article 11 of the Labour Code of Czechoslovakia.
[18] WITZ (1967), p. 99.
[19] Article 74 of the Bases of the Legislation on Labour Law of the Soviet Union and the Federated Republics: Article 173 of the Labour Code of the Russian Soviet Federated Socialist Republic, 1971.
[20] Article 112 of the 1951 Bulgarian Labour Code.

at the completion of the sixteenth year of life according to the respective rule of the positive law.[21] Considering the circumstance, however, that juveniles having completed their fifteenth year of age are already admitted to conclude a labour contract with the approval of the local trade union committee, the date at which the legal capacity and the capacity to dispose will be granted in the field of labour law will present itself as a problem to be solved. Let us take the situation in practice appearing in cases of this kind as a point of departure. A juvenile having completed his fifteenth year of age but not having completed the sixteenth may be employed by an enterprise with the consent of the trade union committee of the plant,[22] that is, the validity of a labour contract bearing upon the employment of a juvenile requires the consent of the local trade union committee. So far as it concerns the terms of Soviet law, persons not having completed their fifteenth year of age are not at all allowed to be the subject of a labour relationship. With the completion of this age, till the completion of the sixteenth year of age they are allowed to conclude such a labour contract the validity of which will require the consent of the local trade union committee. In our opinion this means that, although the legal capacity from the point of view of labour law is granted to juveniles with the completion of their fifteenth year of age, their capacity to dispose is limited till the completion of their sixteenth year of age, as their declaration stating their will to conclude a labour contract will have a full validity only in case of the consent of the local trade union committee.

According to the regulations of the Polish Labour Code, the completion of the eighteenth year of age constitutes a condition of being employed[23], i.e. the legal capacity and the capacity to dispose are granted with the completion of the eighteenth year of age. In case some conditions—specified in the Code—are met, the employment of juveniles not having completed their eighteenth year of age is also admitted, on condition that the juvenile has completed his fifteenth year of age. The employment of persons not having completed their fifteenth year of age is inadmissible.[24] It is a specific feature of the regulation here referred to that although a juvenile with a limited capacity to dispose is allowed to establish a labour relationship even without the consent of his parent or legal guardian, this latter is entitled, with the approval of the competent court of justice, to cancel the labour contract, if the labour relationship seems to be contrary to the interests of the juvenile. This means that, according to the Polish law, the stipulation of the possibility of subsequent intervention is a satisfactory measure for the protection of the juvenile. The regulation of the law of some other countries prefer however to require the declaration of the parent or legal guardian (with its specified, and varying, legal effect)

[21] This is why there is a view claiming that a limited capacity to dispose is something non-existent in the field of labour law, and, therefore the capacity to commit an offence sets in simultaneously with the beginning of the capacity to dispose under labour law. SIROVATSKAYA (1970/1), p. 115.

[22] DVORNIKOV–LIVSHITS–RUMYANTSEVA (1971), p. 17.

[23] Para 2, Article 22 of the 1974 Polish Labour Code.

[24] Articles 22 and 190 of the 1974 Polish Labour Code.

before the conclusion of a labour contract by a future employee with a restricted capacity to dispose.

Finally, the rule of the Yugoslav law should be mentioned, according to which a labour relationship may be established by a person having completed his fifteenth year of age, and being in a health condition appropriate for performing the work.[25] Here the completion of the fifteenth year of age is the crucial point for acquiring the legal capacity and the capacity to dispose in the field of labour law.

By inference it may be stated that the temporal coincidence of the acquisition of the legal capacity and the capacity to dispose constitutes a main rule of labour law; nevertheless, a separation of the two is not excluded in labour law in case of juveniles. Since, however, this separation is only admitted under conditions protecting the juvenile from consequences that might have harmful effects on his interests, the respective legal rules of the individual countries provide for laying down appropriate measures.[26]

2. As is clear from the above-said, the granting of the employee's legal capacity and of the capacity to dispose depends on the completion of a specified age. This condition is motivated, first of all, by considerations related to the protection of health.[27] The setting of the age limit does not, however, depend simply on some physiological and psychological features but is also related to the acquisition of some kind of primary qualification of education. In view of this, the requirements in connection with compulsory school attendance play some role in respect of the regulation of the employee's legal capacity and the capacity to dispose. Simultaneously with the increase of the level of general education, the age limit of the employee's legal capacity will also show an upward tendency, in view of the general requirements of legal policy saying that the entering into a labour relationship should be allowed only after having acquired a specified minimum degree of erudition.

A trend may be observed in the positive law of some countries favouring to set higher the age limit of the employee's legal capacity. The earlier rule

[25] According to Article 10 of the 1973 Act bearing upon the mutual relations of workers engaged in associated work, to qualify as an employee engaged in associated work it is necessary to comply with the conditions laid down by the basic organization of associated work, as well as with the stipulations of the law, the social convention and with the agreement on self-management. Prior to having completed the fifteenth year of age and in case of non-fulfilment of the general sanitary conditions, the employee's qualification for associated work cannot be obtained. A similar disposition is provided in Article 168 of the 1976 Act on associated work.

[26] As for example the requirement of consent; the duty of letting the parent or legal quardian know about the conclusion of the labour contract; the declaration of the invalidity of the labour contract in a given case, etc.

[27] An explicit reference is made to this point in subsection 2, Article 191, Para 1, of the Polish Labour Code, stipulating that the employment of a juvenile is only admissible if ... (2) a medical certificate is presented testifying that the work would not cause any injury to the health of the juvenile applicant. — Regarding Hungary, it is stipulated in Decree No. 12/1972 (VII. 11) Min. of Health that, in order to ensure the increased protection of the health of juveniles, minors to be employed for physical work, or already performing it, have to pass a medical examination.

in the Soviet Union, admitting the employment of juveniles with completed fourteen years of age with the approval of the local trade union committee, was modified in 1956, setting higher the age limit, to fifteen years.[28] — This disposition of the Soviet legislation was followed by the 1957 amendment of the Bulgarian Labour Code, equally setting higher the lower age limit of the employee's legal capacity, to fifteen years.[29] —Similarly, the former lower age limit set for entering into a labour relationship was also modified from fourteen to fifteen years according to a disposition of the 1966 Albanian Labour Code.[30] As was pointed out in the course of the Parliament debate of the Albanian Bill, the age limit had to be set higher as a consequence of the introduction of the compulsory school attendance comprising eight years, i.e. it had to be considered that the end of school attendance coincided mostly with the completion of the fifteenth year of age of juveniles.[31] — Regarding Romania, reference is made to the preceding comments recalling the rule which allows for juveniles being within their fourteenth to sixteenth year of age to conclude a labour contract with the consent of their parents or legal guardian. Taking into consideration, however, the ten-year period of compulsory school attendance,[32] the entering into a labour relationship prior to the completion of the sixteenth year of age has a practical significance only during school holidays.—As regards Poland, the employment of persons not having completed their fourteenth year of age was inadmissible until 1961.[33] Then the age limit was set higher, i.e. to fifteen years, in view of the introduction of the compulsory attendance of the eight-year courses of the secondary school.[34] This concept is clearly expressed in the Polish Labour Code, prescribing the accomplished attendance of the primary school as a condition for the employment of juveniles.[35] The concept to subject the granting of the employee's legal capacity to the completion of the courses of the primary school is expressed unequivocally in the 1969 amendment to the Czechoslovak Labour Code in which, contrary to the basic rule of 1965, the granting of the employee's legal capacity and the capacity to dispose is linked with the first day of the calendar year in

[28] Law-decree of the Presidium of the Supreme Council of the Soviet Union dated December 13, 1956; further: GOLOVANOVA–TROSHIN (1960), pp. 11–12.

[29] *Izvestiya*, No. 92 of 1957.

[30] Article 12 of the Labour Code of the Albanian People's Republic.

[31] *Dreyteshia Popullore*, 1966/5.

[32] "The basic elements of culture are guaranteed for all citizens by means of the ten-year compulsory school attendance." Article 6, Act. No. 11/1968 on education in the Socialist Republic of Romania. See *Official Gazette of the Socialist Republic of Romania*, 1968/12.

[33] Act No. 226/1958 July 2, on professional training, teaching for a specified work, the conditions of the employment of juveniles in their place of work, and the time of entering into labour relationship: Article 2, *Dziennik Ustaw*, 1958/45, No. 226.

[34] Articles 7 and 45 of the Act No. 160/1961 July 15, on the development of instruction and education, *Dziennik Ustaw*, 1961/32, No. 160.

[35] Subsection 1, Para 1, Article 119 of the Polish Labour Code. The minister of labour is authorized to specify the cases in a decree in which it is permitted, exceptionally, to employ juveniles who failed to finish their studies in the primary school, on the one hand, or juveniles having finished their studies in the primary school, but not having completed their fifteenth year of age on the other. Article 191, Para 5, of the Labour Code.

which the citizen finished his/her compulsory studies.[36] Contrary to the earlier regulation (in which the completion of fifteen years of age was laid down as a condition for granting the employee's legal capacity), the lower age limit is not at all mentioned in the amendment which, in turn, contains only a reference to the completion of the compulsory studies. In this respect, MESTITZ remarked that the condition of completed fiften years of age was omitted, essentialy, to make it possible, for the enterprises to conclude apprentice and labour contracts with juveniles prior to the finishing of their compulsory studies, to ensure the necessary manpower recruitment this way. This arrangement must not involve, however, a prejudice to the compulsory school attendance; it is thus laid down in the law that a date preceding the day of the completion of the compulsory school attendance cannot be stipulated as the starting day of entering into work. A juvenile is allowed to conclude a labour contract at the beginning of the calendar year of the completion of his compulsory school attendance but he is not allowed to enter into work before the completion of the compulsory school attendance.[37] Turning to the Hungarian Labour Code, it stipulates also the successful finishing of the primary school or an exemption from regular school attendance, in addition to the completion of fifteen years of age, as the condition for the legal capacity.[38] This stipulation virtually covers the period of school term in the year in which the juvenile completes his sixteenth year of age, taking into account that this is anyhow the end of the period of compulsory school attendance.[39] Apart from what has been said above, it is explicitly allowed by the law that juveniles, having completed their fourteenth year of age, enter into work during their school holdays, without being bound to the condition referred to above.

We come to the general conclusion that the systems of legal norms of labour law and the law of education are related to each other in this field, and they also complete each other. Regarding the situation in the past, as an example reference can be made to the circumstance that until the First World War the employment of children was in general facilitated by the fact that, for juveniles over twelve years of age, compulsory school attendance was either completely unknown or, even in case of legal provisions, these were not put into effect consistently.[40] However, a continuous broadening of the range of dispositions prohibiting the employment of juveniles not having completed their fourteenth year of age is witnessed today, together with the requirement that the period of compulsory school attendance should be extended, put down also in the

[36] Act No. 153/1969 Sb. on the amendment and completion of the Labour Code, Para 1, Article 11. *Sbirka zákonu,* No. 1969/47.

[37] MESTITZ (1970/2), p. 9.

[38] Para 2, Article 18 of the Labour Code.

[39] Para 2, Article 3 Act No. III of 1961 on the system of education of the Hungarian People's Republic.

[40] In France, e.g., the proportion of school attendance of juveniles from 11 to 18 years made out approximately 3.4 per cent in 1901; and, for 10 000 children of 13 years of age, 9 660 failed to continue studying. Substantial changes were achieved in this field only as late as in the years following the First World War. CRÉMIEUX-BRILHAC (1965), p. 97–98.

constitution in the individual countries.[41] The first conventions accepted by the International Conference on Labour Problems set a lower age limit (i.e. the fourteenth year of age) of employment in the areas of industry, transportation, agriculture, fishing etc. The conventions in question were revised several times, with a view to adjusting them to the increasing demands of humanitarian and other topical aspects.[42] — For the time being, it may be regarded as a generally accepted principle that the beginning of the employee's legal capacity should be linked with the end of the compulsory school attendance. Hence, the extension of the compulsory school attendance beyond the completion of the fourteenth year of age will involve setting higher the age limit of the employee's legal capacity.

3. The separation of the legal capacity from the capacity to dispose in the field of labour law may prove to be necessary, in fact, in some cases of guardianship. It was WELTNER who pointed out that the possibility of concluding a labour contract directly, i.e. without the participation of the legal guardian, has to be granted to interdicted majors with a limited capacity to dispose, as the rules of labour law with an indispensable binding force provide, as a rule, automatically also for the protection of the interests of interdicted persons.[43] The provision in Hungarian labour law allowing for persons with a limited capacity of disposal to establish a labour relationship even without the consent of their legal guardian is in conformity with the views explained by WELTNER in this respect.[44]

A regulation of the same kind may be found in the Polish Labour Code, allowing persons with a limited capacity of disposal to establish a labour relationship without the consent of their legal guardian. Nevertheless, as has been mentioned above, the guardian is entitled to cancel the labour relationship, with the approval of the competent court of justice, if it seems to be contrary to the interests of the person with a limited capacity to dispose.[45]

There are regulations with different provisions. The Czechoslovak law provides, e.g., that if the employee's capacity to dispose has been limited by a court of justice in respect of the conclusion of a labour contract, the contract has to be concluded by his guardian.[46] In this case the employee's capacity to dispose is limited from the point of view of labour law, consequently he cannot be the subject of a labour relationship without the specified legal declaration

[41] According to Article 145 of the Weimar Constitution, the primary school of eight years at least ought to serve to realize compulsory school attendance. This was introduced also in other countries.

[42] SZÁSZY (1969), pp. 609 et seq.

[43] WELTNER (1965), pp. 141–142.

[44] First sentence, Para 5 of the Decree relating to the enforcement of the Labour Code.

[45] Para 3, Article 22 of the Polish Labour Code.

[46] According to the stipulations of Article 12 of the Labour Code and Article 10 of the Civil Code, the court of justice establishes the capacity to dispose in civil and labour law simultaneously, and appoints a guardian for both relations; cf. BERNARD–PAVLÁTOVÁ (1979), p. 50. See also Article 12 of the Czechoslovak Labour Code, according to which the court of justice sets the limit of the restriction of the employee's capacity to dispose because the employee is merely capable of performing specified legal acts.

of his guardian. This does not mean that the will of the interdicted person should not be duly considered when concluding a labour contract in the form mentioned above, as even a person with a limited capacity to dispose cannot be forced to carry on work, but formally the guardian acts when a labour contract is to be concluded, therefore, after the conclusion of the contract by the guardian, the interdicted person need not make a formal legal declaration.

It is a more complicated situation if an employee has been interdicted by a court of justice with the exclusion of his capacity to dispose. In fact, the interdicted person is permanently and completely unable, in general, to produce the required understanding in these cases, consequently a legally relevant consent to the conclusion of a labour contract cannot be produced either. In view of this situation, the problem presents itself whether the guardian is then entitled to conclude the labour contract. Considering the 1969 revision of the Czechoslovak Labour Code, the conclusion can be drawn that even a person interdicted by a court of justice with the exclusion of his capacity to dispose may conclude a labour contract through the intermediary of a guardian.[47] Admitting this possibility, the Czechoslovak legislation had in mind some types of simple work, e.g. sweeping, basket weaving, work in agriculture, etc., that can be performed even by interdicted persons with the exclusion of their capacity to dispose. — This possibility is not provided by the Hungarian law, taking as basis the consideration that entering into a labour relationship means always a personal volitional activity of the person concerned. It is another point whether it is correct to exclude interdicted persons with no capacity to dispose left for them from the possibility of carrying on work. The answer should be in the negative, in our view, as the performance of work may contribute to the recovery of a person who was interdicted by a court of justice with the exclusion of his capacity to dispose on account of his mental state of health or mental deficiency. The medical cure performed in an institute specially fit for it is destined to achieve recovery; nevertheless, even if the performance of work is not effected within the framework of a labour relationship in these cases but is based on special sanitary rules, this ensures particular guarantees in so far that the performance of work by the person being cured should not cause any harm to him but, instead, should contribute to his recovery.[48]

---

[47] A disposition is laid down in subsection 1, Para 32 of the Supplementary Act of the Labour Code as follows: "The organization is obliged to conclude the labour contract in writing. Nevertheless, if the period of the labour relationship to be established is not longer than one month, the obligation referred to above will be binding only upon request of the employee concerned or if this latter *was deprived of his capacity to dispose by a resolution of a court of justice* (italics from the author), or his capacity to dispose was restricted by a resolution of a court of justice."

[48] According to the rule laid down in subsection 1, Para 64 of Decree No. 15/1972 (VIII. 5) Min. of Health, the in-patient may be given a reward in each month to the charge of the budget of the hospital (institute for labour therapeutics) in accordance with his capacity to carry on work, revealed in the treatment of labour therapeutics, and in conformity with the work done. The amount of the reward is fixed by the competent head physician of the hospital (head of the institute for labour therapeutics) for each case. The pay for work in labour therapeutics is in the form of a reward and not by wages.

4.3 The employer's capacity to act as subject at law

The employer's capacity to act as subject at law has always been in the closest relation with the conditions of the property of the means of production and following from this, with the given social conditions. With regard to the capitalist social system, anybody having legal capacity is entitled to conclude a labour contract as an employer for, as VINCENTI pointed out,[49] production requires that anybody possessing means of production should also have an employer's capacity to act as subject at law. There is no difference between the capacity to act as subject at law nuder civil law and the employer's capacity to act as subject at law for the very reason that te legal relationhs in connection with the performance of work are in general placed within the framework of civil law in the non-socialist system of law; a separate status to some extent was left only for the sector of civil service but even here the differences are by now far less deep than they were earlier.[50]

As regards the socialist social order, in which, with the collective property of the overwhelming majority of the means of production, the economic organizations can comply with their tasks only if they are granted the employer's capacity to act as subject at law also in the field of labour law (apart from their same capacity in the fields of civil and administrative law),[51] in order to make it possible for them to establish the community of the enterprise, the economic organizations are authorized to employ workers, in conformity with the requirements of production; the more they are obliged to do so, since otherwise they could not comply with the duties and liabilities devolving on them by the stipulation of legal rules. More or less, the said regulations are characteristic of all socialist countries and they may be considered as generally valid regulations.

In a number of countries, the employers are organizations or organs acknowledged as legal entities. In these cases, the employer's legal capacity in labour law is understood to mean that the enterprises, institutions and organizations as legal entities possess the particular capacity to enter into labour relations with their employees by means of their relevant bodies or representatives.[52] Their general problems are regulated in the socialist countries by the rules of the civil or the economic law. In the German Democratic Republic, e.g., the category of legal entities was restituted with the Civil Code of 1975.[53]

---

49 VINCENTI (1942), p. 47.

50 Cf. TRÓCSÁNYI (1975/1), pp. 73 et seq.

51 WELTNER 1964/6, p. 431; SMIRNOV (1971/2), pp. 19–27; GUIMPU–STEFANESCU (1969/1), pp. 41–49.

52 MIRONOV (1975), p. 19: The holder of the legal capacity in the field of labour law is the enterprise proper and not its administration; the enterprise as a whole and not its administration is responsible for all liabilities originating from labour relations. KULIKOVA (1979/6), p. 40.

53 This is also taken into consideration by the Decree of November 8, 1979, bearing upon the combines of State-owned manufacturing (producing) plants, their enterprises, and on State enterprises (*Gbl.* I. No. 38).

There are other socialist countries in which the employer's capacity to act as subject at law is not bound to the institutions of legal entities acknowledged under the rules of positive law. The Polish Labour Code contains, e.g., an explicit rule declaring that a unit of organization, engaging workers, is to be regarded as an employer even if it is not acknowledged to be a legal entity.[54] With regard to Czechoslovakia, the institution of legal entity is beyond the limits of actual legal regulation.[55] Under the terms of Hungarian law, an economic association is not a legal entity but, provided that it disposes of a separate organization, it has the capacity to act as employer.[56] It is however more general that the employers are legal entities.

Attention should be drawn in the following to the problem of the enterprises' varying capacity to act as subject at law in the field of labour law, examining it, particularly in the case of the formation of major groups, i.e. units of organization, associations, etc., on the one hand, and from the point of view of minor units (plants, workshops, etc.), within the framework of an enterprise, on the other. Taking as basis the legal rules of the individual socialist countries, the following inferences can be reached:

1. Regarding the associations of enterprises, the legal rules of the socialist countries show different arrangements. According to the law of the German Democratic Republic, a member enterprise forming part of a combine of industrial plants retains its employer's capacity to act as subject at law i.e. this capacity will not be transferred to the combine itself.[57] Just as the respective enterprises, the combines have an independent status in the field of labour law.[58] In Romania, the central industrial organizations are entitled to claim for the employer's capacity to act as subject at law in respect of the conclusion of labour contracts but this claim is not indispensable.[59] Regarding the regulations in Czechoslovakia bearing upon industrial concerns, they are granted the capacity to act as subject at law, thus in principle, labour contracts are concluded by them. However, the statutes of the industrial concern may stipulate cases in which the member companies of the industrial concern are entitled to proceed in legal relations on their own behalf, in the field of economic, labour, and civil law.[60] Accordingly, the cases in which a member company of an industrial concern is authorized to proceed in relations of labour law on its

---

[54] Article 3 of the Polish Labour Code.

[55] The institution of legal entity ceased to be acknowledged by the Czechoslovak Economic Code of 1964, and it was replaced by the institution of legal capacity.

[56] Decree No. 5/1972 (III. 23) Min. of Lab.

[57] KAISER–KIRSCHNER–SCHULZ (1974), p. 21; KLINGER (1980/3), pp. 194 et seq.

[58] Article 17 of the Labour Code of the German Democratic Republic.

[59] HARAGA (1975/8), pp. 17–21.

[60] As regards statutes, they are issued by the competent minister in respect of the organizations subordinated to the direction of the ministry, in conformity with the principles approved by the government, while in respect of the organizations directed by the national committees they are issued directly by the government. Cf. subsection 1, Para 46, of the Economic Code. Cf. also subsection 2, Para 8 of the Govt. Decree No. 91/1974 Sb.

own behalf are always put down in the statutes of the industrial concern in question and as a consequence the dispositions vary from concern to concern.[61]

In respect of trusts, the regulations are different. The member companies of a trust retain their own capacity to act as subject at law, i.e. a trust does not conclude labour contracts on behalf of the member companies as it has no capacity to act as subject at law in the field of labour law.[62]

Concerning the Soviet Union, the rules of the positive law, on the one hand, know the term legal entity as regards economic organizations—as is put down partly in the Civil Code and partly in the regulations on State-owned enterprises—while in the legal rules bearing upon associations of production, combines of industrial or agricultural plants, on the other, it has not been laid down unequivocally whether or not the individual economic units of the said associations possess legal capacity to act on their behalf.[63] Viewing this situation, disputes emerged in the relevant literature; some of their aspects, related to labour law, will be commented below. As the supporters of one of the disputed views claim, the rights and obligations stipulated in the contracts concluded by the economic associations or combines and workshop units concern only the production association (combine) as legal entity, while the individual internal units belonging to them do not become subjects of the contracts concerned. If a labour contract is concluded by an internal unit it is done on behalf of the association or combine, as the unit does not qualify as a separate legal entity.[64] According to another view, equally represented in the Soviet literature, the unit's individual capacity to act as subject at law in the field

[61] SABOL (1975/4), p. 31; SABOL (1976/1), p. 32.

[62] It is pointed out in the Czechoslovak legal literature that a two-phase control, i.e. that of the competent ministry and the industrial concern, is realized in the case of concerns, while for the trusts the control is effected in three channels, i.e. that of the ministry, the trust, and the enterprise. The legal nature of the member companies of the industrial concern is disputed in the literature. ČAPEK, e.g., questioned SABOL's view claiming for the member companies of the concerns 'to be socialist organizations of a new type' with a specific capacity to act as subject at law, for in such case the three-channel system of control would be effected also with respect to them. Cf. ČAPEK (1976/9), pp. 774 et seq. See also for this sphere of problems TRAVNIČEK (1978/4), p. 125; KALENSKÁ (1979/8), pp. 465–475. The author points out the separation of the capacities to act as subject at law under the labour law and the economic law. In her opinion, an enterprise subordinated to a concern may have full capacity to act as subject at law under labour law, and its capacity as subject at law is merely partial under economic law. This situation may appear just as well in the opposite way in respect of budgetary organs of a narrower range: not all organizations financed from the State budget possess the capacity to act as subject at law under labour law whereas they have full capacity to act as subject at law under economic law.

[63] Cf. the 1961 legislation of the Soviet Union in the field of civil law: 'Regulation on socialist State-owned producing enterprises', approved by Decree No. 731 of the Council of Ministers of the Soviet Union, dated October 4, 1965; see also 'General regulation on the all-union combines and on those at the level of republics', approved by Decree No. 140 of the Council of Ministers of the Soviet Union, dated March 2, 1973; and, 'Regulation on combines of industrial plants', approved by Decree No. 2121 of the Council of Ministers of the Soviet Union, dated March 27, 1974.

[64] YAKOVLEVA–SOBTCHAK (1975/5), p. 87.

of labour law subsists, i.e. the enterprises, scientific research institutes, project or design offices, production units concerned with technology, etc. belonging to the combine are entitled to establish and terminate labour relations. The transfer of an employee from a given production unit to another always means entering into another labour relationship, with another enterprise, and the employee's consent to it is required. The situation is different, however, in the field of trade and services in which the functioning of several branches, separate units, places of work, shops, etc. within one economic organization is usual and the units are not entitled to employ and dismiss employees. Then the problem arises whether or not the employee's consent is required to his transfer to another job. If the labour contract contains a provision according to which the employee will have to perform the contracted work in a specified site (workshop, sale shop, etc.), a transfer to another unit of the employing enterprise needs the employee's consent. In the absence of such provision, the transfer may take place without the employee's consent.[65]

As is clear from the above, the relation between the association of enterprises and the organizational units, or more exactly, the problem of the employer capacity to act as subject at law has not been regulated by the law of the various socialist countries in a uniform way, and a model has not been formulated either. The concept of the so-called partial legal entity has appeared in the Hungarian legal literature, to which we wish to make only a short reference here.[66] Admittedly, the capacity to act as subject at law may be unnecessary in the external economic relations of organizational units, but its existence may be desirable when the issue of organizing the efficient performance of collective work within the unit arises.[67] Therefore the formulations which in relation to the enterprises leave the employer's capacity to act as subject at law untouched also when these enterprises organize themselves into associations seem to be more flexible.

2. Regarding the other problem, i.e. whether or not the various sections of an enterprise should possess the employer's capacity to act as subject at law, a negative answer may be taken for granted as a general rule; accordingly, when concluding a labour contract, they proceed on behalf of the enterprise exceptionally; it may occur that certain industrial workshops possess the employer's capacity to act as subject at law, but only if the internal regulations of the enterprise contain dispositions in this sense.[68]

---

[65] HRUSTALEV (1975/5), p. 61; NIKHITINSKY–GLASURIN (1976/23), p. 724.

[66] PÉTER (1966/1), pp. 1–7. — Comments on the study: *Döntőbíráskodás*, 1966/9, pp. 338–344. According to Para 47, subsection 2 of Act No. VI of 1977 on State-owned enterprises, the trusts and the enterprises working under their direction are legal entities; therefore their employer's capacity to act as subject at law has raised no problems.

[67] EÖRSI (1968), p. 214.

[68] In Czechoslovakia, for example, statutes issued on the basis of the Economic Code may contain dispositions of this character. However, practice has shown that if the employer's capacity to act as subject at law in the field of labour law is granted to internal units of the economic organization, in the sphere of reality it usually happens that it is used only

The requirement of granting the employer's capacity to act as subject at law to the various subordinated sections of an enterprise is usually supported with the argument that the units in question are autonomous within the mechanism of the national economy, their management is based on their own separate economic accounting, they perform the duties conferred upon them by the State at their own responsibility, so, they should be granted the right to establish labour relations. The sphere in which this requirement is enforced in the positive law of the socialist countries has however been rather narrow so far.

Yugoslavia is an exception in this respect. The basic units of associated work organizations became gradually autonomous there and, accordingly, acquired the status of legal entities, therefore, the employees can set up labour relations with them. The extent of the status of legal entity will as far as the associated enterprises, integrated economic groups and the enterprises with separate basic organizational units are concerned depend on the agreement of self-management bearing upon associations joining in the framework of economic organizations.[69]

3. A problem also related to the capacity to act as subject at law in the field of labour law, to which the following comments will briefly refer, is to determine who is/are authorized to conclude labour contracts on behalf of the enterprise.

It is a general rule that the employees of an enterprise authorized to conclude labour contracts are mentioned in the respective legal dispositions, enterprise statutes and working orders, regulations of organization, etc. However, taking into consideration that the establishment of labour relations falls within the sphere of the exercise of the rights of the employer, the authorized person is primarily the director (manager) of the enterprise.[70] Beside the director, his deputy or another leading staff member may be authorized to conclude a contract. It is reasonable to specify in the statutes of the enterprise which are the various spheres of activities concerning which the persons assigned may employ workers.

Regarding the questions of responsibility in cases a contract was concluded, on behalf of an enterprise, by an unauthorized person, the legal rules of the countries considered here contain no dispositions. In the legal literature the view has been expressed that in such cases the enterprise is still liable in

---

in relation to employees performing physical work. Report by MYDLIK, A., Bratislava, September 4, 1976. — With regard to the German Democratic Republic, the point whether an internal unit or a department should or should not be regarded as an 'enterprise', is regulated in the statutes of the combines of industrial and agricultural plants or enterprises concerned (Para 3, Article 17 of the Labour Code of the German Democratic Republic).

69 YOVANOVIĆ (1973/2–3), p. 232. According to Para 45 of the 1974 Constitution, the basic units of associated work organizations are legal entities.

70 Dispositions in this sense are provided in Para 3, subsection (b), Article 12, of the Hungarian Act No. VI of 1977; Article 23 of the Decree issued on March 28, 1973 in the German Democratic Republic, bearing upon the aims, rights and obligations of the State-owned enterprise, combines of industrial enterprises, and syndicates; and, for the Soviet Union, in the Labour Code of the Soviet Socialist Republic of Lithuania.

respect of the employee, adding that there are no obstacles in the way of the enterprise as regards the enforcement of disciplinary or even financial responsibility against the employee who exceeded his authorization. This seems to be reasonable as otherwise the employees would find themselves in a disadvantageous position, i.e. they ought to check the existence of the authorization of the person proceeding on behalf of the enterprise in respect of the conclusion of contracts in each case and, evidently, this could not be expected from them.[71] The same is valid with respect to the later formation of the labour relation, either within the employer's exercising his right to instruction or outside that.

4. As regards the private sector, the question of the employer's capacity to act as subject at law in the field of labour law is to be dealt with separately under the conditions of the socialist society. This is explained by the circumstance that the reasons for the existence of the private sector are acknowledged by the legislations of the various socialist countries within different frameworks and the employer's capacity to act as subject at law is adjusted to the said frameworks. The 1974 Act of the German Democratic Republic bearing upon the amendment and supplement of the 1968 Constitution stipulates, e.g., that economic associations serving to establish economic power, in the private sector, are inadmissible. The smaller workshops of handicraft and other industries based mostly on own work, are established according to the regulations of the positive law, and they enjoy the support of the State in respect of exercising their responsibility towards the socialist society (Article 14 of the Act referred to above). As regards legal policy, the dispositions serve to ensure that the capacity of the private sector could be used more intensively for the fulfilment of the plans of people's economy. In accordance with this principle the district councils are authorized to fix plan targets for handicraftsmen. The targets contain the indices relating to the plans bearing upon services and repair work in particular and fix the number of employees required for complying with the targets.[72]

Turning to Poland, the provisions of the 1952 Constitution, amended and completed by the 1976 Act may be recalled, stipulating that the People's Republic of Poland recognizes and protects individual property, and the right to heritage in respect of land, buildings, and other means of production being in the possession of peasants, artisans and handicraftsmen (Article 17). Within the limits of the said provisions smaller industrial enterprises owned by individuals are allowed to carry on their activities and even the private ownership of major agricultural estates is recognized.[73]

In conformity with these provisions, the owners of the said assets are allowed to employ workers in order to utilize the means of production owned by them,

[71] PRUDINSKY (1974/4), p. 54.

[72] Cf. Decree issued on July 12, 1972, providing support for the handicraft industry in relation of its performance of servicing and repair work, and on the regulation of the private small-scale industry's activities *Gbl*. II. 1972/47, pp. 541 et seq.

[73] SWIECICKI (1969), p. 127.

i.e. they possess the employer's capacity to act as subject at law within the said sphere.[74]

With regard to Hungary, private artisans are allowed to give employment to individuals as follows: (a) six members of their family as aids; (b) three employees or outside workers; (c) three trainees provided that they have a skilled worker's qualification corresponding to their profession or on condition that at least one such worker or assisting family member is employed that has skilled worker's qualification corresponding to the trainees profession.

The total number of employees or outside workers, and the assisting family members must not exceed, however, nine persons.[75]

Private tradesmen running a restaurant, coffee-house, canteen (buffet) and camping, are allowed to employ nine workers, while other private tradesmen are allowed to employ five persons, and family members, as well as three trainees. The total number of employees and assisting family members must not exceed twelve.[76]

With regard to the regulations in Romania, the maximum number of employees of private artisans has been set to three persons, depending on the characteristics of the trade, and the volume of the workshop, but the employment is only permitted in respect of persons who have been trainees with the private artisan and, besides, continue to work in the workshop of this latter after having obtained their professional qualification.[77] On the other hand, the law-decrees bearing upon the regulation of private trade do not contain dispositions concerning the employees of retail dealers.[78] Virtually private trading in Romania is completely negligible, and retail dealers are not allowed to have employees.

In Bulgaria, retail dealers are allowed to employ one assistant, provided that

[74] Regarding the rules relating to private sector's activities see the Act No. 1964 of June 8, 1972 (Dz. U., 1972/23), and the Act No. 158 of July 18, 1974 on trading and other related activities (Dz. U., 1974/27). See also the Decree of the Council of Ministers, dated November 20, 1974 bearing upon the regulation of labour relations within which the employer is a physical person (Dz. U., 1974/45), and the Resolution of the Council of Ministers, dated November 3, 1977, on trading units acting on the basis of a commission contract (Monitor Polski, 1977/29).

[75] Para 10 of Decree No. 4/1981 (IX. 9) Min. of Ind., on the Enforcement of Law-decree No. 14 of 1977, amended by Law-decree No. 16 of 1981 on small-scale industry.

[76] Article 12 of the Resolution No. 10/1982 (V. 14) Min. of Dom. Trade, on the Enforcement of Law-Decree No. 15 of 1977; modified by Law-Decree No. 7 of 1982 on private trade.

[77] Article 6, Act No. 13/1968 on the practice of professions. Buletinul Official, 1968, part I, p. 64. Besides, training in small-scale industry is guaranteed, too, by virtue of Article 11 of the Constitution of the Socialist Republic of Romania, according to which the ownership of the workshops of private artisans is guaranteed by the State. Re-published in Buletinul Official, 1974/56.

[78] Law-decree No. 12, Buletinul Official, January 25, 1952, Cl. 37–38; Law-decree No. 306, Buletinul Official, September 6, 1952, Cl. 59–65; 1972/3; Law-decree on domestic trade, Buletinul Official, 1972/4.

this is justified by their being physically deficient persons. As regards artisans, they are not at all allowed to act as employers in Bulgaria.[79]

Turning to Yugoslavia, it may be noted that, unless an exception is stipulated in the law, the citizens are allowed to carry on own-account private-based enterprising work using their own means of production; the relevant conditions and the spheres of activities in respect of this work are put down in legal rules. Other person's auxiliary work which is permitted, is also regulated by the rules.[80]

On the basis of the respective dispositions of the constitution of the Soviet Union, and also of Czechoslovakia (their constitutions have almost completely identical wording),[81] it is clear that private persons possess the employer's capacity to act as subject at law only in a very limited sphere, and essentially, a labour contract may be concluded only for carrying out household work for the employer, including auxiliary work linked with literary or other creative activities, such as typing, shorthand writing, etc.[82]

After having presented the existing regulations and views bearing upon the employer's capacity to act as subject at law in the individual socialist countries, our summarizing remark would be as inferring that the observance of the limits of the employer's capacity to act as subject at law has always been an obligation binding the employer in relation to the State; if these limits are not observed this must not go together with any prejudice to the employee. An excess of the limits of the employee's capacity to act as subject at law involves the sanction of invalidity; a non-observance of the limits of the employer's capacity to act as subject at law cannot be sanctioned with invalidity, therefore

[79] See: Decree No. 37/1980 (VII. 22) on the carrying on handicraft and small dealer activities of the citizens (*Dr. Vestnik*, 1980/57); see also: Decree No. 2/1981 Min. of Dom. Trade (*Dr Vestnik*, 1981/16) on the retail trade activities of private persons, based on contracts with domestic trade organizations. The regulation of this decree provides further possibilities for private persons to carry on commercial activities.

[80] See Articles 64 and 68 of the 1974 Constitution of the Socialist Federative Republic of Yugoslavia; see also Article 165 of the Act on associated work; the labour relationships between citizens having the right to dispose of their own means of production and individuals working for these citizens, in the frameworks of the private sector, are to be regulated in conformity with the provisions of this Act.

[81] By virtue of Article 9 of the 1936 Constitution of the Soviet Union, small-scale private economic activities based on the own work of privately farming and working peasants and handicraftsmen are permitted, excluding, however, the exploitation of other persons' work. Article 9 of the 1960 Constitution of the Czechoslovak Socialist Republic permits small-scale private economic activities, based on the citizens' own personal work, and excluding the exploitation of outside labour, within the frameworks of the socialist economic system. The only difference between the dispositions of the two constitutions is that privately farming and working peasants and handicraftsmen are mentioned in the Soviet Constitution, while this is missing from the Czechoslovak Constitution.

[82] Accordingly, there is no prohibition for the citizens in either State to employ a domestic aid, a driver, a caretaker, a nurse, etc. As for the Soviet Union, see ALEK-SANDROV, ed. (1966), p. 229. — Other forms of private-based contracting (entrepreneur) activities are penalized in the Soviet Union. Cf. BERTNOVSKAYA (1972/9), pp. 52–53. Under the terms of the Czechoslovak Labour Code, a labour contract between private citizens may be concluded only for rendering services that meet own personal needs.

a labour relationship within this sphere may be terminated only by giving notice bearing upon the future.[83]

The extent of the employer's capacity to act as subject at law has always depended on the given social and economic systems; it is another point that, using its specific means, the law may also contribute to the formation and development of social and economic conditions. Having in mind, e.g., the requirement of the satisfaction of the increasing demands of the population, the increasing significance of raising the standard of services on a broad range appears as a natural consequence, and the private sector of economy may fill an actual gap when meeting these requirements. As a matter of fact, the role of the law is not restricted here merely to comply with them but, by making use of its regulating role, it may contribute indirectly to increase the standard of services, e.g., by ensuring, among other points, the employer's capacity to act as subject at law within the appropriate limits.

[83] WELTNER (1964/6), p. 341.

5. THE ESTABLISHING OF EMPLOYMENT RELATIONSHIPS

5.1 Forms of the establishing of employment relationships

In the socialist countries, with the exception of Yugoslavia, the most important forms of establishing labour relationships, are the various labour contracts. There is a view claiming for the contract to be the only basis of the establishing of labour relationships,[1] nevertheless, the institutions of appointment and election together with commission, appear in almost all countries reviewed here, beside the contract, as acts leading to labour relationships.[2]

---

[1] By Romanian law, according to Act 1 of 1970 on the organization of labour and labour discipline, one can enter into a labour relationship only by means of a contract. Theoreticians hold that possible appointments or elections can only be considered as preconditions of entering into a labour relationship. According to Para 64 of the Romanian Labour Code of 1972, the form of instatement in work (incadrarea in muncă) is the conclusion of labour contracts. See MILLER (1967/2), pp. 46 et seq.—It is only to be mentioned that the terms labour relationship and labour contract are in some legal rules frequently used alternatively, i.e. considered as synonyms, although they have different meanings and implications. In a great majority of the cases a labour contract is a legal act establishing a labour relationship. Nevertheless, a labour relationship may come into existence from other juridical facts as well, as will be demonstrated in the discussion below. Besides, the contentual elements of a labour contract and of a labour relationship are not identical. In fact, they have a much narrower scope in the case of a labour contract than in the labour relationship. Numerous rights and obligations become *ex lege* contentual elements of a labour relationship in respect of which the relevant labour contract do not—or cannot—contain agreements. It is the termination of a labour relationship that represents a closer link between the two institutions, as a cancellation of a labour contract implies the termination of the respective labour relationship. For a comprehensive and fairly demonstrative study on this problem in the Soviet literature see SHAKHOV (1980/6), pp. 133–136.—For a detailed and thorough comparative analysis of labour contracts see NOVOTNÁ (1979/1), pp. 75–89.—Recently the significance of labour contracts as means of the realization of the right to work has been emphasized in several authors. See PIATAKHOV (1980), pp. 4–10.

[2] According to Article 2 of the Polish Labour Code, the coming into existence of a labour relationship may have five different forms, viz. (i) the contract *(umowa)*, (ii) election *(wybor)*, (iii) nomination *(nominacja)*, (iv) invitation *(powolanie)*, and (v) the labour contract of co-operatives *(spoldzialcza umowa o prace)*.—The difference between invitation and nomination is that, in the case of a post obtained by invitation, the person may be relieved of his post at any time. It is characteristic of these posts that confidence plays an important part when they are to be filled, as is the case, e.g., with directors of enterprises, deputy directors, senior chief accountants, senior civil servants holding leading posts, etc. In the case of relieving someone of his post, the person concerned may be transferred to another post or his/her labour relationship may be terminated in conformity with the general rules, i.e. by giving notice or by dismissal with immediate effect, unless a particular disposition with another content is applicable. The relieving of someone of his/her post may be of an immediate

According to the dispositions of the Hungarian Labour Code, appointment and election, after acceptance, are to be regarded as labour contracts.[3] This rule is based on the view that the agreement of the parties is taken for granted also in the cases of appointment and election, for a labour relationship may be established only in the case of its previous or subsequent acceptance by the employee concerned.[4]

An appointment or election cannot become effective without the will of the interested party. This principle speaks for itself and is fundamental, so much so that it is particularly emphasized, e.g., in Article III of the Czechoslovak Labour Code as one of the Fundamental Principles, pointing out that labour relations, through which the workers take part in the work of society, may be established only with the understanding of the persons concerned and the relevant socialist organizations. The only disputed point is whether this understanding or agreement is to be regarded as a contract and, if so, the legal institution of the contract should be considered as the collective (general) term of all acts leading to labour relations.

Our point of departure is here that, in the case of the conclusion of a labour contract, the subjects of the labour relationship are the contracting parties, that is, the persons whose contractual act of will leads to the establishment of a labour relationship. The question is whether the situation is the same in the case of an appointment or election, i.e. whether the contractual act of will bearing upon the establishment of the labour relationship comes from the enterprise with which the person concerned will establish a labour relationship.

A particularly close attention was paid to this problem earlier in the legal literature of the German Democratic Republic. The problem was raised with a particular sharpness in connection with the labour relations of leading State officials working in the sphere of economy, in view of the circumstance that

effect, or linked with a term of relieving but the labour relationship itself is not affected by it.—As regards the regulation of nomination in the Polish law, this way of the establishment of a labour relationship is justified by the special character of the work to be performed; it is actually established by dispositions taken on the basis of Article 298 of the Polish Labour Code or other decisions provided for special cases, primarily in the civil service. As regards the coming into existence of a labour relationship by means of election, this is established for the case in which the election implies the duty of performing work as an employee (cf. Para 1, Article 73 of the Polish Labour Code). For these two cases, the general rules bearing upon the cancellation of a labour contract are to be followed. As is clear, these cases constitute separate grounds for the establishment of labour relationship in Polish law.—Turning to the Czechoslovak labour law, it should be noted that appointment has a particular character meaning that a labour relationship established by appointment is not terminated as a consequence of recalling someone from his post or the resignation from it; the organization or body that effected the recall of the appointed person will have a discussion with him about his transfer to another kind of work in conformity with his qualification (Article 65, subsection 2, of the Czechoslovak Labour Code). A recall from a post may be effected also without letting the person know what the motives are, and with immediate effect. See HANZLIK (1977/8); BERNARD-PAVLÁTOVÁ (1979), p. 333.

[3] See subsection (1), Article 22 of the Labour Code.
[4] WELTNER–NAGY (1974), p. 148; WELTNER (1965), p. 197.

the office holders concerned had to work for the enterprise which possessed an independent legal entity even though it was subordinated to the body that effected the appointment. According to supporters of another view, one of the subjects of the labour relationship, the employer, is the superior body that effected the appointment.[5] Others were of the opinion that the appointing body could not be regarded as subject of the labour relationship as it stood for the legal status of a third party placed beyond the labour relationship and so, this latter was to be established with the enterprise.[6]

The supporters of this view emphasize, e.g., that the director (manager) of an enterprise performs his/her work for the enterprise and not for the superior body; his/her right to work is realized in his/her relation to the enterprise named in the document of appointment, his/her activity is determined by the targets of the respective plain, in place of instructions of the superior body; the director is a member of the community of the employees, that is, s/he belongs to the staff of the enterprise. The internal organization of labour is applicable also to the director and puts obligations on him/her. In case of disputed problems affecting the enterprise, the director is not entitled to represent this latter, i.e. the representative of the enterprise will be appointed by his/her superior body. This view conforms to that expressed by SCHLEGEL. According to his opinion, the subjects of a labour relationship are always the employee on the one hand, and the enterprise or administrative body for which the former carries on his/her activities, on the other. Even if the body effecting an appointment is not the employing enterprise or subordinated administrative body but the respective superior administrative body, the labour relationship in question will be established between the employee and the enterprise for which the former will work.[7]

The problem involves also the question of whether or not the parties are bound to conclude, additionally, a contract in the case of an appointment or election. Evidently, this has been dealt with in the legal literature several times. According to PASHKOV's opinion, the administrative body is not the subject of a labour relationship in the case of appointment; instead, it represents the interests of the subordinated economic enterprises, and the administrative act carried out by it, i.e. the appointment proper, constitutes a particular condition of concluding a labour contract.[8] The employee-to-be and the employing

5 KIRSCHNER (1957/11), p. 289.

6 KIRMSE (1958/9), pp. 267–270.

7 SCHLEGEL (1959), p. 163. – The institution of the so-called special contract *(Einzelvertrag)* is also accepted in the law of the German Democratic Republic. Contracts of this kind are concluded with professionals, members of the educated layers of society, intellectuals, the members of the intelligentsia, acknowledging thereby their important contribution to progress in the field of science, engineering, arts, etc. Contracts of this kind may have sponsorial stipulations concerning the creative activity of the person involved in the specified scope. The conclusion of a special contract is subjected to the consent of the competent central State authority.—According to the views expressed in the recently published GDR legal literature, the special contracts cannot be regarded as a separate type of the labour contracts. See PÄTZOLD–VOGLER (1980/8), pp. 350–351.

8 PASHKHOV (1966), pp. 120–121.

economic enterprise are bound to conclude a contract with each other, in addition to the appointment; taking into consideration, furthermore, that the administrative body authorized to appoint is not the subject of the labour relationship to be established, it is the employing economic enterprise that will appear as subject and the opposite party to the employee; hence, the enterprise will be a party to the contract to be concluded. In ALEKSANDROV's view, a labour relationship for specified categories of office-holders is established on the basis of a compound state of facts, *replacing* a labour contract (italics from the author), and consisting of:

(a) a preliminary agreement bearing upon the acceptance of the appointment in question, and

(b) a disposition of appointment in respect of the post in question.[9]

Under the terms of Czechoslovak labour law, the contract, appointment, and election constitute independent grounds for the establishment of a labour relationship.[10] A separate contract is sometimes concluded in the case of election, this however only serves to confirm the conditions of the labour relationship which has already been established by virtue of the appointment.

As regards the earlier Romanian theory of labour law, it was essentially based upon PASHKOV's views. Appointment or election constituted a condition of concluding a labour contract, as was pointed out by MILLER and GHIMPU. The body effecting the appointment or election had an *ad hoc* role in respect of the establishment, modification, or termination of the labour relationship, but a labour contract had to be concluded in all cases.[11] According to a more recent view, an appointment demonstrates the agreement of the employer to the conclusion of the labour contract; together with the simultaneous agreement of the appointed person, the labour contract is then concluded. In case of leading staff members appointed by the competent superior authority, this latter demonstrates its agreement to the conclusion of the labour contract.[12] Continuing to comment the views of the Romanian legal literature and turning to the case of election, it may be read that a distinction should be made according to whether the election was initiated by a body which is the superior authority of the enterprise as a legal entity and therefore is just one of the parties to the labour relationship in question, or it is another, outside body. In the first case, election is nothing but a specific case of the agreement to the conclusion of the labour contract and, together with it, of the establishment of the labour relationship, provided, of course, that the approval of the body in question coincides with the consent of the subject of the election. As for the second case, the will of the electing body (e.g. the National Assembly, in the case of election of the judges of the Supreme Court), taking shape in the act of the election, produces for the interested parties the obligation to conclude a labour contract with the elected person; the consent of this latter is, of

9 ALEKSANDROV, ed. (1972), p. 246.
10 Article 27 of the Czechoslovak Labour Code.
11 MILLER–GHIMPU (1966), pp. 118–120.
12 STANOIU (1974/5), p. 5.

course, always required. Thus, the necessity of a labour contract as the source of labour relationship cannot be doubted even in the cases of this category.[13]

As for the views discussed in the German Democratic Republic, it was first disputed whether the conclusion of a labour contract in addition to the act of appointment was necessary. KOWOLLIK represented the opinion that a labour contract had to be concluded with the respective enterprise even in the case of an appointment.[14] As regards the recent developments, the view has come to the fore—although it had earlier advocates as vell—that in the case of an appointment the conclusion of a labour contract is not necessary as the appointment itself establishes the labour relationship.[15] In his textbook on the labour law of the German Democratic Republic, MICHAS also accepted this view.[16] As a complementary remark the Decree (issued in 1961) on the procedure of appointment and recall of employees should be mentioned which was in force till the coming into force of the 1977 Labour Code.[17] According to the Decree of 1961, a separate agreement in writing could be concluded with the employee concerned, in addition to the appointment, in which the conditions of labour were laid down in detail, in conformity with the relevant dispositions of the labour law. The agreement was not a labour contract, it did not establish a labour relationship, but served only to give a closer definition of the labour relationship established by appointment.[18] Under the terms of the new, 1977 Labour Code, appointment or election by itself constitutes the right to establish the labour relationship.[19]

In the Polish legal literature, SWIECICKI pointed to the different legal nature of labour relationships that come into existence by means of appointment and election; in his view, a distinction has to be made between appointment or election and contract. Agreements bearing upon the performance of work based on appointment or election do not belong in the category of contract.[20]

Summarizingly it may be stated as an established view that if an appointment or election is concerned with the performance of work for another body than the one effecting the appointment or election, the subject of the labour relationship thus established will always be the body or organization for which the work in question has to be performed.[21] There have been differences in views, however, in so far whether a labour contract has to be concluded

[13] STANOIU (1974/5), p. 7.

[14] See in KIRSCHNER (1957/11), pp. 289.

[15] Fiege (1957/11), pp. 285–289; SCHLEGEL (1959), p. 161.

[16] MICHAS (1970), p. 176.

[17] *Gbl.* II (1961/38), p. 235.

[18] MICHAS (1970), p. 177.

[19] See subsection 2, Article 38; and Articles 61 and 66 of the Labour Code of the German Democratic Republic.

[20] SWIECICKI (1969), p. 134.

[21] Let us note here that reference was made already in the pre-war Hungarian literature to the circumstance that the employer was not always identical with the person who effected the administrative act required to the employment of a civil servant. See MAGYARY (1942), p. 376.

too, in addition to an appointment or election. The opinion arguing that, given the existence of an appointment or election, the conclusion of a separate labour contract is not required has gained predominance. Nevertheless, if a labour contract is still concluded, as is the case in Romanian law, the opposite contracting party of the future employee will be the organization for which, appointed or elected, the person in question will perform work.[22]

The establishment of a labour relationship based on appointment or election needs the consent of the person concerned. It is explicitly laid down in Article 11 of the Polish Labour Code that the establishment of a labour relationship always requires the concordant declaration of the employer and the employee, *regardless of its legal form* (italics from the author). It may be disputed, however, whether the consent should be qualified as a contract, and there are different opinions in this respect.

In our view, the contract-based concept of a labour relationship originating from appointment or election is substantially coupled to the effort of the legal policy claiming for labour relations to be volitional relations in which parties of equal rights participate. However, considering that the act of appointment or election cannot become effective without the consent of the appointed or elected person, the transfer of the contract-based concept to labour relations established on the basis of appointment or election seems to be unnecessary.

As regards labour relations established by means of appointment or election, their character is different from those constituted by a labour contract. ALEK-SANDROV points out in this respect that the act of appointment is needed in all cases when the sphere of activity of the person entering into work is in connection with the exercise of rights of authoritative dispositions either within the enterprise or institution, or in respect of organizations or persons coming into contact with the given enterprise or institution. In cases of this character, the person in question is entitled to effect the acts of disposition just on the basis of the appointment.[23] This regulation at the same time represents an acknowledgement of the office-holders charged with special tasks in connection with the fulfilment of the State targets. A recourse to appointment is made when the employee (office-holder) in question has to face special responsibility in performing his tasks, therefore, it seems to be fully justified to lay down special regulations for the establishment of such distinguished labour relationships.

As regards the procedures of establishing the labour relationship there are differences between contract-based or appointment-based procedures. In case of a labour contract a labour relationship is recognized as established with the very conclusion of the contract, regardless of any separate disposition in

---

[22] In case the election was carried out not by the body for which the elected person will perform work, the very fact of the election always brings about an obligation for the bodies concerned to conclude a labour contract with the subject of the election. The existence of a labour contract as source of labour relationship cannot be denied even in these cases. See STANOIU (1974), p. 6.

[23] ALEKSANDROV, ed. (1972), p. 245.

writing concerning the employment of the person in question, while in case of appointment the person concerned is not allowed to occupy his post until the appropriate act is effected. According to PASHERSTNIK's wording the act of will of one of the parties constitutes a condition for the act of will of the other party, i.e. first the act of will of one of the parties takes an objective form with the forwarding of his application, and this is followed by that of the other party, in the form of the appointment. Thus, legal consequences ensue only with the act of will of the other party.[24]

Turning now to the labour relations established as a consequence of an election, their characteristics equally show differences as compared to labour relations established by means of a labour contract. The complex character of the procedure results here from the circumstance that the primary condition of being elected for a given post or job is that the consent of the person concerned is given beforehand. This is followed by the actual election on the part of the respective organ, or the persons entitled to elect. In some cases specified in normative acts, this series of procedure is completed by the confirmation in the post. With an absence of the consent of the party concerned, the act of election would become void and a labour relationship could not be established. It is a further characteristic feature of elections that the delegates of the workers or the citizens who participate in the election will not become thereby subject of the legal relationship established as a result of the election; however, the elected person is submitted to a supervision exercised by them, for he is obliged to report on his activities from time to time. Elections take place for a specified period of time. In view of this particular point, there is an opinion that apart from the election, a labour contract for a specified period of time has to be completed as well. According to another view, which may be regarded as generally accepted, the labour contract is not needed because the consent of the candidate to his nomination for the post expressed, too, his agreement with the conditions of work specified for the post.[25]

The way of the establishment of labour relations has always to be determined by the content of the legal relation. For this reason, we are of the opinion that it is not necessary to apply the contractual form to labour relations constituted by means of appointment or election, because it would lead only to a dissolution of the required harmony between form and content. Taking into account this point, it seems to be more appropriate, on the side of theory, to support the view claiming that the juridical acts serving as basis for the establishment of labour relations, e.g. contract, appointment, election, etc. are juxtaposed to each other, as the individual acts giving birth to rights have different legal characteristics. At most, their common feature is that the consent of both parties is indispensable to achieve the legal effect they are aimed at. By this we expressed also our opinion that, in the case of appointment or election, no separate labour contract is needed in view of the circumstance that the labour

[24] GHEIKHMAN (1973/5), p. 108.
[25] This opinion is generally accepted in the socialist countries.

relationship is established without the conclusion of a labour contract, but with the appointment or election and the acceptance thereof by the interested party.[26]

Even though we have taken stand for the independent existence of acts establishing labour relations, nevertheless, we are far from claiming the same importance for all of them. In our firm view it should be emphasized that the labour contract continues to represent the most important form of establishing a labour relationship; the other acts establishing labour relations should be regarded as of exceptional nature, therefore, in the comments which will be presented below attention will be concentrated principally upon problems that are in connection with the establishment of labour relations by means of a contract.

To complete our survey, attention should however be paid here briefly to the Yugoslav concept, too. The labour relations of all those engaged in work carried on in associations are to be understood to comprise the mutual relationship of those working in basic organizations (economic units) or working communities, established by them in the process of realizing their right to work, in the frame of common work performed with the use of the means of production in collective property. By the application of the general acts on self-management, in which the individual and collective rights, duties, and liabilities are laid down, the relations in question are regulated and put into practice in conformity with the dispositions of the act on associated work. Observing the stipulations of the law and proceeding as prescribed by the respective act on self-management, everybody is free to establish labour relations with the workers of basic organizations (economic units) with equal rights and under equal conditions. It is allowed to establish labour relationships for all those who comply with the conditions put down by the employees of a basic economic (work) unit based on the general act on self-management and observing the rules of the law, in line with the requirements of the working process, the conditions of work, and in view of the actual targets. The conditions with which applications have to comply in order to establish a labour relationship, with an aim to perform a specified work or fulfil a target, are announced by the basic organization (economic unit) in the form of a competition or advertisement. The selection from the candidates who presented themselves upon the advertisement or in the frame of a competition will be then made by the worker's council or a committee appointed by the same worker's council proceeding in the way set out in the general act on self-management in conformity with the law. A labour relationship will then be established upon a declaration in writing of the future employee, confirming his knowledge of the self-management agreement bearing upon the association of the work of the employees of the basic organization (economic unit) in question, and of the general act on self-management regulating labour relations, the other acts on self-management regulating

---

[26] In the case of labour contracts depending on consent, there is a different situation, as, depending again on the structure of the contract, the granting and the refusal of the consent constitutes two different conditions, the one preceding, the other following the coming into existence of the labour relationship concerned.

the employees' rights, obligations, and responsibilities, as well as the statutes of the basic organization.[27]

The essential point in the Yugoslav concept is the omission of the labour contract as an act establishing the labour relationship. Consequently, the conclusion of a contract with the basic organization will not result in the establishment of a labour law relationship, instead, a civil law relationship will be constituted.[28]

Evidently, the dispositions described above have been motivated by the intention to emphasize the importance of the functional relationship which, as far as the relations between employees and economic organizations are concerned, is characteristic of the self-management system serving as basis for the Yugoslav socio-economic structure.

5.2 Time of the establishment of the labour relationship

The various socialist States are, in general, unanimous in their view that a labour contract may be regarded as established from the time of the agreement of the parties concerning the conditions thereof, still, the actual time of the beginning of a labour relationship, from the viewpoint of the labour contract, may be disputed. Three different views may be distinguished, viz. (1) the conclusion of a labour contract involves the establishment of a labour relationship with immediate effect, (2) the establishment of a labour relationship is set to the date agreed upon by the parties as a starting date of the performance of work, (3) a labour relationship starts to exist only at the moment of the actual beginning of work.[29]

Joining to these main views, there exists a further approach arguing that the formation of a labour relationship represents a process and is established not at a given moment for, although the constitution of a labour relationship presupposes an agreement of intentions coming into existence between the subjects of the labour contract, which is obviously related to a specified portion of time, the formation of a labour relationship involves the taking into consideration and the fulfilment of several other legal requirements, conditions, and technicalities.[30]

(1) The view claiming for the coming into existence of a labour relationship by virtue of the conclusion of a labour contract with immediate effect has supporters in almost all countries. As for the Soviet literature, the problem

[27] Articles 161, 167, 170, 172, and 173 of the 1976 Act on associated work.

[28] On the basis of a contract, provisional or seasonal work may be performed for the basic organization; nevertheless, the employee performing this kind of work is not within a labour relationship. The conditions of contracts covering the performance of work of this kind as well as their contents are laid down in Article 175 of the 1976 Act on associated work. For the relevant legal literature see TRÓCSÁNYI (1969/3), p. 528.

[29] For a summary of the complex of problems see WELTNER–NAGY (1974), pp. 139 et seq.

[30] STANOIU (1974/5), p. 3.

was raised whether a labour relationship started to exist from the time of issuance of the disposition on the employment or at an earlier date. In a university textbook, edited by PASHKHOV, the opinion according to which an actual labour relationship is established with the issuance of the disposition on employment, is treated as incorrect, as this disposition is issued subsequently to the contractual act of will of the worker to enter into work for the enterprise or more exactly it is not an act bringing about a legal relationship, it only follows the conclusion of the labour contract.[31] Similarly, the disposition of the enterprise is considered in the textbook edited by ALEKSANDROV as a posterior document of the concluded labour contract, which is needed in registering the employee in question in the staff of the enterprise, for specifying his actual conditions of work, etc.[32] ALEKSANDROV expressed similar views in another work, laying down that, as soon as the agreement concerning the employment and the actual entering into work is reached, the labour contract has to be regarded as concluded, in conformity with general rules, and the contract becomes then effective, irrespective of the date of the disposition on employment.[33] According to SMIRNOV's view, a labour contract comes into effect and is to be regarded as concluded from the date of the agreement covering all essential points. In case of an opposite opinion, a conclusion could be drawn as if the enterprise were allowed to conclude a labour contract also with another person, prior to the actual entering into work of the employee concerned, as the relevant mutual rights and obligations would not come into being before the date in question. However, this could lead, easily, to abusive administrative methods and contravention of the right to work. In avoidance of these, the mutual rights and obligations should come into existence with the day of the conclusion of the labour contract.[34]

The issuing of a disposition on employment, in verbal form or by means of an instruction or advice in writing, has its own importance. On the basis of a concluded labour contract, the management of the enterprise concerned is obliged, in fact, to issue a disposition in writing concerning the employment; notwithstanding, the employee is allowed, indeed, to proceed to actual work upon a verbal instruction of the management. If the management fails to issue a disposition in writing on the employment or to give a verbal instruction concerning the beginning of actual work, then the employee will not be in a position to proceed to the fulfilment of the labour contract as a result of a fault of the management, in spite of the effected conclusion of the labour contract. In such cases the employee cannot be held responsible for the non-fulfilment of his obligation of performing work and by making recourse to a competent court of justice. This latter will oblige the management of the enterprise to comply with the respective stipulations of the contract.[35]

---

31 PASHKHOV (1966), pp. 112–113.
32 ALEKSANDROV, ed. (1966), p. 235.
33 ALEKSANDROV, ed. (1972), p. 245.
34 SMIRNOV (1964), pp. 124–125.
35 ALEKSANDROV–MOSHKALENKO (undated), pp. 114–115.

Under the valid rules of Soviet law, an employment has to be laid down in writing by the management of the enterprise in the form of an instruction (disposition), and the employee shall acknowledge its receipt also in writing. Nevertheless, an actual entering into work should be regarded as the conclusion of the labour contract, irrespective of the circumstance whether or not the employment has been laid down in the above form.[36]

As regards the Bulgarian law, essentially it accepts the contract-based view.[37] The conclusion of the labour contract is considered to be the date of the labour relationship coming into existence.[38] The entering into work results in an actual state implying the coming into existence of certain rights and obligations, nevertheless, some rights and obligations start to exist as early as the moment of the conclusion of the labour contract. The period from the date of the conclusion of the labour contract to the actual entering into work is neither determined nor limited by the respective legal rules. Furthermore the Bulgarian legal rules provide no binding rule concerning the fixed date of entering into work; it occurs very frequently that the parties omit to agree concerning the precise date of entering into work. This does not at all mean a renouncing of the obligation of entering into work or placing applicants in jobs. Hence, the fact of the conclusion of the contract implies for the employees the obligation of entering into work. Since the legal rules do not contain provisions as to the date within which the employee is obliged to enter into work following the date of the conclusion of the contract, this lack of dispositions, in the absence of a relevant agreement, can cause troubles in practice.[39]

Looking at the law of the German Democratic Republic, it appears that the contract-based theory was first represented by SCHLEGEL. In his view, the conclusion of a labour contract is to be understood so that, with the realization of the employee's right to work, a labour relationship comes into being between the parties with immediate effect, even if actual work does not begin at the same time.[40] WASSMUND is also supporter of the view that a labour relationship is established simultaneously with the conclusion of the relevant contract. In his opinion, this concept is an assurance for the employee that the post will be reserved for him/her by the enterprise up to the time when the previous labour relationship becomes terminated. In case of an agreement of the enterprise and the employee on fixing the actual entering into work at a subsequent date it is beyond any doubt, in his view, that the intention of the parties with the subsequent fixation was only concerned with the actual entering into work, leaving untouched the effect of the legal relationship as a whole. He firmly

[36] Article 18 of the Labour Code of the Russian Federation of Socialist Soviet Republics. BARINOV (1978/2), pp. 44–49.

[37] We do not wish to deal here with the question whether in the literature of labour law the contract is regarded as concluded at the date of the signature of the document of employment by the head of the institution or organization or only when the employee has learned about it. See in MRATCHKHOV (1965/3), p. 38.

[38] MRATCHKHOV (1965/3), p. 42.

[39] MRATCHKHOV (1965/3), p. 44.

[40] SCHLEGEL (1959), p. 158.

represents the view that a labour relationship is established with immediate effect both by the conclusion of the relevant contract and by an appointment or election. These acts giving birth to rights are not only needed for the establishment of a labour relationship but also they are sufficient at the same time. The actual entering into work by the employee is only a fact of fulfilment, to meet his obligation of performing work for the employer. Hence, this act is a consequence of the already existing labour relationship.[41] Reference should be made here to FÖRSTER's argumentation. He mentions certain season-bound activities, occurring chiefly in the field of catering, agriculture, and forestry in which a delay of more than 14 days between the conclusion of the labour contract and the actual entering into work is usual. In these cases there are already some kinds of binding relations between the parties, and they can only be interpreted as rights and obligations resulting from an already established labour relationship.[42]

HANTSCH, although he took in a given sense different position, should also be considered as belonging to the supporters of the contract-based theory.[43] In his view, it is the intention of the partners that determines whether they prefer to see the immediate coming into existence of the legal effect of a labour contract or they are in support of the arrangement that its establishment should be bound to the day of actual entering into work. In the first case, the labour relationship comes into being with the conclusion of the contract, while with the actual entering into work, the phase of performance begins.

Let us mention here that the Supreme Court of the German Democratic Republic has also taken stand upon the contract-based opinion, with its declaration that a labour relationship starts to exist with the day of the conclusion of the labour contract and, following from this, a labour relationship can be terminated in the period between the conclusion of the contract and the employee's actual entering into work only in a legally admitted way. In this view, in the absence of a special disposition, the 31st and subsequent Articles of the Labour Code were applicable.[44] The recent legal literature unequivocally infers that a labour relationship is established with the conclusion of the labour contract.[45]

The authors of the Czechoslovak legal literature are more inclined to hold the view that the day specified in the labour contract as the day of entering into work is to be regarded as the starting day of a labour relationship.[46] However, in the opinion of NOVOTNÁ, the coming into existence of a labour relationship has to be linked to the conclusion of the labour contract, and a distinction should be made between the coming into being of a labour rela-

---

[41] WASSMUND (1958/1), pp. 16–17.
[42] See in WASSMUND (1958/1), pp. 16–17.
[43] HANTSCH (1957/4), pp. 92–93.
[44] MICHAS (1970), p. 102.
[45] KIRSCHNER–MICHAS (1978), p. 37.
[46] FREUND (1980), p. 63.

tionship and the date of actual entering into work, which does not necessarily coincide with the date of the conclusion of the labour contract.[47]

The earlier Polish legal literature seems to have favoured the contract-based theory. According to SWIECICKI, a labour relationship comes into being by virtue of the simple fact of the conclusion of the contract irrespective of the circumstance whether or not the employee concerned entered into work actually.[48] Identically a labour relationship is existing regardless of the fact whether or not the employee complied with his obligation to perform work, as WALAS put it down. He adds the remark, however, that a labour relationship is merely *in statu nascendi* at the conclusion of the contract by the parties. If an employee fails to enter into work, his labour relationship may be terminated *ex tunc*, while subsequently to the entering into work, termination may only be effected *ex nunc*.[49] In the view of JONCZYK, a labour relationship is established at the moment of the conclusion of the contract, only the beginning of the fulfilment of the obligation to perform work may be postponed. In this latter case, the labour relationship is regarded to be in a latent state up to the time when the employee enters into work actually. If he fails to do so, his labour relationship may be terminated with immediate effect, viewing the fact that the employee failed to comply with an essential obligation resulting from the labour contract. The fact of entering into work in itself does not mean the existence of the labour relationship.[50]

It should be noted here that the stipulations of the 1974 Labour Code of Poland differ from the views of Polish jurisprudence referred to, and commented, above. (We shall return to this later on.)

Under the terms of the Romanian Labour Code, the placing of applicants in job is the fact constituting a labour relationship, with the labour contract serving as its basis.[51] Being attached to a unit of socialist work, the person becomes a member of the working community of the unit, with rights and obligations resulting from this link. He is thus entitled to have a job in conformity with his abilities, professional qualification and, of course, the demands of the working unit.[52] The establishment of a labour relationship coincides thus with the conclusion of a labour contract under the rules of the Romanian law.

With regard to the Hungarian literature, the problem of the starting date of a labour relationship led to dispute. WELTNER put it down in details that a labour relationship started to exist with the conclusion of a labour contract; besides, as he pointed out, the date fixed for taking up work and the actual date of entering into work had also their respective significance. Nevertheless, these two dates had this significance not as facts constituting a legal

[47] NOVOTNÁ (1975/8), p. 777.
[48] SWIECICKI (1969), p. 140.
[49] WALAS (1961), p. 193.
[50] Standpoint set forth at a consultation held at Wroclaw on October 30, 1969.
[51] Article 64 of the Romanian Labour Code.
[52] Articles 8 and 19 of the Romanian Labour Code.

relationship, but only in so far as a distinction had to be made between the various phases of a labour relationship.[53]

According to a Hungarian textbook of labour law, theoretical distinction should be made in relation of: (a) the legal coming into existence of a labour relationship, (b) the date of the 'legal beginning' of a labour relationship, i.e. the date fixed for the beginning of employment or the performance of work, and (c) the date of the actual beginning of work.

In view of this, two main phases may be distinguished within a labour relationship, viz. (i) the phase from the conclusion of the labour contract to the date when, according to a stipulation of the labour contract or a disposition of the relevant legal rule, the employment or the actual performance of work, constituting the labour relationship, has to be started with the full legal effect; (ii) the phase of legal relationship which starts to run at the moment when, under the stipulations of the labour contract or by virtue of the relevant legal rule, the employment or the actual performance of work has to be started with full legal effects. If the enterprise failed to put into practice the employment at the provided date, on the one hand, or the employee failed to start to perform the work, on the other, the labour relationship legally comes into being but actually it will not and its subsequent fate will depend on the circumstance whether the conditions contrary to the dispositions presented themselves through the conduct of the one or the other party, and whether this conduct is imputable to one or the other party.[54]

In his work 'International Labour Law', SZÁSZY also takes the view that a labour relationship is established with the conclusion of the contract, and it is only the legal effect of the contract that is not complete until the actual beginning of the work. Some of the rights and obligations comprised by the legal relationship come into being already with the conclusion of the labour contract while other points become fully effective only with the actual beginning of the work. In his view, the rights and obligations of this latter group exist only in the form of an expectancy until the actual beginning of the work, similarly to the rules of civil law in which, for contracts subjected to a condition, the legal effects enforce themselves only with the realization of the stipulated condition. Thus, the actual beginning of the work is an act having real legal effects within a labour relationship.[55]

The substantial features of the contract-based theory show that a labour relationship is established, under the respective rules of the law, on the day of the conclusion of the contract and its legal effects come into existence from the moment they are laid down by the parties or fixed by a legal rule. Clearly, a link between the establishment of a labour relationship and the date of conclusion of the labour contract does not imply the obligation of the employee to enter into actual work immediately, as the contracting parties are free to agree upon this point also at a later time. Besides, a way of regulation is also

[53] WELTNER (1958/7), p. 30.
[54] WELTNER–NAGY (1974), p. 140.
[55] SZÁSZY (1969), pp. 431–432.

usual in which the date of actual entering into work is fixed by a disposition of the enterprise, within the frame of an already established labour relationship; this is not equal, however, to the establishment proper as the relationship did already come into being with the conclusion of the contract.

(2) According to other views, a labour relationship comes into existence at the moment which has been agreed upon by the parties as the starting date of the performance of work. Contrary to his previous opinion, PÄTZOLD represented the view that the beginning of the existence of a labour relationship can be put only to the day fixed for the actual entering into work by the mutual agreement of the parties. The fact that a later date is agreed upon by the parties for the actual entering into work should thus be explained by the agreement of will of the parties in the direction that the rights and obligations become effective not immediately but only from a subsequent date on. He is namely of the view that a labour relationship is nothing other than the totality of mutual rights and obligations becoming effective between the parties.[56] Pätzold's views have been shared by FRANKE, too. As he pointed out, in case the actual entering into work should be subsequent to the conclusion of the labour contract, under the terms of this latter one, the labour relationship comes into existence only at this later date.[57]

As for the Romanian law, MILLER represents the opinion that a labour relationship comes into being with the day which was agreed upon by the contracting parties as the date of entering into work.[58]

Turning to the Czechoslovak literature, BERNARD and PAVLÁTOVÁ should be mentioned who set out that a labour relationship does not come into existence with the mere conclusion of the labour contract; in view of the conditions, also a longer period may become interposed between the conclusion of the labour contract and the actual entering into work of the employee, therefore, the day of the actual entering into work of the employee should always be fixed in the labour contract; as a rule, the labour relationship comes into being only with this day. A labour contract is only the legal basis of the establishment of a labour relationship, nevertheless, from the very moment of its conclusion, some legal consequences are linked with it.[59] In KOVÁŘIK's view, the establishment of a legal relationship is a coherent process which is brought to completion by the employee's actual entering into work.[60] Essentially, the same approach is expressed in Article 33 of the Czechoslovak Labour Code, ruling that a labour relationship based on a concluded labour contract comes into existence on the day fixed in the labour contract for entering into work. Consequently, the agreement bearing upon the day provided for entering into work is a substantial element of the labour contract.[61] As is laid down in

---

[56] Cited by WASSMUND (1958/1), p. 16.

[57] Cited by HANTSCH (1957/4), pp. 92–93.

[58] Standpoint set forth at a consultation held in Bucharest on October 21, 1970; see also, MILLER–GHIMPU (1966), pp. 215–218.

[59] BERNARD–PAVLÁTOVÁ (1979), p. 92; see also PAVLÁTOVÁ (1977), p. 111.

[60] KOVÁŘIK (1963/8), pp. 42 et seq.

[61] Article 29, Para 2.1, subsection (c) of the Czechoslovak Labour Code.

Article 65 of the Czechoslovak Labour Code, a labour relationship constituted by virtue of appointment or election comes into existence with the day fixed for occupying the post.

According to Article 26 of the Polish Labour Code, a labour relationship comes into existence at the date fixed for entering into work or, in the absence of a fixed date with this effect, the day of the conclusion of the relevant contract. Contrary to the Czechoslovak regulation with its compulsory provision for setting the date of entering into work, the Polish legislation constituted thus an undisputable presumption in respect of the coming into existence of a labour relationship.

The essential features of the views referred to above may thus be summed up in a way that, in case of an agreement of the parties stipulating in the labour contract a later date for entering into work, the basic structure is, in fact, a labour contract with a delaying force, i.e. its effect is pending till the date fixed for entering into work. The parties can enforce their rights only from the said date on and, vice versa, they are bound to come up to their obligations equally from the date in question on. Accordingly, no notice to quit is permissible prior to the date fixed for entering into work; if notice is given, irrespective of this rule, the period of notice starts to run not earlier than the date fixed for entering into work.[62] If the employee fails to enter into work on the day fixed for that, without being prevented from doing so by an obstacle concerning the work, or if he fails to let the enterprise know the obstacle of this kind within a fixed period, the enterprise will be entitled to abandon the contract.[63] As a consequence, the labour contract loses its validity *ex tunc*, i.e. the situation will be as if a labour contract had never been concluded.[64]

(3) According to a further opinion, a labour relationship comes into existence only from the date of the actual beginning of performing the work. The so-called theory of the applicants' actual entering into job, serving as basis for this concept, has also supporters and the respective legal rules of some States reflect also this approach.

Essentially, two variants of this concept presented themselves so far. According to the first view, there is no need at all to conclude a labour contract. This is the Yugoslav regulation. Thus the contract-based theory as the fundament of the establishment of a labour relationship was rejected by the Yugoslav legislation.[65] The 1966 Basic Act on labour relations already contained a disposition in its Article 2 that the workers were free to enter into a labour organization and, accordingly, to quit it on their own free will.[66] Furthermore, as is laid down in Article 15 of the 1973 Act bearing upon the mutual rela-

---

[62] HANTSCH (1957/4), pp. 92–93.
[63] Article 33, Para 2 of the Czechoslovak Labour Code.
[64] BERNARD–PAVLÁTOVÁ (1979), p. 92.
[65] KYOVSKY (1967), p. 9.
[66] *Služebni List*, No. 43, 1966.

tions of the employees engaged in associated work, the employees are 'co-workers' in the basic organization of the association.[67]

Under the terms of the Yugoslav legal rules in force, a labour relationship is established with a declaration in writing of the workers and employees stating their knowledge of the self-management agreement bearing upon the association of work of the working members of the basic organization; of the general act on self-management character regulating the labour relations; of the other general acts regulating rights, duties, and liabilities; as well as of the statutes of the basic labour organization. Nevertheless, if the employee fails to proceed to work in the basic labour organization on the specified day, then his rights, duties and liabilities in connection with his labour relationship come into existence with the day of entering into work actually, in conformity with the general act on self-management regulating labour relations. If the employee fails to enter into work on the specified day without reason, it is to be regarded as if no labour relationship had been established.[68] Thus, the actual entering into work continues to have a decisive significance also under the terms of the new regulation.

Another view accepts the contract as the basis of the establishment of a labour relationship but claims for the day of actual entering into work to be the beginning of a labour relationship. As for the Hungarian legal literature, in a debating paper published as early as 1958, NAGY accepted the theory of the applicants' actual entering into job. According to his view, the arrangement stipulating the establishment of a labour relationship with the conclusion of the contract instead of the actual entering into work makes it possible for an employee to enjoy, for some time, the advantages provided for the workers without performing work; moreover he may even obtain double remuneration if he happened to be employed elsewhere for the same period. According to NAGY's opinion, these possibilities are not in accordance with the concept of not allowing for anybody to have an income without performing work, or with the principle of distribution by the quantity (and quality) of the work performed.[69] In order to support the way of regulation that the day of actual entering into work should be regarded as the starting date of the existence of labour relationship, several examples are cited by NAGY; for the cases dealt with here, it is worth mentioning the one when a State farm concludes a labour contract, with a provided fulfilment during the summer season, already in springtime. In the author's view it does not seem to be justified to keep the employees concerned within a labour relationship in this case for some months. In view of FÖRSTER's opinion, arguing in favour of the contract-based theory, this example is worth particular mentioning.

Considering the relevant Hungarian legislation of labour law, there was no unequivocal standpoint of principle in this respect for a long time, which is

---

[67] *Službeni List,* No. 22, 1973.
[68] Article 173 of the 1976 Act on associated work.
[69] NAGY (1958/11), pp. 9–13.

shown also by the fact that the Labour Code could be interpreted by the authors of various studies in different ways.[70]

Under the terms of the valid rules of the Hungarian labour law, a labour relationship is established upon the agreement, i.e. the labour contract, between the enterprise and the employee (cf. subsection 1, Para 22 of the Labour Code); nevertheless, the beginning of the existence of a labour relationship is the day of actual entering into work, unless the relevant legal rule provides in a different sense. Unless the contracting parties agreed in a different way, the employee is obliged to enter into work the first working day following the date of the conclusion of the labour contract (see Para 19 of the Labour Code). Having applied the mentioned regulation, essentially, the Hungarian legislation accepted the theory based on the applicants' actual commencing work, presumably favouring the concept that the primary consequences of a labour relationship, i.e. the performance and the remuneration of work, come into being and application with the day of entering into actual work.[71]

It should be noted here that, even accepting the contract-based theory, there is an exceptional possibility to arrange that a labour relationship should come into existence only with the actual entering into work. Thus, if an employee enters into work without having concluded a labour contract earlier, the labour relationship will start to exist also with the day of the actual entering into work. As was pointed out in the Soviet legal literature, the labour contract has to be considered as concluded in this case, however, with effect from the date of actual entering into work, i.e. the labour contract is then concluded *per facta concludentia*. A subsequent issuance of a disposition concerning employment or the omission thereof is irrelevant in this case from the point of view of the establishment of the labour relationship.[72]

By inference it may be stated that the differences of principle that present themselves between the various theories, are, in fact, considerable, and arguments may be brought forward in support of each of them; the more, it occurs that the same arguments are advanced in support of even opposing theories. Nevertheless, at a closer look it will be clear that the practical effects of the differences are less sharp. Putting aside the Yugoslav concept, all of the three views discussed above have the starting point that a labour relationship is established by a labour contract, i.e. an agreement between the

[70] WELTNER came to the conclusion that a labour relationship is already established with the conclusion of the labour contract, even if the parties provided for the actual beginning of the work at a subsequent date, in view of the circumstance that the parties were subjected to various liabilities already in the course preceding the date fixed for the actual beginning of work. See, WELTNER (1958/7), pp. 29–33.—NAGY opposed this view and referred in his reply to the essay to the point that, as is laid down in the rule, a labour relationship starts to exist with the day of entering into work, unless a different starting date was stipulated in the labour contract (see Article 18/A of the Labour Code that was in force prior to the present Code, i.e. Act No. II of 1967).

[71] WELTNER–NAGY (1974, p. 19), wrote that, in the case of the regulation concerned, practical aspects were considered when formulating the decree on the enforcement of the Labour Code, however, the authors did not elaborate on this.

[72] DVORNIKOV–LIVSHITS–RUMYANTSEVA (1971), p. 19.

employer and the employee, irrespective of the date which will be considered as the starting date of the established labour relationship. It is thus beyond doubt even for the contract-based theory that the parties are obliged to render the substantial services only following the date fixed for entering into actual work, i.e. to perform work, on the part of the employee, and to secure employment and to remunerate the work on that of the employer.

Similarly, the supporters of the theory based on the applicants' actual entering into job do not bring in question that the conclusion of the labour contract or the date of this conclusion implies some liabilities. Regarding the labour contract, the partners are bound by virtue of it to establish the labour relationship, and to create the conditions which are required in order that the labour relationship can be effective. Accordingly, the enterprise is obliged, under the terms of the theory of the applicants' actual entering into job, to place the employee in job or to demand his commencing work, already by virtue of the labour contract, and the employee is equally obliged to enter into work or to demand the creation of the conditions enabling him to commence work; then it is only a matter of the starting point of principle or the foundation for the given view whether the relevant rights, duties and liabilities exist as the labour relationship has already been established with the conclusion of the contract, or as they are the consequences of the obligations stipulated in the contract with a view to establish a labour relationship. Anyway, we are of the opinion that the contract-based theory seems to be more suitable to ensure the collective and individual interests linked with the realization of a labour relationship, in view of the circumstance that, in case of a debate, this theory is fairly convenient to eliminate any doubt whether the relevant rules of civil law or labour law are applicable when the rights, duties and liabilities arising in the period from the conclusion of the contract till the actual beginning of the work are to be judged and settled.

Accepting the contract-based theory, it is beyond any doubt that labour relations are governed by the rules of labour law from the date of conclusion of the labour contract. Nevertheless, if a later date is fixed for the coming into existence of the labour relationship, the problem may arise whether the legal acts effected by the contracting parties prior to the later date in order to realize the legal relationship are governed by the rules of this or that branch of the law. Similarly, problems may also arise in the latter case whether the time running from the conclusion of the labour contract, on the one hand, and the day fixed for the beginning of work, on the other, or the latter and the date of the actual entering into work, respectively, should be regarded as covered by the labour relationship from the point of view of holidays, rewards for a prefixed longer period of service, the national health services, etc. Also, it may be a disputed point whether the responsibility of the employee and the enterprise is based for the mentioned transitory period on the rules of labour law or those of civil law bearing upon financial responsibility and, furthermore, whether the disputes arisen during the mentioned period are to be regarded as 'labour law disputes' to be submitted to a board of arbitration proceeding under the rules of labour law or they belong to the field of civil law, within the competence of the relevant ordinary court of justice.[73]

In fact, it is not in contradiction to the contract-based theory if one realizes that the establishment of a labour relationship is a process within which the various dates, i.e. the conclusion of the labour contract, the date fixed for the beginning of the performance of work, and the actual entering into work, have their particular significance. The coming into existence of the labour relationship should, however, be examined in its total scope, taking into consideration all three elements of the state of facts. The particular legal consequences linked with them must not be disregarded. Essentially, the point is a series of states of facts in which, taking the normal course of the establishing of the labour relationship, the previous chains of the series are always presupposed in the subsequent ones. However this is not an exclusive rule, for there are cases in which some elements of states of facts coincide or do not appear. Ultimately, all these points depend on the concrete regulation which puts to the fore such solutions that vary from country to country and according to phases of development.

5.3 Duration of the validity of labour relationships

By their very nature, labour relations are of a lasting duration, therefore, labour contracts are in general concluded for an unspecified period of time, unless they contain a disposition stipulating the duration of the labour relationship concerned. The legal systems of various countries permit for the contracting parties to establish a labour relationship for a specified period of time. With regard to the respective conditions, various arrangements have been developed.

(1) The conditions of concluding a labour contract for a specified period of time are less strictly stipulated by the legal rules of some countries, while there are more restricting provisions in the law of other countries. In some of them, these restrictions may have an objective character, i.e. a contract for a specified period of time can be concluded only in the existence of certain specified conditions, while restrictions of this kind are non-existent in other countries, and limits are set only to the extent that the maximum duration of a labour relationship established for a specified period of time is fixed by the law.

According to the law of the German Democratic Republic, a labour contract may be concluded for a specified period of time, i.e. a maximum duration of six months, if an enterprise needs manpower temporarily on a larger scale, or, if its employees have to be replaced, for a certain period, as e.g. in case of some seasonal work, or because a high number of employees are on the sick-list or rendering their military service, etc.[74] Besides, particular rules may be instituted by the law for specific fields of work or groups of individuals. No

---

[73] WELTNER (1965), pp. 212–213.
[74] MICHAS (1970), p. 170.

written form is required for the establishment of a labour contract with a maximum duration of two weeks; for all other cases, the establishment in writing is indispensable for the conclusion of labour contracts.[75]

In the Yugoslav law, the existence of seasonal work and the increase in the workload to be performed give a legal basis for establishing labour relationships for a specified period of time. Nevertheless, the respective organizations of associated work, performing their activities in the field of agriculture, trade, building industry, etc. have to specify precisely in the general acts on self-management the targets requiring a definite duration of labour contracts, and they are then bound to observe the same consistently.[75/a]

Regarding the rules of Soviet law, the possibility of concluding labour contracts for a specified period is limited only from a temporal point of view. According to Article 10 of the 1970 Fundamental Statutes of the labour law legislation of the Soviet Union, and the member republics of the Union, the maximum permissible duration of a labour contract for a specified period of time is three years. According to Article 17 of the Labour Code of the Russian Soviet Federated Socialist Republic, a labour contract may be concluded for a maximum duration of three years or for the period of the performance of a specified work. In the latter case, the duration of a labour contract concluded for a specified period of time may exceed three years. As is expressed by some authors in the Soviet legal literature, labour contracts for a specified period of time are concluded only in case of employment in territories of the Far North, in the frame of organized recruitment of manpower or for seasonal work.[76] Nevertheless, a more general practice has been established in the sense that labour contracts of this type are concluded in the field of such professions or branches that show the highest rate of fluctuation, in view of the circumstance that a labour contract for a specified period of time may be cancelled upon the initiative of the employee only for strictly specified reasons.[77] These contracts and the stabilization of cadres have been the subject of combined examinations in the recent legal literature.[77/a]

According to Para 27 subsection (b) of the Bulgarian Labour Code, a labour contract may be concluded also for a specified period of time, with a maximum duration of three years.

The exceptional character of this type of labour contracts is evident also in the legal systems in which the respective rules have no explicit restrictive dispositions. It is thus laid down in the Czechoslovak Labour Code that a labour relationship has to be regarded as established for an unspecified period of time, unless its duration is expressly fixed in the relevant labour contract. This provision demonstrates the unequivocal intention of the legislation to consider

---

[75] Article 47 of the Labour Code of the German Democratic Republic.

[75/a] BOZOVIC (1979/271).

[76] ZAGUMENOV (1975/17), p. 31.

[77] Article 32 of the Labour Code of the Russian Soviet Federated Socialist Republic.— As regards the termination of a labour relationship established for a specified period in Czechoslovakia, see PAVLÁTOVÁ (1976/9), pp. 850 et seq.

[77/a] SHLEMIN (1980/18), pp. 14–15.

labour relations established for an unspecified period of time as of primary importance, because they are suitable to secure a constant supply of manpower for the enterprises, on the one hand, and a solid basis of existence for the employees, on the other.[78] There are no limits in the Czechoslovak law in respect of the conclusion of labour contracts for a specified period. In practice, the maximum period for which a labour relationship of a definite duration may be established is of ten years. This is linked with certain specific financial rules according to which the reimbursement of a loan granted to an employee by his employer for house-building on co-operative basis is remitted upon the obligation of the former to work for the enterprise in question during the period concerned and to use the flat for which the loan was granted. A similar regulation is applied, with minor differences, in the case of loans granted by the enterpirse for house-building on private basis.[78/a] According to some other views the conclusion of a labour contract for a specified and excessively long period of time is contrary, however, to the provisions of Article III of the Labour Code ruling that the enforcement of the rights, duties and liabilities resulting from labour relations has to be co-ordinated with the rules of socialist coexistence. Supporting this view, it may be said that the interests of the employee may suffer a prejudice in case of labour relations established for a specified period of excessively long duration, i.e. by the abandonment by the employee of the possibility to terminate his labour relationship in case of subsequent changes in his private conditions of living. A specified period of time may be stipulated also repeatedly, both by taking calendar days or by specifying the work to be performed.[79]

Under the terms of the Polish law, a labour contract may be concluded for a specified period of time, an unspecified period of time or for such that is required for the accomplishment of a specified work. Within this scope, there are no special restrictions in the relevant legal rules.[80]

With regard to the Romanian labour law, a labour contract may be concluded also for a specified period of time in specified cases, e.g. an employee is temporarily absent from service but his post has to be reserved by the unit concerned, thus he has to be substituted; or the accomplishment of a job of seasonal character or of other kind of activity of provisional nature must be ensured. The rules of the Labour Code are equally applicable to persons employed for a specified period of time, taking into consideration, however, the specific features of their activity and the duration of their employment.[81]

In the Yugoslav law, labour relations are established both for a period not

[78] BERNARD–PAVLÁTOVÁ (1979), p. 72.

[78/a] VAŠEK (1978/1), pp. 25–29; DUBENSKY (1979/2), pp. 63—67; JÁGERSKY (1980/7), pp. 644–648.

[79] FREUND, M.: Consultation on September 3, 1976.

[80] Article 25, Para 1 of the Polish Labour Code.

[81] Para 70, subsection 2 of the Romanian Labour Code. From the Romanian legal literature, see to this point MILLER–FLORESCU (1970/1), pp. 133–145. In respect of persons within the limits of a specified category and particular situations, e.g. artists, the conclusion of labour contracts for a specified period of time is permitted by a special legal rule. See BELIGRĂDEANU (1978), p. 62.

specified in advance, and for a specified period of time. As was mentioned above briefly, the workers employed by the basic labour organization of associated work may put down, on the basis of the general act on self-management regulating labour relations, the targets and the cases in which an employee may establish a labour relationship for a specified period of time. On account of their character, the following types of work belong here: seasonal work, tasks to be performed in case of an accumulation of work lasting for a shorter time, or the necessary substitution of employees performing their military service, public services, holding social offices or being absent for a longer period of time for some other reasons. If a worker establishes a labour relationship for a specified period of time, he will enjoy the same rights, perform the same duties and assume the same liabilities as the employees working within a labour relationship concluded for an unspecified period of time; of course, the extent of the rights will be determined by his contribution to work or the duration of his working time or, in other words, the rights in question should be fixed depending on the above details.[82]

Regarding the Hungarian law, there are no restricting provisions in it in respect of the conclusion of a labour contract for a specified period of time; it only states that the maximum duration of the legal relationship may be limited by legal rule.[83] Thus, as regards the research posts of the Hungarian Academy of Sciences, the maximum duration of employment for senior research officers has been fixed for five years, and for junior research officers for three years, in case of a first employment by the academic body in question. In the case of employment of research officers, a labour relationship established for a specified period of time may be prolonged upon its expiration even several times. As regards junior researchers, they may be transferred to the category of research officer upon the termination of the three-year period of practice, continuing the labour relationship as established for a specified period of time, provided that they complied with the conditions laid down in the respective legal rule.[84] As for artists a maximum duration of five years is fixed for their employment contracted for a specified period of time.[85]

Labour relations established for an unspecified period of time represent the general type also for Hungary. Unless agreed upon in the opposite sense, a labour contract has to be regarded as concluded for an unspecified period of time.[86] Besides, an intended duration of a specified period of time, exceeding

[82] Para 174 of the 1976 Act on associated work.
[83] Para 23, subsection 1 of the Labour Code.
[84] Instruction No. 5/1971 MTA–F (A.K. 7) of the Secretary-General of the Hungarian Academy of Sciences, bearing upon the enforcement of Decree No. 7/1969 (XI. 4) Min. of Lab., on the employment of persons engaged in specific fields of research work, for a specified period; and Instruction No. 101/1971 (1–2) Min. of Lab., on the introduction of regular supplements for leading office-holders, further, on some problems of employment in scientific work, and the regulation of competences regarding appointments (employments).
[85] Para 3 of Decree No. 5/1965 (VII. 16) Min. of Educ. was left unchanged by the subsequent Decree No. 1/1969 (I. 15) Min. of Educ.
[86] MIHOLICS (1969), p. 35.

30 days, has always to be stipulated in writing, otherwise the labour relationship will be considered as established for an unspecified period of time.[87]

(2) In respect of the requirements set for the contractual stipulation of the duration of a specified period of time, the differences appearing in the statutes of the various States have a nuance character at most. The duration of a labour relationship can be determined by calendar terms, by specifying the contracted work, or by laying down other conditions that give an objective basis. Most frequently, the duration of a labour relationship of such kind is fixed by calendar days, weeks, months, sometimes by years. The setting of the limit for duration of a labour relationship by specifying the work to be performed is particularly convenient if the accomplishment of a task of urgent or extraordinary character seems to be necessary, therefore the number of the employees has to be increased temporarily, e.g. in case of seasonal or occasional work. The labour relationships established for a specified period of time to substitute the work of other employees being absent for a long time form a separate group. The period of the labour relationship may be determined either by such factors the duration of which is known in advance, e.g. maternity leave, military service etc. of the employee, or by factors with an unknown duration, such as the substitution of an employeee put to the sick-list, etc.[88]

If the labour relationship is concluded for the period of the accomplishment of a specified work, it is justifiable if the employee is advised of the probable date of the completion well in advance of the work. Considering this, the Labour Code of the German Democratic Republic (Article 22, subsection 2) e.g., stipulates that the enterprise is obliged to advise the employee of the planned termination of the work one week ahead of the date concerned. With regard to Hungarian positive law, this requirement is compulsory only in cases of substitution.[89] Information relating to the probable duration of the work concerned, made at the conclusion of the contract, is one point, and giving advice before the termination of the labour relationship is, as a matter of fact, another. In all cases when the duration of the labour relationship is determined by the period needed to perform the work in question, giving information to the employee on the date provided for the termination of the work is required, in our view, already by the demand of the mutual co-operation of the parties; besides, it is needed to make it possible for the employee to look for an appropriate other employment in due time. *De lege ferenda* it is desirable to stipulate in such cases the obligation of giving preliminary advice within a specified term.[90]

(3) The consideration that, as regards labour relations, social interests favour their stabilization has led to a trend in the various States so that their statutes promote the transformation of labour relationships concluded for a specified

---

[87] Para 13, sbusection 2 of the Decree on the Enforcement of the Labour Code.

[88] The latter category is specially emphasized in Hungary; cf. Para 17, subsection 2 of the Decree on the Enforcement of the Labour Code.

[89] Para 17, subsection 2 of the Decree on the enforcement of the Labour Code.

[90] According to Para 48, subsection 1 of the Labour Code of the German Democratic Republic, this period is one week.

period of time to such that bind for an unspecified period of time. Several methods have been applied to this end. The Labour Code of the German Democratic Republic, e.g., contains a provision for the case if an employee, substituting a fellow worker, is prepared to continue to work for the employer also upon the expiration of his labour contract concluded for a specified period of time; then, a labour contract for an unspecified period of time is to be concluded replacing the previous contract. In case the continued employment cannot be arranged, the enterprise has to give support to the worker in order to facilitate his employment with another enterprise.[91]

If a worker employed for a specified period of time continues to work upon the expiration of the contracted period—with the consent of the employer—the duration of the labour relationship transforms from a specified to an unspecified period of time. As is stipulated, e.g., in Soviet Law, the expiration of the term laid down in the labour contract does not automatically involve the cancellation of the contract. Unless one of the parties acts in a contractual sense to cancel the labour relationship in question, the labour contract has to be considered as prolonged for an unspecified period of time.[92]

The Bulgarian law has a similar provision, i.e., a labour contract has to be regarded as prolonged for an unspecified period of time with unchanged conditions if the labour relationship in question continues to exist, on condition, however, that the prolonged performance of work has lasted for at least three days.[93]

As regards the Polish law, there are no provisions of general character concerning the prolongation of the duration of labour contracts concluded for a specified period of time; however, the view has been prevailing that a labour relationship with a specified duration will be transformed, without any particular agreement of the parties, so as to be in existence for an unspecified period of time, if the employee continues to work upon the expiration of the contracted specified period. This arrangement is to be observed unless, taking into consideration all of the relevant circumstances, the duration of the work is evident from the nature of the work in question, which is nothing other than some auxiliary or supplementary work.[94]

The Czechoslovak law has similar regulations, i.e. if the employee continues to perform work upon the expiration of the contracted period of time, with the approval of the enterprise, the labour relationship will be transformed into such that is valid for an unspecified period of time, unless the enterprise and the employee agree differently.[95]

According to the practice established in the German Democratic Republic, a labour relationship contracted for a specified period of time is transformed, too, to a labour relationship for an unspecified period of time, if the employee

91 Para 48, subsection 2 of the Labour Code of the German Democratic Republic.
92 Article 30 of the Labour Code of the Russian Soviet Federated Socialist Republic.
93 Para 28 of the Bulgarian Labour Code.
98 MICHAS (1970), p. 171.
95 Para 56, subsection 2 of the Czechoslovak Labour Code.

84

continues to work upon the expiration of the contracted period for the enterprise with the consent of this latter.[96]

The Government Decree on the Enforcement of the Hungarian Labour Code contains a provision in a similar sense (Para 17, subsection 3).[97]

To some extent it is a disputed problem, whether the labour contracts concluded for a specified period in succession several times of time, i.e. the so-called chain contracts, are valid. According to MICHAS, the possibility of concluding labour contracts for a specified period of time in succession is given if the duration of the contract does not exceed the maximum fixed in the legal rule. With regard to all subsequent contracts, it has to be examined whether the conditions fixed in Para 22, subsection 1 of the Labour Code of the German Democratic Republic for labour contracts concluded for a specified period of time are met.[98]

The possibility of the subsequent prolongations of a labour relationship established for a specified period of time is not excluded also in the Romanian law, provided that it is justified by objective factors, otherwise an abuse of the law is established.

According to the rules of the Hungarian law, there is no obstacle for the parties to conclude labour contracts in succession for a specified period of time; the more, this is just a generally established method in some branches. Supposing, however, that an enterprise tries to make use of this practice with the intention to circumvent the rights of an employee, e.g. to shorten the period of giving notice, the employee is entitled to ask the board of arbitration of the enterprise to declare his labour relationship to have been concluded for an unspecified period of time.[99]

Finally, it should be noted that subsequent prolongations of labour relationships for specified periods of time do not lead *ipso facto* to the transformation of the labour relationship from one kind to another, ie., specified to unspecified, period of time of validity; it is terminated with the expiration of its validity, possibly prolongated repeatedly, unless the transformation is in conformity with the provision of some legal rules.[99/a]

[96] Consultation with PAUL on November 30, 1970 in Budapest.

[97] A labour relationship established for a specified period, exceeding 30 days, will be transformed to a labour relationship for an unspecified period if the employee continues to work for the enterprise for a period of a minimum duration of one day, after the lapse of the period specified in the labour contract, and with the approval of the person charged with the supervision of his work. As regards a labour relationship established for a maximum 30 days of duration, or for even a shorter period, it will be prolonged in such cases only with the same length of time as was the original term.

[98] MICHAS (1970), p. 171.

[99] MIHOLICS (1969), p. 37.

[99/a] As regards the Yugoslav law, the court of justice took the stand that a repeated prolongation of a labour relationship, e.g. in case of substitution for an ill employee, would not involve the transformation of the labour relationship of the substitute to a relationship for an unspecified period. See SZÉKELY (1976).

5.4 Scope of the parties' right of disposal in concluding a labour contract

It is one of the essential consequences of the conclusion of a labour contract that the rules of labour legislation are then applicable to the parties. This binding application is of particular significance in respect of the socialist States for, as KERTÉSZ set forth it clearly, the cogent aspect and not the dispositive aspect is the main rule when laying down the content of socialist labour relationships.[100] Naturally, there have been differences in the legal rules of the various contries in respect of the degree of the cogent element.

As regards the concept of Soviet labour law, some doubts were raised by the provision of Para 28 of the 1922 Labour Code of the Russian Soviet Federated Socialist Republic according to which the stipulations of a labour contract were null and void by virtue of which the conditions of labour of the workers and employees proved to be worse in comparison to the provisions laid down in the legislation on labour, the collective agreements or the internal regulations of the enterprise or institution. This provision permitted namely to draw the conclusion that all agreements made between the contracting parties were valid unless the labour conditions of the employees were deteriorated by them. According to the view evidently to be considered as predominant in the Soviet legal literature, the interpretation referred to above should have been in contradiction to the principle of the primacy of the law.[101] Thus, it must be emphasized that even though—by concluding a labour contract—the parties only undertake the obligation, in terms of Soviet law, to subject themselves to the conditions of labour and wages, they are notwithstanding allowed to put to actual terms the mentioned conditions only within the frames laid down in the law, e.g. by specifying the payable wages, within the limits of the various categories prescribed by law.[102] The terms of a labour contract that are contrary to the law are considered to be null and void also in Soviet jurisprudence, even if the respective provisions do not result in the deterioration of the labour conditions of the workers.[103] As a matter of fact, the contracting parties are free to agree upon complementary conditions such as term of probation, assuming more than one post in work, guaranteeing an official residence, etc.[104] In conformity with the established practice in the Soviet Union, the Fundamental Rules of Labour Legislation contain the provision (Article 5) that the conditions of a labour contract by virtue of which the workers' and employee's conditions of labour proves to be deteriorated in comparison to labour legislation or are contrary to the law are null and void. A similar

---

[100] KERTÉSZ (1964), p. 24.

[101] KARPUSHIN (1958), p. 105.

[102] DVORNIKOV–LIVSHITS–RUMYANTSEVA (1971), p. 13.

[103] Thus the Civil Law Department of the Supreme Court of the Soviet Union declared null and void an agreement in which a legal representative undertook to proceed in a case for a specified percentage of a sum payable by the defendant, instead of a remuneration fixed against the quantity and quality of his accomplished work. See KARPUSHIN (1958), p. 106.

[104] DVORNIKOV–LIVSHITS–RUMYANTSEVA (1971), p. 12.

provision is laid down in Article 5 of the Labour Code of the Russian Soviet Federated Socialist Republic, declaring null and void the conditions of a labour contract by virtue of which the worker's and employee's conditions of labour prove to be deteriorated in comparison to the labour legislation of the Soviet Union and the Russian Soviet Federated Socialist Republic or contravene labour law rules in some other way.

Under the labour law regulation of the German Democratic Republic, labour contracts must comply with the provisions of labour law. Accordingly, points of agreement or stipulations integrated into a labour contract not meeting the mentioned requirement, are to be considered as null and void, and they will be replaced by the rights, duties and liabilities conforming to the provisions of the labour law legislation. If, in the course of the discussions aimed at the conclusion of the labour contract, the enterprise offered the prospective employee remuneration in a higher wage bracket in relation to that admitted by the legal rule, it is then obliged to offer, without any delay, another acceptable job that would conform to the category of wages offered previously. If it is needed the enterprise is obliged, furthermore, to propose a professional training course. Besides, the enterprise is also obliged to pay the employee the wage difference between the admitted and offered category, prior to entering to actual work. Nevertheless, if the employee refuses to accept the alternative job as offered or the professional training as proposed, he will have no more claim for a compensation. With regard to managers of the enterprises, they bear the financial liability for having granted wage categories contrary to the respective legal rules.[105]

As regards the problem of cogency in the Czechoslovak Labour Code, the formulation in the Code cannot be considered as consistently unequivocal, and this statement is valid to the legal rules of other States as well. In fact, the text of the law is frequently not clear enough to permit to state unequivocally whether this or that provision can be regarded as a cogent or a dispositive one. Of course there are cases in which the law-maker's positions are beyond any doubt; e.g., it is clear from the wording of Para 112 of the Czechoslovak Labour Code that, as regards the wages as fixed in the respective regulations or the collective agreements, no deviation is allowed, neither in favour nor to the disadvantage of the employees. In other cases, few in number, anyhow, the law contains prescriptions of explicitly dispositive nature.[106] Nevertheless, the possibility of an arrangement admitting to incorporate provisions into a labour contract favouring the status of the employee and consituting a difference from the general rules, may be envisaged in the field in which the parties' freedom to dispose is not excluded by the law explicitly or, the other way round, it is made possible not explicitly.[107] Agreements *contra legem* are,

[105] Para 44 of the Labour Code of the German Democratic Republic.
[106] Para 51, subsection 2; Para 57, subsection 2; Para 245, subsection 2 of the Czechoslovak Labour Code.
[107] MESTITZ (1968/1), pp. 27–28.

however, not permissible even in these cases; what is allowed, is to come to agreements in favour of the employee *praeter legem*.[108]

The views reflected in the Polish law are worth of interest, too, from this point of view. SZUBERT pointed out, e.g., that—taking into consideration the requirements of the planned economy—all efforts that would have made it possible for the contracting parties to depart from the provisions of the respective legal rules, e.g. in respect of wages, were strictly opposed in Poland. Nevertheless, the view arguing for the admittance of departures from the respective legal rules in labour contracts, in favour of the employees, has gained more and more ground in the judicial practice. The employee is thus entitled even to demand the enforcement of the more advantageous conditions of labour and can by no means be deprived of the rights that have been ensured for him in the labour contract.[109] This means that the upper limit of the wages ceased to be of a cogent nature in all aspects, as far as the employee was concerned. It should be noted, however, that cases of this kind present themselves exceptionally rarely, as also SZUBERT hinted to this circumstance, in view of the fact that wages are regulated and fixed by collective agreements and not by the various labour contracts. Reference is made by him to that with the protection of the contractual rights of an employee proceeding in a benevolent way the financial responsibility of the manager of the enterprise is not excluded at all, provided that he has consented to an agreement concluded on an unjustifiably high level of wages.[110]

In this respect, the relevant provision of the Polish Labour Code of 1974 reads that the stipulations of labour contracts and other acts constituting a labour relationship must conform to the rules of labour law. If the stipulations of labour contracts and other acts constituting a labour relationship are less favourable for the employees than the respective rules of the labour law, they are then null and void, and they have to be replaced by stipulations more in harmony with the relevant provisions of the labour law. So the Code contains no provisions in respect of the case of departures from a legal rule which are in favour of the employee, i.e. sanction of invalidity deals only with the case of departure which are to the prejudice of the employee.

The views expressed in the Romanian legal literature are worth being commented as well. MILLER pointed out that stipulations of a labour contract being more favourable for the employees than those contained in the general provisions of the Labour Code are not inadmissible provided that they are not contrary to the law. The parties are thus free e.g. to exclude the application of the Labour Code rules bearing upon commission or delegation; similarly, an employee has the right to stipulate his exemption from night shift or overtime work.[111]

---

[108] As it is not prohibited by the law, the parties are free to agree in the labour contract that the employee will not perform overtime work.

[109] SZUBERT (1965).

[110] A view set forth in a consultation held on July 19, 1970.

[111] MILLER (1969/1), p. 104.

According to the Hungarian Labour Code (Para 22, subsection 3), labour contracts that are concluded not conforming to the rules relating to employment shall be null and void. Nevertheless, if it is only one clause or some of the clauses of a labour contract that violate the rules relating to employment, only this particular clase or clauses will be null and void, and the contents of the remaining part of the labour contract will be regarded as complying with the rules. As WELTNER remarked in this respect, a labour contract or a stipulation thereof is only null and void if it violates a prohibition with a compulsory force or if a condition of validity qualified as indispensable is not fulfilled. A labour contract or a clause thereof continues to be valid if the violation concerns a rule permissive in nature, for the departure from that rule is permissible in this case.[112] Thus in case a departure from a rule is permissible there is no implication of invalidity if the actual agreement remains within the permitted range.[113]

As regards the law of the various socialist countries, the possibilities of the establishing of labour relations by means of contracts are different in so far as, under the law of some countries, an explicit provision of the respective legal rule permits it, while under the law of other countries, the parties are free to act unless it is prohibited by a positive legal rule. Thus, the role of a labour contract is less to lay down labour conditions, instead, it should serve as a means to ensure the prevalence of the effect of labour law rules for the case of the parties' conforming acts of will to establish a labour relationship. The conditions of labour are laid down in the rules bearing upon labour relations with a compulsory force; in view of this, the most that can be said of the possibilities of the parties reads that they are allowed to constitute their positions in the field of labour law within the limits of the relevant legal rules; in other words, their possibilities in this range are set to limits by the cogent provisions of the law.[114]

5.5 Content elements of the labour contract

The predominantly cogent character of the rules of labour law does not mean as if the will of the parties did not play any role in respect of the conclusion of a labour contract. On the contrary, it is just the parties proper who have to come to an agreement concerning the most essential elements of a labour

[112] WELTNER–NAGY (1974), p. 159.
[113] MIHOLICS (1969), p. 41.
[114] This problem was presented by KERTÉSZ (1964) in a sense that, although the labour contract has an important role within a labour relationship, nevertheless the liabilities resulting directly from the legal rules and independent of the will of the parties are mostly preponderant in respect of the content of a labour relationship; in other words this means that the content of a labour relationship is determined by the rules relating to labour relationships with an absolute character, and on a broad scale, irrespective of the will of the parties, the rules concerned become elements of the content of the respective labour contract or labour relationship, even against the intention of the parties; accordingly, the parties are not allowed, as a rule, to disregard the content elements in question, not only during the existence

relationship, i.e. the sphere of work, wages, etc. — The conditions laid down in the legal rules of the socialist States, and considered to be indispensable for the establishment of a labour relationship, without which no labour contract can come into existence will be the subject of our discussion in this subsection. These conditions are called the necessary (indispensable) contentual elements of a labour contract. It is a different question that the parties are free to agree also upon various other conditions (e,g. stipulation of a term of probation, of premises placed at disposal by the enterprise in its building to be used as a flat, etc.).

(1) Under Soviet law, it is an indispensable requirement of the conclusion of a labour contract that an agreement should be reached in respect of the kind of work to be performed by the employee for the enterprise, on the one hand, and the place of work, on the other.

The agreement upon the kind of work comprises the specification of the job of the employee to be performed. For example, the branch or field in which he will be employed is the professional field of a construction worker, physician, etc., or he will be working as a carpenter, a mason, a house-painter, a surgeon, an oculist, etc.; in other words his trade or specialization will be put down; the degree of training required for the work to be performed (e.g. locksmith of the 3rd or 5th category); the post determined on the basis of professional knowledge, experiences, rank (e.g. in case of employees, head of department, head surgeon etc.). The employee's tasks may also be determined by establishing in detail the various phases of the job. Essentially, we deal here with the scope of the liabilities undertaken by the employee when he enters into the labour relationship.[115]

The agreement concerning the place of work constitutes an indispensable requirement of content of the labour contract as well.[116] According to the rule an agreement is to be reached in respect of the enterprise where the employee will enter into work; essentially, this means the establishment of the place of work. To make it clear, the entire site of the enterprise is considered as place of work under the rules of Soviet law. In view of this, the place of work is to be understood as an enterprise, institution or organization situated in a given place.[117]

There has been a view in the Soviet legal literature claiming that the agreement concerning the place of work need not constitute, essentially, an indispensable contentual element of the labour contract, considering the circumstance that an employee may be put into work, within a given community, in any unit of the structure of an enterprise (e.g. department, section, etc.). Conse-

---

of their labour relationship but even after its termination; similarly, they are not entitled even to renounce of same with legal effect; cf. WELTNER–NAGY (1974), p. 152.

[115] Article 8 of the Basic Rules of Labour Legislation; Article 15 of the Labour Code of the Russian Soviet Federated Socialist Republic.

[116] PRUDINSKY (1974/4), p. 54.

[117] ALEKSANDROV, ed. (1972), p. 241. For the Hungarian literature of this problem see ROMÁN (1972), pp. 373 et seq.

quently, the place in which the work will be performed has to be exactly laid down in the labour contract only if the various units of the enterprise are situated in different communities. It is thus this latter case in which the actual fixation of the place in which the work has to be performed will become an indispensable element of the content of the labour contract; in this case a modification of this point will then be admitted only with the mutual agreement of the contracting parties.[118]

According to the views of some Soviet authors, the setting of the day (time) of entering into work[119] or, in case of labour contracts concluded for a specified period of time, the exact fixation of the termination of the work[120] is also to be regarded as an indispensable element of content.

According to the partisans of another view, the agreement upon wages has to be laid down in the labour contract as well. A stipulation of Article 8 of the Basic Rules of Labour Legislation of the Soviet Union, and the member republics, seems to have been worded in support of this view, qualifying a labour contract to be'an agreement between an employee and an enterprise, institution or organization under the terms of which the employee takes the obligation to perform work related to a definite profession, qualification or function, on the one hand, and the enterprise, institution or organization takes the obligation to pay the employee *wages* (italics from the author) and to ensure labour conditions in conformity with the labour legislation, the relevant collective agreement, and the contractual agreement of the parties, on the other.' The same provision is laid down in Article 15 of the Labour Code of the Russian Soviet Federated Socialist Republic. Nevertheless, a view was also expressed, claiming for the agreement concerning wages to be regarded as an indispensable element of content only for cases in which the legal rule determines the upper and lower limits only of the wage category.[121]

It is a general rule that an agreement concerning the elements of the content of a labour contract must not be contrary to the dispositions of an act or another normative rule. For cases in which an essential condition of labour is not laid down in the labour legislation for an employee of a given labour category, the scope of the indispensable elements of content will be appropriately extended, e.g. with the specifying of time of work for employees performing a secondary job.

As for the various complementary conditions, the stipulation of a term of probation should be dealt with in particular. According to Article 11 of the Basic Rules referred to above, a term of probation may be stipulated in the agreement of the parties when concluding a labour contract, in order to make it possible for the employer to obtain experience concerning the qualification of the employee or worker, with special regard to the performance of the

[118] SMIRNOV (1964), p. 122.
[119] ALEKSANDROV, ed. (1972), p. 241; PASHKOV, ed. (1966), p. 107; SMIRNOV (1964), p. 123.
[120] *Kommentary* (1975), p. 35.
[121] SMIRNOV (1964), p. 125.

work at his/her charge. The limits of a term of probation are laid down in the relevant legislative rules of the Soviet Union and the member republics. It is stipulated in Article 21 of the Labour Code of the Russian Soviet Federated Socialist Republic, that, when concluding a labour contract, the parties may agree upon stipulating a term of probation, with a view to permitting the employer to check whether the worker or employee concerned is suitable to perform the job at his charge. Unless different provisions were laid down by the legislation of the Soviet Union and the Russian Soviet Federated Socialist Republic, the term of probation must not exceed one week for workers, two weeks for employees, exception made for those charged with holding an office of a higher responsibility, and one month for this latter group of high-ranking employees. These terms cannot be prolonged, neither by an administrative disposition or by an agreement of the parties; on the other hand, it is permissible to set shorter the duration of the term of probation.

The employment of a person for a term of probation is not regarded as a definite one during the term of probation, i.e. it will become a definite one or will result in dismissal, depending on the judgment of the quality of his work performed during the term of probation. Similarly, the labour relationship is transformed so as to being concluded for a specified period of time in case the term of probation was prolonged contrary to the provisions of the rules. Then the employer is no more entitled to dismiss the employee on the basis that he failed to come up to the requirements during the term of probation. On the other hand, the enterprise is entitled to terminate the labour relationship of the employee during the course of the term of probation at any time. Contrary to this, the employee has the right to terminate his labour relationship only in conformity with the relevant rules of general character.[122] If the labour relationship is not terminated by the parties until the expiration of the term of probation, the labour contract will assume a definite character.[123] According to the views prevailing in Soviet jurisprudence, the labour contracts concluded for a term of probation are considered to be contracts concluded under a condition of avoidance.[124] In case of an unsuccessful outcome of the term of probation, the labour contract may be cancelled without the obligation of letting the employee know the cause of cancellation. Otherwise, the rights, duties and liabilities arising from a labour contract concluded for a term of probation are equal to those following from a contract concluded without this condition. A term of probation cannot be stipulated in a labour contract concluded for a specified period of time. The respective provisions of the legislation of the other member republics of the Soviet Union are similar to those mentioned and commented above. The categories of work in which a term of probation

---

[122] According to a provision laid down in Article 23 of the Labour Code of the Russian Soviet Federated Socialist Republic, if workers and employees carry on work after the termination of the term of probation, they are regarded as having passed the term of probation successfully; accordingly, the labour contract may be terminated subsequently only in conformity with the respective general rules.

[123] DVORNIKOV–LIVSHITS–RUMYANTSEVA (1971), p. 22.

[124] KARPUSHIN (1958), pp. 106–107.

cannot be stipulated are also laid down in the labour codes of the member republics.

(2) As for the law of the German Democratic Republic, the work tasks, the work place, and the specifying of the beginning of work (day of entering into work) constitute the indispensable elements of the content of a labour contract.[125]

A stipulation concerning the day of beginning to work has to be included into a labour contract in view of the circumstance that this day need not necessarily coincide with the date of conclusion of the labour contract, i.e. a labour contract may be concluded prior to take up work actually; moreover, this is so of necessity in some cases, e.g. if the previous labour relationship of the employee has not yet been terminated.

The work tasks should be determined in the way they occur in reality, taking into consideration the distribution of work within the enterprise and the various registers of the enterprise in which they figure, e.g. workshop certificates and reports, wage lists, directions for qualification, etc. In addition to these, the dispositions of the skeleton collective agreements are also taken into account. It is insufficient to denominate the work categories in the labour contract in a generalizing way, e.g., locksmith, clerk, secretary, etc. for this is not equal to the definition of the actual work tasks; what is required means to specify them just as they are registered with the enterprise, on the basis of the actual distribution of work.[126] It is important to comply with this requirement for it involves essential consequences governed by labour law and relating to such as the remuneration for work, supplementary holidays, liabilities, etc.[127]

---

[125] Para 40, subsection 1 of the Labour Code of the German Democratic Republic.

[126] Accordig to the original wording of the first (1961) Labour Code of the German Democratic Republic, spheres of work *(Arbeitsbereiche)* should have been formed in each enterprise, and these would have comprised the place of work and the tasks equally. Nevertheless, the supplementary 1963 Act to the Labour Code stipulated that tasks and not spheres of work should be determined so as to have a narrower and more concrete category. Report by PAUL from March 15, 1973.

[127] According to Para 100 of the Labour Code of the German Democratic Republic, the competent central State organs and the central committees of the competent trade unions have to agree in respect of the wage categories for the tasks of work, in the form of wage guidelines forming part of the skeleton collective agreements. According to Para 101, the wage category guidelines refer to the work categories included in the collective agreements. If the guideline does not refer to a given category of work, the respective wage or salary category to be applied has to be fixed with the consent of the head of the enterprise and the local trade union committee, in accordance with the stipulations of the collective agreement. The problem of the categorization of wages was dealt with the previous judicial practice as well. It was thus stated that, when determining a job, the global volume of the work performed had to be the point of departure. Let us take an example from the field of the building industry: an assembly carpenter, categorized into the 5th wage group, is more and more assigned to carry on work which, as a result of technical development, belongs already in the limits of 6th wage category, and his increased work constitutes as much as 70 per cent of his activity; a tension will arise between the amount of work laid down in the labour contract, and his actual output. In such cases, the labour contract has to be modified, in compliance with the actual situation. Note that it will be an inappropriate arrangement if the difference of work is reflected only in the wages, i.e. 70 per cent of the

The work tasks as stipulated have to be laid down in the labour contract very clearly, so that their content should be unequivocal for the employee concerned.

The place of work has always to be determined in the labour contract explicitly. It is the enterprise proper that should be designated as the place of work; in case it has several, locally separated, district plants, the one should be designated in the contract as the place of work in which the employee will perform his work actually. The designation of more than one, locally separated, district plant or regional unit of the enterprise as the place of work is admitted if this is required to fulfil the tasks of work as contracted by the parties.[128]

As a rule, wages do not constitute an essential element of the contract; according to the views prevailing in the German Democratic Republic, the agreement upon the tasks of work means that the fixing of the respective category of wages or salaries becomes thus an element of the content of the labour relationship, and this results, in fact, from the provisions of the acts and collective agreements. Some exceptions are made for the cases in which the upper and lower limits of the wages are put down in the skeleton collective agreement, i.e. it is insufficient that only reference is made to the relevant category of wages or salaries. An agreement on wages serves then to complete the fixing of the category of wages or salaries. Nevertheless, a complementary agreement of this kind can only be concluded if it is permissible under the terms of the skeleton collective agreement.[129]

Apart from the indispensable elements of the content of labour contracts, the law of the German Democratic Republic also permits to come to agreements on complementary conditions, bearing upon, e.g., partial employment, undertaking full financial liabilities, etc. within the limits laid down in the legal rules. The stipulation of a term of probation in the contract is inadmissible for it would make the position of the employee uncertain. A 14-day period of notice is applied, unless otherwise agreed upon and, upon the expira-

---

work of the employee would be remunerated according to the 6th, and 30 per cent according to the 5th wage category. Cf. Judgment No. 16/17 of the Supreme Court, dated September 29, 1967. *Arbeit und Arbeitsrecht,* 1968/8, pp. 206–208.

[128] Para 40, subsection 2 of the Labour Code of the German Democratic Republic. It should be noted here that the labour law of the German Democratic Republic distinguishes between the terms *Arbeitsplatz* and *Arbeitsort,* both meaning place of work. Nevertheless, the first is understood to mean the place in which the employee gets in direct contact with the means and objects of work, i.e. the local appearance of the task of work (e.g. in case of more than one post of secretaries in an enterprise, locally at various places, the employee in question may be required to perform the work at any of the places concerned); the second term represents the section, workshop, department etc. of the employing enterprise, locally specified in the respective labour contract. It is the second term *(Arbeitsort)* which has to be agreed upon in the labour contract. See KIRSCHNER–MICHAS (1978), p. 27.–It should be noted, too, in this respect that, unless a contrary provision exists, decision with respect to choosing the *Arbeitsplatz* is within the employer's capacity to dispose. See GERULL (1981/3), p. 131.

[129] With regard to setting the wage limit in the labour contract, see KIRSCHNER–MICHAS (1978), p. 33.

tion of this period, the employment may be cancelled on account of the unsuitability of the employee. It should be noted, however, that the judicial practice has taken a strict stand in respect of the inspection of unsuitability, i.e. it represents the view that the enterprise is obliged to make its best in order to ensure the employment of the person or persons concerned.[130]

(3) According to Polish law, the indispensable elements of the content of a labour contract comprise the fixing of the kind of work, the date of its beginning, and the remuneration for it, according to its kind.[131] Regarding the kind of work, this term is understood to comprise not only the kind and the scope of the actual work as undertaken by the employee to be performed, i.e. the kind of work in its closer sense but every point that determines the character of the employee's conduct at work. Hence, other circumstances such as the character of a leading function, the degree of responsibility, the intensity of the required physical force, e.g., depending on the number of the operated machines, etc., are taken into consideration. The principle saying that—in case the kind of work to be performed is laid down in the labour contract only in general terms—the statutes or the general rules of the enterprise in question are applicable in order to clarify the kind of work continues to be valid. Accordingly, the employer may concretize the kind of work only within the limits laid down in the labour (employment) contract, the statutes of the enterprise or within the general rules as developed there. Nevertheless, the possibility is given for it also within the limits of various kinds of work with a close specific setting, and the sort of work should not be interpreted in a narrow sense.[132]

When fixing wages and salaries, not only the relevant category has to be specified but its components, the modes of payment, etc. as well. With regard to the duration of work, i.e. the time which has to be spent at work, it has to be fixed explicitly only in case of a working time shorter than the maximum working time as laid down in the legal rules, e.g. for half-day employment.[133]

A labour contract may comprise a clause concerning the place of work, and even though its stipulation is not compulsory it is laid down frequently. In the absence of a clause of this kind, the locality in which the work has to be performed for the employer is considered to be the place of work. Hence, the modification of the contract is usually not necessary in case an employee is transferred from a given place of work to another within the territory of the same district, with the employing enterprise left unchanged. Exception is made, however, for cases in which a transfer of an employee within the territory of the same district would result in a substantial deterioration of the living and working conditions of the employee, for transport etc. reasons. In this latter case, the respective labour contract needs to be modified. Furthermore, a

---

[130] Consultation with PAUL on November 30, 1970, in Budapest. Essentially, the district court of Gera took the same stand in its judgment of February 25, 1966. *Arbeit und Arbeitsrecht*, 1966/17, p. 398.

[131] Para 1, Article 29 of the Polish Labour Code.

[132] SZURGACZ (1976), p. 58.

[133] SWIECICKI (1969), pp. 177–179.

labour contract is bound to be modified in case of a transfer from one district to another, even if the employing enterprise remains the same.[134]

Besides, a term of probation may be stipulated in the labour contract with a maximum duration of two weeks; for senior employees, managers performing their work at their own liability, or being financially liable for goods or property remitted to them, the said duration is of three months at most.[135] A labour contract concluded for a term of probation or training in practice expires with the lapse of the period in question; also, it can be cancelled by giving notice prior to its expiration.[136]

(4) Under the rules of the Czechoslovak law, the indispensable elements of the content of a labour contract comprise agreement on the kind of work, the place in which the work has to be performed (district, plant or place otherwise specified), and the day of entering into work.[137] In the absence of an agreement upon all the indispensable elements of the contract, this latter loses its validity, and a labour relationship is not established.[138]

As regards the kind of work to be performed, it can be specified by indicating the trade, e.g. smelter, toolmaker, mason, carpenter, gardener, etc.; or the trade and the category of wages, e.g. metal turner of the 6th category of wages; or the function to be held by the employee.[139] This latter is the usual way of indicating the kind of work for employees in technico–economic posts or working for State bodies (in the civil service).[140] According to a view, a function is to be understood as an assignment to a long-lasting task and some sort of a directing activity, i.e. involving a major degree of responsibility, unless the employee is in a leading post. In this view, the activity of a foreman

---

[134] WALAS (1968/19), pp. 130–138; LEWANDOWSKI (1972/10–11), p. 28.

[135] A person undertaking to perform work for the first time, and he who has not been employed by one single enterprise, institution or body, etc. for one year at least, may be employed by means of a labour contract concluded for an unspecified period only following his/her employment for a term of probation and, subsequently to it, for a term of practice with a complete duration of one year. If the labour contract was concluded for a specified period or a period required for the performance of a specified work, and the employee continues to be employed by the same enterprise, institution, body, etc. even after the expiration of the labour contract which was shorter than one year, another labour contract has to be concluded for a term of practice to compensate the difference of time, consequently, the period of one year should be filled. This term of practice may be shortened to a minimum duration of three months by the head of the employing body upon his/her own initiative or upon the suggestion of the works' council provided that it seems to be justified by the good results achieved by the employee in question in his/her work. However, the establishment of a term of probation or term of practice is not required, if the employee undertook the job with a view to obtaining professional qualification; if the employee continues to be employed by the same enterprise, institution, body, etc.; and if the employee graduated in a specialized primary or secondary school or in a high school, and will be employed in the branch in which he graduated. Paras 1–4, Article 28 of the Polish Labour Code.

[136] Para 2, Article 30 of the Polish Labour Code.

[137] Para 29, subsection 1 of the Czechoslovak Labour Code.

[138] WITZ (1967), p. 109.

[139] WITZ (1971), pp. 26–27.

[140] HOLUKA (1971/6), p. 612.

is also a function.[141] The kind of work may be determined also in a broader sense than according to only the degrees and classes, or categories, e.g., driver entitled to drive various sorts of vehicles for which he holds a licence; on the other hand, a driver may be classified as driver of a car, of a lorry, or, even stricter, driver of lorries of the type 'Tatra 111'.[142]

Employment in more than one profession is also admitted, supposing that the employee may reckon with the possibilities of meeting the requirements, eiher simultaneously, as e.g. a mason and a rough-caster, or alternatively, e.g. gardener in the summer and fireman in the winter season.[143]

As regards the determination of the sort of work, or a function, the Labour Code contains no provisions, therefore the parties' agreement is to be observed. No definition is given with respect to the content of the term 'sort of work' or 'function'. Thus the determination of the sort or function of work either in a narrower or a broader sense depends only on the act of will of the parties. Furthermore, this depends on the needs and possibilities of the employing enterprise and, not least, on the kind of work as provided, on the one hand, and the demands, professional qualification and abilities of the employee, and last but not least on the interests attaching to the precise determination of the obligations concerning the work to be performed, on the other.

A transfer to another sort of work or function is bound, as a rule, to a modification of the labour contract. Nevertheless, in case of a transfer to another particular job within the same sort of work category, the employee may be assigned to do this within the frames of his existing labour contract. Thus, the frames of the sort or function of work as laid down represent at the same time the frames of the enterprise's authority to instruct.[144] Therefore without a change in the sort of work, no unlawful transfer to another kind of work can occur.[145]

Similarly, the relevant legal rules contain no dispositions as to the way according to which the place of work should be fixed in the labour contracts. Practically, this is effected by denominating the district or the enterprise in, or for, which the work has to be performed.

For the interests of the employees the determination of the place of work in a very broad sense may be prejudicial, e.g. in case of enterprises functioning on a district or regional scale, i.e. with a field of activity covering the entire territory of a district or region, resulting in the circumstance that enterprises having such structure are almost free to dispose of their employee's geographical placement, therefore they need not have recourse to a transfer.[146] It would be appropriate in these cases to put down in the contract the town

[141] BIL (1972/7), pp. 412–414.
[142] BIL (1972/7), p. 414.
[143] BERNARD–PAVLÁTOVÁ (1979), p. 65.—With respect to the elaboration of the kind of work (or function) and its alternative definition see also PUDIK (1973/7), pp. 406–411.
[144] HOLUKA (1971/6), p. 613.
[145] SABOL (1970/9), p. 852.
[146] PADELOVÁ (1972/6).

or village (district) of the employee's place of regular work or from which he is sent on official journey.[147]

If the place of work is not laid down in the labour contract, it should be presumed that it is the place at which the employing enterprise has a plant; in case of several plants, the one in which the worker has been employed.[148]

The place of work may be fixed more precisely, by denominating the relevant unit or workshop of the enterprise; for example, Machine shop No. 11, or Shop No. 37 of the Catering Enterprise No. 1 of Prague.[149]

The labour contract usually contains the parties' agreement on the wages category in which the employee will belong, in conformity with the sort of work, or bearing upon other conditions the setting of which is in the interests of the parties.[150] A labour contract may, however, be concluded without an agreement on the wage category, as it follows from the sort of work which has to be performed by the employee under the terms of the labour contract.[151]

Thus, according to the Czechoslovak Labour Code, the concrete establishment of the wage category or of the basic wage is not an essential element of a labour contract. The labour contracts of employees working in technico–economic fields usually contain the denomination of the wage category applicable to the sort of work or function in question, including in some cases the respective upper and lower limits of the salary as well. Nevertheless, the actual amount of the basic salary within the respective two limits is frequently not indicated in the contract for practical reasons, e.g. with respect to wages policy, etc. In such cases the actual amount of the basic salary is laid down in a separate written notice of the employing enterprise. If the basic salary is not fixed in the labour contract, this latter need not be modified in case the amount of the salary is changed. It should be emphasized, however, that the parties are free to lay down the actual amount of the basic salary in the labour contract.[152]

The parties are entitled to stipulate in the labour contract the duration of the labour relationship, particular rules concerning the beginning and the end of the working time, training to a special work, etc. According to the prevailing view, a provision of this kind is admitted in case of an explicit approval of a relevant legal rule (e.g. for shortened working time, cf. Para 86 of the Labour Code) or if it is not explicitly prohibited by a legal rule (e.g. particular rules for working time). Reference should be made in this respect to the preceding chapter in which the possibilities of agreements *praeter legem* are dealt with.

Under Czechoslovak law, a term of probation may be stipulated in the labour contract, with a duration of one month unless the parties agree in a shorter term. A subsequent prolongation of a stipulated term of probation is impermissible, even if its duration is established in shorter than one month.

---

147 For the place of regular work see more details in FREUND (1971/3), pp. 266 et seq.
148 *Sbirka rozhodnuti a sdelini soudu CSSR* (1969/7), Decision No. 7.
149 BERNARD–PAVLÁTOVÁ (1979), p. 67.
150 Para 29, subsection 2 of the Czechoslovak Labour Code.
151 BERNARD–PAVLÁTOVÁ (1979), p. 62; (1980/10), pp. 23, et seq.
152 BRYCHA (1976/1).

Nevertheless, if the employee is not in a position to perform work during the term of probation as a consequence of obstacles beyond his responsibility, for six working days at least, the duration of the obstacles in question has to be excluded from the term of probation.[152/a] The stipulation of a term of probation is not excluded even in case of a labour relationship concluded for a specified period of time; nevertheless, it is an exceptional case that a term of probation is stipulated in a contract of this type.[153] The labour relationship may be terminated by the enterprise or the employee at any time during the term of probation, without the obligation of giving its reason.[154]

(5) According to the Romanian Labour Code, a labour relationship (instatement) is established by concluding an individual labour contract.[155] An individual labour contract contains the obligation of the employee to perform the tasks assigned to him, by observing order and discipline and respecting the law, on the one hand, and the obligation of the employing body to ensure the conditions that are convenient for the employee to perform his work, to remunerate the employee in proportion to the performed work, and to give him all the emoluments that are due him. One of the elements of a labour contract, i.e. the function to be fulfilled by the employee, is thus set and clarified between the parties with the act of the instatement; this element includes the wages, going together with the fulfilment of the employee's function, as well as the other relevant consequences.[156]

It is the instatement in work *(incadrarea in muncă)* of the employee by which he is granted the frame making him a member of the community of the enterprise, with all consequences of this membership. Skilled workers are grouped into categories of special qualification or into various degrees of a particular category.[157] The conditions under which the employees may be instated in various medium-level economic, social, cultural or administrative functions, such as book-keeper, statistician, clerk charged with cultural affairs, filing of documents, archivist, cashier, typist, etc., or as high-ranking office-holders (e.g. economist, legal adviser, editor), are laid down in the relevant legal rules.[158]

The employee is obliged to carry out any activity in compliance with his instatement, conforming to his qualification and the demands of the employing unit.[159] Particular statutes are to be elaborated in sectors in which this is required by the nature of the activity to be carried out there, and the criteria of instatement may be laid down in details in these statutes.[160]

[152/a] PAVLÁTOVÁ (1976/10), pp. 519 et seq.

[153] BERNARD–PAVLÁTOVÁ (1979), p. 77.

[154] Para 58, subsection 1 of the Czechoslovak Labour Code.

[155] Para 64, subsection 1 of the Labour Code of Romania.

[156] GHIMPU–MARMELIUC (1972/2), pp. 42–53.

[157] Act No. 12/1971 on the instatement and the promotion of persons employed by State-owned socialist units; Para 22 of the *Bul. Of.*, 1971/131.

[158] Paras 38, et seq. of Act No. 12, 1971.

[159] Para 20, subsection 2, item(c) of Act No. 10, 1972.

[160] Para 22, subsection 2 of Act No. 10, 1972.

Furthermore, it has to be put down in the labour contract whether the employee will perform his work in a specified region or in a district to which he will be sent on official duty.[161] In view of this, the place in which the labour contract is fulfilled is to be understood at the place of work, i.e. the geographical place that was stipulated as the regular place of performing the work. This is in conformity with the rules bearing upon detached duty, sending the employee to a post, and transfer.[162]

The stipulation of a term of probation is explicitly admitted by the Romanian Labour Code, too; its duration is of fifteen days in general, or 90 days at most for employees in leading posts.[163] A labour relationship may be terminated by any of the parties and at any time during the course of the term of probation, without an obligation to indicate the reason of the termination. At the expiration of the term of probation, the labour relationship has to be regarded as definitely concluded. A term of probation may be stipulated in case of a labour contract concluded for a specified period, in view of the fact that no difference is made between the two types of labour relationship in the relevant legal rule.

(6) According to the stipulations of the Bulgarian Labour Code, the place and the kind of work to be performed have to be laid down in a labour contract; besides, other conditions concerning the utilization of the employee's availability for work may be fixed as well.[164]

As regards the place of work, it may be delimited to a particular district (city, town, village) as the site of the enterprise, or to a section of the enterprise. According to the practice of the Supreme Court of the Bulgarian People's Republic, the enterprise as a whole is to be understood as place of work within the district in question, unless it was restricted to a particular unit of it by the parties at the conclusion of the contract or at a subsequent date.[165]

Regarding the kind of work, i.e. the job or function, it is understood to be a determined variety of work, performed by the employee for the enterprise, institution or organization. The job or function may be determined in various ways, e.g. by specifying the profession or trade (e.g. engineer or engineer engaged in construction work with reinforced concrete), by indicating the degree of skill (e.g. spinner remunerated in the 6th wage category), by giving the post held by the employee (e.g. archivist), or by denominating the working operation (e.g. weft selector).[166]

(7) Turning to the view that may be regarded as established in the Hungarian literature of labour law, agreements on the establishment of a labour relationship, the scope of activity, and the basic salary constitute the required elements of content of a labour contract. Nevertheless, only the two latter

---

[161] Para 64, subsection 2 of Act No. 10, 1972.
[162] MILLER–GHIMPU (1966), p. 21.
[163] Para 63 of the Romanian Labour Code.
[164] Para 15 of the Bulgarian Labour Code.
[165] Information received from MILOVANOV, K., on May 9, 1973.
[166] RADOILSKI (1957), pp. 253 and 262.

points are specifically mentioned in the Labour Code.[167] No mention is made in the Code of the act of will to establish a labour relationship, as the legislator takes it for granted that a labour relationship can only be established if the act of will of the parties is directed towards it.

The place where the work is to be carried on may also be laid down in a labour contract. In the absence of an agreement of the parties on this point, the employee is obliged to perform the work on the site of the enterprise where the labour contract was concluded.[168] If the enterprise has no headquarters or premises at the site where the labour contract was concluded, the site of the enterprise closest to the place at which the labour contract was concluded is to be regarded as the place of work.[169]

The parties are free to agree upon the day of entering into work in the labour contract. Unless an agreement in the opposite sense has been concluded, the employee is obliged to enter into work on the first working day following the day of conclusion of the labour contract.[170]

The parties are entitled to stipulate a term of probation in the labour contract. The normal duration of this term is 30 days; nevertheless, the parties may agree in the labour contract upon a different, i.e. shorter or longer duration, the maximum length being three months. Any party is entitled to terminate the labour relationship in the course of the term of probation with immediate effect. A term of probation may be established even in the case of a labour relationship concluded for a specified period of time. If the labour relationship is not terminated by any of the parties on the last day of the term of probation, the labour contract will have a definitive character from that day, and the labour relationship will be considered as concluded for an unspecified period of time. If the labour contract was concluded for a specified period of time, the labour relationship will exist until the end of the period laid down in the labour contract.[171]

(8) As regards Yugoslavia, labour relations are established there not by means of a labour contract, and the scopes of work, or the particular kinds of work pertaining to the frame of a specific scope of work, are determined by a general act of self-management. The employees are entitled and obliged to perform the scope or task of work that conforms to the purpose for which the labour relationship concerned has been established. In conformity with the law and the respective general act of self-management governing reciprocal relations, the employee may be assigned to any scope of work within the basic economic unit in the course of the duration of the labour relationship, in compliance with his professional qualification or capacity to work.[172]

---

167 Para 22, subsection 2 of the Labour Code.
168 Para 35, subsection 2 of the Labour Code.
169 MIHOLICS (1969), p. 35.
170 Para 15 of the Enforcement Decree of the Labour Code.
171 WELTNER–NAGY (1974), p. 176.
172 Para 177 of the 1976 Act on associated work. Besides, the term of probation is also established in Yugoslav law. At the expiration of a term of probation of three months, the

Summary.—Concerning the positive laws of the various countries, it may be stated that the specification of the work to be performed by the employee constitutes an indispensable element of content of a labour contract, without exception. This may be realized by specifying the scope of activities, function and target, or the kind of work to be performed. In the absence of an actual specification, the establishment of a labour relationship is out of question.[173]

As to the requirement concerning an explicit agreement upon wages, it is not a general stipulation (it is only laid down in the Hungarian and Polish law), for wages are considered by the legislations of some countries as depending on the scope of work, etc. Accordingly, the definition of the scope of work involves, they hold the view, the specifying of the wages as well; a separate agreement upon the wages is thus only necessary if the definition of the scope of work does not cover the specifying of the wages.[174]

An agreement upon the place of work may also be an indispensable content element of the labour contract, as is the case in the positive law of Bulgaria, Czechoslovakia, and the German Democratic Republic. With respect to putting down in writing the beginning of work as an indispensable element of the conclusion of a labour contract, see the law of Czechoslovakia and the German Democratic Republic.—Regarding the agreement upon the establishment of a labour relationship as an indispensable content element of the labour contract, it appears only exceptionally, in the Soviet law, although it is beyond any doubt that, taking the legislation of any country, a labour relationship may come into existence only upon the agreement of the parties in respect of its establishment.

An ordinary existence of a labour relationship seems to be unthinkable without the above elements having been concretized. The only point is to make it clear that some of them are required by the respective legal rule to be laid down in an agreement of the parties, so that if the parties failed to do so a labour contract will not be regarded as established or, if laid down, it will have no validity. The concretization of some other elements may be effected by means of a legal provision, i.e. a subsidiary rule is constituted for the case if the parties failed to come to an agreement upon a condition.

The definition of the scope of work to be performed is by all means an indispensable content element of the labour contract. Here belongs the specifying of wages, too, if the definition of the scope of work did not mean

---

employee becomes member of the respective basic organization of associated work for an unspecified period of time. See SZÉKELY (1977).

[173] This rule was firmly established in the old Hungarian civil law, too. As VINCENTI (1942, p. 68) writes: "the parties have to agree, anyhow, upon the kind of the work or service to be performed by the employee, in general terms at least."

[174] An interesting comparison can be made here again with the old Hungarian civil law according to which the compulsory content of a contract does not comprise an agreement upon the extent of the countervalue to be given by the employer to the employee; the more, not even its kind need be determined in the contract. In case of the absence of a relevant agreement of the parties and, unless another provision is given by a particular rule, the wage is payable in money, and its amount is precised by the court. See VINCENTI (1942), p. 69.

it at the same time. In order to avoid possible uncertainties, with disputes resulting from them, it seems to be a more appropriate approach if the precise assignment into a wage category is considered as an element of the conclusion of a labour contract, which is subject to the agreement of the parties proper. The beginning of work and the place of work may be laid down also by means of a subsidiary rule in the absence of a respective disposition of the parties in the labour contract. An agreement on the establishment of a labour relationship can be disregarded as an indispensable element of content of the labour contract, since it is not so much an element as is a precondition of the setting out of a labour contract.

As regards the auxiliary elements of content of the labour contract, the only remark worth mentioning is that they may appear in varying forms. Nevertheless, more detailed rules bearing upon the said elements may be found only in respect of the stipulation of a term of probation in some legal systems. It is characteristic of these rules that the maximum duration of a term of probation is limited without exception; different rules exist, however, concerning the possibility of stipulating a term of probation or the termination of a labour relationship in the course of a term of probation.

It should be noted finally that the agreement upon the required elements of content of a labour contract should be laid down, as a rule, in an explicit form. An agreement on the scope of work to be performed may come into existence, exceptionally, also tacitly, i.e. in an indicative way; nevertheless, this is only acceptable if, in the absence of an explicit agreement, there is no doubt whatsoever in respect of the scope of work in question. Accordingly, a labour contract will not be established if at the conclusion of the contract the parties failed to come to an agreement, explicitly or tacitly, upon the scope of work to be performed.[175]

5.6 Forms of the conclusion of labour contracts

As regards the formal rules of the conclusion of labour contracts, the regulation is not uniform in the law of the socialist countries. It may be noted that the main trend of development has been, increasingly, the conclusion of labour contracts in writing. The problem is not regulated by the Basic Rules of Labour Law Legislation of the Soviet Union, i.e. its arrangement has been relegated to the legislation of the individual member republics. The labour codes of the member republics contain then, in general, a rule saying that a labour contract may be concluded either orally or in writing. There are cases, nevertheless, in which a labour contract has to be concluded in writing, e.g. in case of employment within the frames of an organized manpower recruitment, employment in the regions of the Far North, etc. As is laid down in some acts of the member republics, the fact of the permission

[175] WELTNER–NAGY (1974), pp. 145–146.

to enter into work has to be regarded as the conclusion of a labour contract. Nevertheless, labour contracts are concluded in the Soviet Union in writing.[176]

Under the provisions of the 1965 Czechoslovak Labour Code, a labour contract could be concluded, as a rule, in a verbal form. This arrangement was modified with the 1969 Amendment of the Code, therefore labour contracts are now concluded in writing, and contracts concluded verbally are only the exceptions. As a rule, labour relationships with a maximum duration of one month could be established in verbal form: notwithstanding, a written form of the contract to be concluded was required in some cases even within the group of the labour contracts with a shorter duration. The validity of a labour contract concluded only in verbal form was not affected by the Amendment, and this meant that a labour contract concluded in verbal form could not be sanctioned by voidness.[177] The employee may claim to conclude the labour contract in written form; the more, he may also claim for indemnification in case of damages suffered as a consequence of the omission of the written form. Moreover, the competent council bodies may impose a fine on the enterprise for the non-fulfilment of the obligations prescribed by the relevant rules of the law.[178]

According to the Romanian Labour Code,[179] a labour contract may be established either in a written or in a verbal form. This rule was modified by Para 6, Act 1 of 1970, providing that a labour contract is to be concluded in writing. Since the previous disposition was not invalidated by the Act and, in view of the circumstance that its field of application covered only socialist (collective) organizations, excluding private employers, the latter continued to be allowed to conclude a labour contract in verbal form. (Practically, this was understood to be applicable mainly to labour contracts concluded with domestic servants.) Owing to the absence of a positive rule declaring labour contracts concluded only in a verbal form to be null and void, the requirement of the written form was understood not to be a condition *ad validitatem* but merely *ad probationem*. Hence, labour contracts continued to be based upon consent.[180]

According to the stipulations of the Labour Code of the German Democratic Republic,[181] a labour contract has to be concluded in a written form. The Code also prescribes that at least the category of wage or salary as stipulated and the duration of holidays for recreation must be indicated in the written con-

---

[176] Furthermore, the labour codes of the member republics may contain dispositions providing that employment can take effect through an instruction (disposition) of the board of directors of the employing enterprise. This is laid down in the model regulation issued by the State Committee for Labour and Wages, attached to the Council of Ministers of the Soviet Union, dated from September 29, 1972. See PRUDINSKY (1974/4), p. 54.—The view was expressed also in the legal literature that the inadequate way of formulating the content of a labour relationship may well have an influence upon its course. See ARDZINBA (1980/4). p. 78.

[177] Cf. Paras 32 and 242 of the Czechoslovak Labour Code.

[178] MESTIT (1970/2), p. 10; PUDIK–BENES(1974), p. 54.

[179] Para of the 1972 Romanian Labour Code.

[180] BELIGRĂDEANU (1971/6), p. 71; STANOIU (1974/5), p. 10.

[181] Para 42 of the Code.

tract. The contract text has to be delivered to the employee without delay, but on the day of entering into work at the latest. The situation is not completely unequivocal for the case if the parties failed to observe the written form. It is beyond doubt that any of the parties is entitled to terminate the labour relationship by giving notice. Our view that in the absence of giving notice the labour relationship continues to be existing, seems to be supported by the opinion expressed in the relevant literature arguing that it would be unreasonable to terminate a labour relationship, constituted by the consent of the parties, merely on account of the absence of a contract in written form.[182]

As regards Poland, the conclusion of a labour contract in writing was required by the legal rules in force prior to the enactment of the present Labour Code only in few cases. Even so, the conclusion of labour contracts in written form was a fairly general practice. It was thus just the confirmation of the already established practice that the Labour Code prescribed the conclusion of a labour contract in written form, requiring explicitly to specify the type and conditions of the contract concerned.[183] In case a labour contract was concluded not in writing, the employing enterprise was obliged to confirm the type and conditions of the contract to the employee, in written form and without any delay.[184] Just as in the Romanian law, the significance of the written form is limited to the point of evidence, and the failure of using the written form does not involve prejudicial legal consequences automatically.[185]

As is laid down in the Bulgarian Labour Code, a labour contract has to be concluded in a written form.[186] According to the prevailing view, expressed in Bulgarian jurisprudence, this is a requirement *ad validitatem* and not *ad probationem*, i.e. its non-observance implies the voidness of the contract in question.[187] Nevertheless, this opinion of principle was made more elastic by practice, i.e. the requirement of the written form for the conclusion of a labour contract has to be regarded as met if the employing enterprise issued a written document on the entering into work of an employee, even in the absence of a written application for employment of the worker.[188]

Concerning Hungary, a labour contract may be concluded both in verbal and in written form; it may come into existence even tacitly, on the basis of an indicative conduct. There are two cases, however, in which

---

[182] KAISER–KIRSCHNER–SCHULZ (1974), pp. 47 and 84. Even if the parties failed to use the written form the labour relationship is established, as a labour contract concluded only in verbal form also has a legal effect. The existing defect may be remedied, as the contract may be put into a written form subsequently. KIRSCHNER–MICHAS (1978), p. 36.

[183] A labour contract may be concluded either for an unspecified period, or for a specified period, or for a period required for the performance of a specified work; cf. Article 25, subsection 1 of the Polish Labour Code. This is understood to mean the types of the contract.

[184] Article 29, Para 3 of the Polish Labour Code.

[185] It should only be noted that the same principles are applicable in relation to the form of giving notice. See SALWA (1974/8–9), p. 24.

[186] Para 16 of the Bulgarian Labour Code.

[187] RADOILSKI (1957), p. 255.

[188] MRATCHKHOV (1965/3), p. 48.

a labour contract has to be concluded in writing, i.e. in case of a specific stipulation of a legal rule or if the employee requests it. Furthermore, distinction should be made whether the entire labour contract has to be put down in writing or it is only for specific stipulations that their validity depends on their written form. If the written form is prescribed by a legal rule as a condition of validity and, irrespective of this stipulation, a labour contract was concluded only in verbal form, recourse may, or should, be made to remedy. Nevertheless, the labour contract becomes valid with the lapse of a period of thirty days, even in the absence of a realized remedy. Essentially, it is a similar situation if the party requested its being put down in writing; with the lapse of a period of thirty days, the remedy will be made automatically, for it would be against the interests of the parties if reference could be made to the invalidity of a labour contract of this kind even after the lapse of a longer period. Different sanctions are applied in case a contract was not put down in writing but the written form was declared as a condition of validity only for some of the stipulations. Thus, a labour relationship concluded for a specified period of time and longer than thirty days but not put down in writing will be considered as concluded for an unspecified period of time; if the employment was stipulated for various places of work and the parties failed to put down this in writing, the stipulation of various places of work will be regarded as null and void.[189]

Summary.—Labour contracts may generally be concluded in both verbal and written forms; nevertheless, their conclusion in writing are regarded as being increasingly brought into practice. For most countries, the absence of a written form does not involve the voidness of the contract because the fundamental principle is to respect the intention of the parties concerning the legal act in question. Accordingly, a labour relationship must be regarded as duly established in the presence of the consent of the parties, irrespective of the form of the contract in question. Therefore, the written form has not been a condition of validity in general, although there are cases supporting this view. Furthermore, a *stricti juris* judgment of the form of a contract seems to be inadequate, all the less so, since in case of a complaint of the employee, the respective rules of procedure make it possible for the competent bodies anyway to take a stand in respect of the existence or non-existence of the labour relationship in question; the relevant rights, duties and liabilities may then be fixed in case of doubts.

[189] WELTNER (1960), p. 132; Paras 17 and 18 of the Decree of Enforcement of the Labour Code.

6. MODIFICATIONS OF LABOUR RELATIONS

6.1 Scope of the modifications of labour relations

When analysing these problems first and foremost the concept of the modification itself should be considered. It is a conceptual element of modifications of labour relations that in their case the labour relationship continues to exist but a change takes place in some of its original relevancies. Contrary to the termination of a labour relationship, a modification thereof has only partial effects. Changes may take place in respect of either the subjects, or the objects, and the contents of a labour relationship.

A change in the subjects of a labour relationship means that on the employer's side it is replaced by another subject at law. In fact a change in the person of the employee is beyond the scope of modifications in labour relations, for a change of this kind involves the termination of the labour relationship. The obligation of the actual performance of work by the employee constitutes, necessarily, an essential element of a labour relationship. In view of this, if an employee fails to meet some obligation for any reason whatsoever, the labour relationship has to be terminated except for such circumstance that receives legal protection. No possibility exists for the employee to get somebody to do his job, even temporarily.

Consequently, if the work is taken over from the employee figuring in the respective contract by another person, the work of the latter will be performed within the framework of a new labour relationship, and not the previous relationship will be continued with another subject at law in the position of the previous employee.

As regards the employer's side, a change of the subjects at law in general takes place in the case of the termination of the existence of the employing enterprise.[1] Two cases should be distinguished here, viz. (1) reorganization; when a legal successor is given, this, too, has two variants: (i) fusion (merger) meaning the unification of two enterprises, and (ii) division, when two or more enterprises are established from a preceding one; it is a general rule that the content of labour relations is not affected by reorganization; admittedly, some modifications—for example, in the work tasks—may become necessary as a result of a reorganization, notwithstanding, in cases of this kind a particular disposition is required, usually in the form of an agreement with the employee con-

---

[1] Existing labour conditions are not affected by changes in the property of the employer, i.e. the new proprietor enters into the labour relationship. Of course it is a different point that a change of the owner of the enterprise (employer) may induce the employee, or the

cerned; (2) when a legal successor is not given, ie. in case of liquidation, the labour relationship of the employee or employees has to be terminated in the prescribed way, usually by means of joint consent or by giving notice.

It may thus be stated that the modifications of labour relations, changes occurring in the person of the subjects of a labour relationship, may only be of significance if the changes take place on the employer's side. A modification of a labour relationship may occur not *ipso facto* but upon the agreement of the parties, in compliance with the legal provisions applicable to the case. Accordingly, from the viewpoint of the modification of the labour relationship, a change in the subjects of a labour relationship may only have an indirect effect.

As regards the changes in respect of the objects of a labour relationship, these do not present any considerable problem, either, for the modification of a labour relationship. It should be remembered to this point that the object of a labour relation is understood to be a specified conduct (performance of work) and the employee is obliged to come up to it so that direct or indirect sanctions are applicable if the employee fails in performing the relevant conduct or fulfilling some obligation in an adequate wwy. The employer is obliged to keep to an appropriate conduct as well, principally to pay wages, and his failure to keeep to the respective conduct, or an insufficient fulfilment of his obligation, implies sanctions equally. In fact the appropriate conduct is in an inseparable relationship with the exercise of the rights and the fulfilment of the obligations constituting the content of labour relationships. Any change taking place in the content elements of a labour relationship has necessarily an effect on the conduct that form the object of the labour relationship, irrespective of the circumstance whether the conduct is related to the employer or the employee. A change in the object of a labour relationship cannot be examined under labour law if it is isolated from the content elements of the labour relationship. This is the reason why the modifications in labour relations are not dealt with separately in the literature on labour law. The changes in the content elements in question are examined as being necessarily constituting parts of the conduct. This method is more appropriate for grasping the principal problems bearing upon modifications in labour relations than the one starting from changes that take place in the object of labour relations. It should be remarked here that the problem of modifications in labour relations are dealt with in the legal literature through examining the modifications of the labour contracts, since the basis of a labour relationship is usually the labour contract and the modification of a labour relationship takes place, as a rule, in the form of the modification of the labour contract. The changes are mostly related to content elements of the labour relationship (for example, especially, the scope of work, and the place of work). In general, this view is also expressed in the positive rules of law, but, as a matter of fact, not without

employer as well, to modify or even to terminate the labour relationship. NAGY (1975/7), pp. 379–380.

exception. In the Czechoslovak Labour Code[2], e.g., the point of departure is the modification of the labour law relation, and the question of modifying the stipulated labour conditions is dealt with within the modification of labour law relations, which comes to realization by means of modifying the labour contract.[3]

6.2 Modification of the content elements of the labour relation

In the majority of cases, a labour relationship is continuous; nevertheless, the necessity of changes may present itself during its course in respect of the activity, technology, the number of the staff of the employer, on the one hand, and the personal, family or other circumstances of the employee, on the other, which may make it impossible or difficult to maintain the legal relationship with an unaltered content. The content of the legal relationship has to be coordinated with changed situations, and the juridical means for that is given by modifying the labour relationship. A modification of a labour relationship may be made necessary for highly different reasons.

It is general rule that all content elements of a labour contract may be modified in respect of which the parties were free to come to an agreement at the conclusion of the labour contract. Within this range, a modification may concern any condition laid down in the labour contract, but it may extend even to such a case in which—although no explicit arrangement was laid down in the labour contract concerning a given condition—it is apparent that one of the parties has concluded it only because he paid regard to the condition in question, and the other party had been advised of it.[4-7] The modification of a labour relationship may be required also by the deterioration of a condition of work, even if this condition was not laid down explicitly in the contract.[8-9]

[2] Para 36 of the Czechoslovak Labour Code.

[3] It should be mentioned that a labour relationship established by appointment and election may be modified, as a rule, with the consent of the employee and by means of the appropriate acts; in view of this, it seems to be correct to take the regulation on modification of the labour relationship as starting point.

[4-8] This is the situation, e.g., when an employee concludes the labour contract only in the supposition that his work will be linked with a specified type machine or a given section of the enterprise, and the employer has no doubt concerning this point. MILLER (1964/2), pp. 182 et seq.

[8-9] It is a disputed problem whether the reduction of the basic salary, within the upper and lower limits of the wage category concerned, has to be regarded as a modification of the labour relationship. According to a view expressed in the Czechoslovak legal literature, this measure cannot be considered as a modification of a legal relationship, provided that the relevant labour contract has a clause saying that the enterprise is authorized to reduce the basic salary by a unilateral act, within the limits of the relevant wage category in case the performance drops below a specified rate. In the absence of a disposition of this kind of the labour contract, the enterprise is not allowed, however, to reduce the fixed basic salary by a unilateral act. It should be added to the preceding that, as is laid down in the Chechoslovak law, an agreement on the wages does not institute a compulsory content element of a labour contract. In practice, the parties agree on the assignment of an employee to a

Similarly, it is beyond any doubt that, in a given case, the modification of the labour relationship may be required even in the case of the amelioration of a condition of work, when the consent of both parties is absolutely necessary to carry it out.[10]

There is no possibility of modifying the content of a labour relationship in cases which are beyond the competence of disposition of the parties. These cases comprise those content elements of the labour contract which are declared to be absolutely necessary by a legal rule. The bans of employment represent also restrictions in this respect.

It is inadmissible to assign an employee to a category or place of work for which a valid labour contract cannot be concluded as a consequence of a ban of employment; if an assignment is carried out to a function or place of work of this kind, in spite of the ban, the employee in question must be re-assigned to his original function or place of work after the facts of the case have been established.[11]

The modification of the content of a labour relationship is possible primarily by means of the joint consent of the parties. This is the principal form of modifying the labour relationship. Even though this concept is expressed in different ways by the legal rules of the various countries,[12] the fundamental

wage category which is in conformity with the kind of work to be performed. Anyhow, this is also not a required way of settlement, taking into account Czechoslovak jurisprudence, in the view of which the assignment to a wage category is always related to the actual work under the terms of the contract. BRYCHCA (1976/1), pp. 61–65.

Another example: the transfer of a locksmith from an indoor to an outdoor place of work within the same enterprise has to be regarded an actual transfer, i.e. a modification of the relevant labour contract, according to the views expressed in the Soviet legal literature; accordingly, a mutual consent of the parties is required, even if the transfer would not mean an assignment to another scope of work. PIATAKHOV (1970/4), p. 83.

10 In the Romanian legal literature MILLER (1964/2. p. 184) mentions the cashier of a shop of a co-operative as an example. The employee has to be transferred to the centre of the co-operative, again as a cashier, and with a higher salary, still he refused to accept the transfer, although the district in which the work should have been performed was the same. Since the execution of the tasks of a cashier in the given shop was of a decisive importance for the employee when the labour contract was concluded, and this circumstance was known to the co-operative, a unilateral transfer to the centre of the co-operative was impermissible.

11 Para 19, subsection 2 of the Decree on the Enforcement of the Hungarian Labour Code.

12 As is laid down in Article 12 of the Basic Rules of Labour Law Legislation of the Soviet Union and the 1971 Labour Code of the Russian Soviet Federated Socialist Republic (Article 24), an enterprise, institution or organization is not entitled to demand the performance of work from an employee in the absence of a relevant agreement on this particular work. As is put down in Article 24 of the Bulgarian Labour Code, the sort (nature, content) of the work specified in the labour contract, in another word the function of work can be modified only with the consent of the employee. According to the Chechoslovak Labour Code (Para 36, subsection 1), the content of a labour contract as specified can only be changed with the mutual consent of the enterprise and the employee. According to the Labour Code of the German Democratic Republic (Para 49), the clauses of a labour contract can be modified only in contractual way. The respective provision of the Hungarian Labour Code (Para 24) reads that the labour contract can be modified only with the mutual consent of the enterprise and the employee. For more details from the Hungarian literature concerning

principle is the same, i.e. the conditions laid down in a labour contract may be modified, as a rule, with the bilateral consent of the parties only.

As an exception, some content elements of a labour relationship may also be modified by a unilateral act of the employing enterprise. Thus, the employer is entitled to modify the basic salary (wage) of an employee unilaterally, with regard to an alteration of the relevant wage system. The provisions of the content of a labour contract which are contrary to some newly-issued rules, bearing upon wages, cannot be compulsory for the enterprise from the day of the latter entering into effect, i.e. *ex nunc*. Accordingly, the enterprise is obliged to observe the new provisions on wages as cogent legal rules, and to modify the relevant provisions of the content of the labour contract, bearing upon wages, by a unilateral legal declaration of constituting character.[13]

Under given conditions, the employer is entitled to modify an employee's category and place of work by means of a unilateral act. This modification may take place with a provisional or continuous effect or in a compulsory or facultative way. The point here is whether the modification of the labour contract, serving as basis for the labour relationship, is thus concerned, or such situations presented themselves which had already been taken into consideration by the parties at the conclusion of the contract and, as a consequence, they became content elements of the labour relationship in a way that their realization did not require such modification of the labour relationship that could be subjected to the consent of the other party. Under Hungarian law, e.g., an employee may in a justified case be obliged to perform work even beyond his function of work; furthermore, he may be obliged to carry on work in the same premises of the plant, within the same function of work, and with his basic wage unchanged but in a place of performance other than stipulated in his contract.

The following comments will be limited to the problem of assignment to another function or place of work, as this represents a typical case of the modification of a labour relationship, in our view, and is the source of the most numerous disputes. Thus the cases of the transfer of an employee should be examined in detail in which the labour relationship concerned has to be modified in fact, on the one hand, or the function or place of work of an employee may be changed without modifying the labour relationship, on the other.

---

the modification of a labour contract with the mutual consent of the parties, see WELTNER (1965), pp. 412 et seq.

[13] There is an explicit provision in this sense in the Hungarian positive law (Para 24, subsection 1 of the Labour Code), but similar provisions may be found in the law of other countries as well. BRYCHCA (1976/1), pp. 61 et seq.

6.3 Transfer from one function or place of work to another as the basic case of the modification of the content elements of the labour relation

In view of the circumstance that the transfer of employees from one function or place of work to another proved to be a means enabling the management of enterprises to carry out rearrangements in the most efficient way, that ensure the most appropriate utilization of the manpower, enterprise managements make use of this possibility relatively frequently in the course of their operative activities. However, dispositions of this kind by the management may affect the employee in a very sensible way. Consequently, it is not indifferent whether the employer is entitled to order a transfer by means of a unilateral act, within the range of his power of instructions or this possibility is only given by means of the modification of the labour relationship when the consent of the employee is indispensable.

Taking a different approach, the acts may also be grouped so that the transfer of an employee from one function or place of work to another may present itself in some cases as the employer's right, whereas in other cases the employee has a legal right to be employed in a function or at a place of work other than that in which he works at present. In this latter case, the employer is under the obligation of affecting the transfer. Finally, it may also occur that, in case of the existence of specified conditions, the enterprise is under the obligation of effecting a transfer even in the absence of a claim for it on the part of the employee. This rule is linked usually with the protection of female employees having children.

The transfer of an employee from one place of work to another may be effected within one enterprise and more than one enterprise. In the comments that follow we shall be concerned only with the possibility of a transfer within the enterprise and so the cases of inter-enterprise transfer will be disregarded.

In this respect it should be recalled that, as far as the Hungarian law is concerned, an enterprise is not entitled to transfer an employee to another enterprise permanently, without the employee's consent. Similarly, this rule occurs only exceptionally in the law of other States.[14]

As a matter of fact, a provisional delegation of an employee to another enterprise is admitted both in Hungarian law and in the law of other countries. This case needs, however, only to be indicated here.

The parties may agree that the employee transferred enters into a labour relationship with the other enterprise. This, however, belongs in the scope of

[14] As is laid down in the Romanian Labour Code (Para 69), a person assigned to a labour relationship may be transferred to another economic unit within the same branch, as a rule, being in the interests of the employer, in order to improve the operation of the unit in question. However a transfer serving the interests of the employer is inadmissible if the employee does not agree with the transfer for causes affecting his state of health (and he confirms this by a medical certificate) or from other appropriately justified motives. The competent supervising body will then decide on the well-foundedness of the motives. BELIG-RĂDEANU (1978), pp. 123 et seq.

termination, and not in that of modification, of a labour relationship, consequently it is dealt with in the part bearing upon the termination of labour relations.

6.4 Transfer from one function or place of work to another as the employer's right

The employer's right to transfer an employee from one function or place of work to another may be attributed to causes that present themselves either on the employer's or the employee's side. The transfer may be carried out with a continuous or a provisional effect. It should be emphasized here again that, as a rule, the legal rules do not entitle the employer to transfer an employee from one function or place of work to another indefinitely, i.e. continuously, for a cause emerging on the employer's side and with a unilateral act of this latter, without the employee's consent.[15] A transfer linked with a cause on the employer's side may be effected only provisionally but a transfer linked with a cause that presented itself on the employee's side may be carried out with both a continuous and a provisional effect.

6.4.1 Transfer of an employee on account of a cause emerging on the employer's side

Under Hungarian law, an employee may provisionally be obliged to perform work beyond his scope of activity, for a cause arising on the employer's side and in a justified case. With regard to his function, age, state of health or other conditions, the work must not cause him, however, disproportionate prejudices, and must not affect his right to salary, according to his previous (original) function.[16] Performance of work beyond the normal scope of activity may be justified by various causes, e.g. substitution, unexpected accumulation of work, elimination of a trouble in operation, etc. Furthermore, an employee may be obliged to perform work outside the place of his permanent work with a provisional effect.[17] Unless otherwise agreed upon, the duration of the work beyond the contracted field of activity of the person, or ordered so as to be performed outside the place of his permanent work must not exceed three

[15] ALEKSANDROV (1972, p. 261) emphasized in particular that the transfer of an employee was inadmissible without his consent, even if the enterprise was anxious to effect it. The only exception is Romania, where the transfer with permanent affect does not depend on the consent of the transferred person. Cf. BELIGRĂDEANU (1978), p. 124.—In the law of the socialist countries this is a special regulation, therefore in our generalizing remarks it is not dealt with.

[16] An employee performing an easier type of work on account of an organic disease would suffer an injury if the enterprise might decide to transfer him to another kind of work that involves a considerable physical burden.

[17] Para 35 of the Labour Code. The collective agreement elaborates on what should be understood under a transfer having transitory or provisional effect in this respect.

months per calendar year, except if a longer period of performance is justified by extraordinary circumstances or it is provided for in the collective agreement.[18]

According to the Soviet law, an employee may be transferred, provisionally, to a work other than his contracted one, by a unilateral act of the employer if it is required by the needs of production and in case of idle time in his permanent work.[19] The first point covers the cases of natural disasters, the prevention or elimination of damages in production, the ruining of State or collective property, as well as the substitution of absent workers and employees. In these cases, a provisional transfer from one work to another is admitted with a duration of up to one month at most. In case of the suspension of work (idle time), the transfer is applicable over the entire duration of the suspension of work (idle time).[20]

Under the provisions of the Bulgarian law, an employee may be transferred from one work to another,[21] for the needs of production, the suspension of his contracted work, and as a result of unavoidable circumstances. The duration of transfer effected for the needs of production may be longer or shorter, and the task to be performed may take a permanent character as well; nevertheless, the transfer of an employee to another work without his consent must not exceed 45 days per year.[22] The suspension of work is a provisional phenomenon; nevertheless, if it turns to take a permanent character, the consent of the employee is required to his transfer to another work of permanent nature.[23] Finally, the duration of the existence of unavoidable circumstances depends on the actual factors. Taking into consideration, however, that unavoidable circumstances frequently arise from production needs, an employee who has already been transferred to another work for the reason of production needs for a period of 45 days cannot be transferred any more for the reason of production needs in the course of the same year.[24]

As for the Czechoslovak law, the placing of an employee from one work to another is permissible in the case of idle time, the prevention of a natural disaster or other imminent danger or for the lessening of the conditions or

[18] Para 37 subsection 13 of the Decree on the Enforcement of the Hungarian Labour Code.

[19] A transfer to a kind of work other than contracted but required to meet production tasks is permissible, irrespective of the trade and professional qualification of the employee concerned. Nevertheless, the interests of production and the employee, i.e. the necessity of the reasonable employment of the cadres in particular, require not to allow the existence of a striking controversy between the work after transfer and the professional qualification of the employee concerned. In the field of substitution, a skilled worker cannot be required to perform a work not bound to a professional qualification. NIKHITINSKY–GLASURIN (1976/ 23), p. 725.

[20] Para 14 of the Basic Rules; Paras 26 and 27 of the Labour Code of the Russian Soviet Federated Socialist Republic.

[21] A transfer to another job is understood to mean a change of the content of a labour contract as a result of which the workers and employees will carry on another kind of job or will work at another place than contracted, or the change will take place in both senses. RADOILSKI (1957), p. 262.

[22] MILOVANOV (1972), p. 96.

[23] MILOVANOV (1972), p. 104.

[24] MILOVANOV (1972), p. 122.

consequences of same, or for another inescapable industrial need; nevertheless, a maximum permissible duration of 30 days is set for the latter case.[25] An employee's transfer from one place of work to another is only permissible within the employing enterprise, and in the case of industrial need occurring in the relevant plant, and with a maximum duration of 90 days per calendar year.[26]

According to the Yugoslav law, an employee may be assigned to any work or task of work within the basic economic organization for which he works, in the course of the duration of his labour relationship, in conformity with the general act of self-management and the law, in compliance with his professional qualification or ability to work, on the basis of the fixed demands of work, and in accordance with the factors laid down in the act. Exceptionally, an employee may be assigned, with his consent, to a category of work or tasks which require a qualification lower than his actual one. This transfer may be of provisional or permanent effect.[27]

As regards Poland, employers are also entitled to give orders to their employees, in cases justified by the needs of the enterprise, such as acts of God, replacement of an absent employee, idle time, etc., to perform a kind of work other than that specified in the labour contract.[28] This right is limited to a period of three months at most within a calendar year, provided that this act does not imply the decrease of the earnings of the employee and complies with his professional qualification.[29]

In this respect reference should be made to a specific institution of the Polish law, i.e. giving notice with a modifying character. The relevant dispositions of the Labour Code give precise rules on the principles of giving notice with a modifying character,[30] thus filling the gap which existed in this respect in the previous rules. This means that the provisions bearing upon the termination of the labour contract are appropriately applicable if the employer proposed the employee new conditions of work or wages, and the employee refused to accept them. In the latter case, the labour contract is terminated with expiration of the period of notice. If the employee did not declare his refusal to accept the proposed conditions before the expiration of the first

[25] Para 37, subsection 3 of the Czechoslovak Labour Code. The mentioned provision is worded in the Czech version of the Code as *prevedeni*, while in the Slovak version as *preradenie*.

[26] Para 38, subsection 23 of the Czechoslovak Labour Code. The mentioned provision is worded in the Code as *prelozeni* and *prelozenie*.

[27] Para 177 of the 1976 Act on associated work. According to a provision laid down in Para 179, the employees are obliged to regulate, by means of a general act of self-management, the cases and conditions the existence of which allows that an employee may or must perform other tasks or jobs than contracted, either provisionally or with a permanent effect (transfer of an employee).

[28] According to the Polish Labour Code (Article 29, Para 1), the parties should agree on the kind of work *(rodzaj pracy)*.

[29] Para 4, Article 42 of the Polish Labour Code. In the previous regulation, a period of six months was also provided in case of substitution. LEWANDOWSKI (1972–10/11), p. 28.

[30] Articles 42 and 43 of the Polish Labour Code.

half part of the period of notice, he has to be regarded as having consented to the conditions in question.[31]

According to the law of the German Democratic Republic, an employee may be assigned to an activity beyond the category of his specified tasks of work, or an activity to be performed at a place of work other than the contracted one, only in exceptional cases, taking into consideration the social and personal interests as well as the qualification of the employee.[32] Accordingly, an employee may be assigned to perform a work other than his contracted one, or at another department or section in the community as contracted originally, or for an enterprise other than specified in his original contract, if this seems to be necessary to meet requirements considered as important for the enterprise or for the national economy. In cases of this kind, the duration of the assignment, i.e. to perform a work differing from the contracted one, must not exceed four weeks within one calendar year. An order to perform a work other than the contracted one but for the original enterprise is permissible only with the consent of the employee, in case its duration would exceed a period of four weeks. An order to perform a work differing from the contracted one and to be effected at a department or section of the enterprise in a district other than the one named in the original contract, is only permissible with the consent of the employee. An approval of the local trade union committee is required to an assignment when the work to be performed differs from the contracted one, and it should be made continuously and for a period of more than two weeks. Finally, the consent of the local trade union body is absolutely necessary if the work is other than the contracted one and it has to be performed for an enterprise other than the contracted one but in the district named in the originally concluded contract.[33]

With the consent of an employee to a commission to perform a work other than the contracted one, in a case specified in the legal rules, no contract modifying the preceding one will come into existence for, having accepted the commission, the employee does not yet undertake an obligation to perform the work permanently.[34]

According to the Romanian Labour Code, each employee is obliged to participate in carrying out any kind of work and executing any measure required by the interests of the enterprise, irrespective of his function and

[31] ZIELINSKI (1975/5), pp. 640–658.

[32] In case of catastrophies, the provisions relating to the performance of work with a provisional effect do not apply; then the provisions of the Decree February 28, 1963 (Gbl II. 139) are decisive, binding all State and economic bodies, institutions, and the citizens to participate in the prevention of and fighting against catastrophies as well as in the elimination of their direct consequences.

[33] Paras 84–88 of the Labour Code of the German Democratic Republic. For the literature, see LANGANKE (1980/4), pp. 173–175.

[34] ADLER (1973/17), pp. 523–524; furthermore, judgment of the Supreme Court of the German Democratic Republic, passed on November 10, 1972; *Arbeit und Arbeitsrecht*, 1973/ 17, p. 533.

field of activity; this obligation is applicable to extraordinary cases, according to the needs of the required operation of the enterprise.[35]

Summing up, it may be stated that the right of an enterprise to provisionally transfer an employee to another category of work or a particular work or to another place of work, for a cause which presented itself on the employer's side, is limited to exceptional cases related to the functioning of the enterprise; as for the duration of a transfer of this kind, it is made dependent on the supposed duration of the exceptional circumstances which provoked it, or it is exactly fixed. The provisional or transitory nature is understood to be the decisive element in the transfer of employees. In case of a probably longer duration of a transfer, the consent of the employee is indispensable.

6.4.2 Transfer on account of a cause emerging on the employee's side

The transfer in these cases may be of a provisional or a permanent nature.

Under the rules of Hungarian labour law, an employee may be transferred to a category or place of work other than that laid down in his labour contract for a specified or an unspecified period of time, as a result of a disciplinary procedure. In the latter case, the transfer may take place with his category of work left unchanged, as well. The Hungarian labour law admits transfer to another, but identical, category of work, provided that the transfer of the employee to another worker's community within his employing enterprise ensures his training to a higher discipline.[36] In case of a transfer to a category of work differing from the previous one, as far as possible this new function should be chosen so that the person in question should be allowed to make use of his specialized qualification or professional experiences efficiently.[37]

In case of a transfer ordered for a specified period of time, the employee has to be restituted to his previous category or place of work with the expiration of the period. In case of a transfer ordered as a result of a disciplinary procedure and for an unspecified period of time, the employee will have no

---

[35] Para 20, subsection 2, item (c) of the 1972 Romanian Labour Code.

[36] An employee is, e.g., held responsible disciplinarily on account of his unsociable conduct and, in view of his slandering assertions, his continued employment in his originally contracted place of work turns out to be inconvenient, with regard to the unbearable conditions thus created. DEÁK (1969), p. 42.

[37] Para 55 of the Labour Code; Para 72, subsection 3 of the Decree on the Enforcement of the Labour Code. In case of a transfer pronounced as a disciplinary measure, the person or body authorized to proceed in a disciplinary procedure is obliged to put down in the respective disciplinary decision the new category of work of the person subjected to the disciplinary procedure. Beyond this obligation, the new place of work and the date of the transfer have to be laid down in the disciplinary decision as well. The more, it is also convenient to determine the new amount of wage (salary). Cf. Stand No. 89 of the Labour Law Department of the Supreme Court. Casebook of Labour Law Decisions. Vol. II, Közgazdasági és Jogi Könyvkiadó, Budapest 1980, pp. 374–375.

claim to be restituted to his previous category or place of work, even if he was dispensed from the disciplinary punishment imposed upon him.[38]

Under the rules of Soviet law, a transfer ordered as a result of a disciplinary procedure is admitted for a maximum period of three months; besides, the transfer should be aimed at an assignment to a work with a lower remuneration compared to the preceding one or to an inferior post of work.[39]

The transfer to a work with a lower remuneration compared to the preceding one, ordered as a result of a disciplinary procedure, with a provisional or a permanent effect is also known in the Bulgarian law.[40] The maximum duration of a provisional transfer is of three months. In practice, this punishment is imposed with a duration of one, two, or three months. A transfer to a work with a lower remuneration compared to the preceding one, decided in a disciplinary procedure and having a punishment character, may be ordered also to a place of work other than the preceding one, but within the same community.[41] Besides, it is permitted in the Bulgarian law to transfer an employee to a work differing from the preceding one also in case of the non-fulfilment of the norm binding for him or for producing inferior work.[42]

Under the rules of the Czechoslovak law, a transfer to a work with a lower remuneration compared to the preceding one, ordered as a disciplinary punishment, may have only a provisional effect, i.e. a maximum duration of three months.[43] In these cases the place of work, as laid down in the labour contract, must be left unchanged; the change of the work premises, e.g. a workshop of a textile mill, the sales shop of a trading company, a department of an institution of health welfare, etc., is permissible depending on the way of definition of the place of work in the relevant labour contract.[44] It should be considered here that the purpose of the disciplinary measure is to subordinate

---

[38] WELTNER–NAGY (1974), p. 186.

[39] Article 56 of the Basic Rules; and Article 135 of the Labour Code of the Russian Soviet Federated Socialist Republic. Within a limit of three month the actual duration of the transfer is determined in an instruction of the manager of the enterprise, who takes into consideration the degree of gravity of the disciplinary offence, the circumstances under which it was committed, and the previous performances of work of the employee. With the expiration of the period of transfer, the employee has to be re-installed to his previous place of work. As regards provisional degradation, it is only applicable within the enterprise; the profession and trade of the employee will have to be taken into consideration. An engineer or a foreman must not be assigned to a work categorized for a worker. In case of the absence of a suitable scope of work of inferior degree within the enterprise, disciplinary measure other than degradation has to be applied against the employee. NIKHITINSKY–GLASURIN (1976/23), p. 726.

[40] Para 130, subsections (d) and (e) of the Bulgarian Labour Code.

[41] MILOVANOV (1972), p. 128.

[42] Para 31, subsection (c) of the Bulgarian Labour Code, taking into consideration Article 10 of the Regulation of Wages. Cf. MILOVANOV (1972), p. 134.

[43] Para 77 of the Czechoslovak Labour Code.

[44] A change of the place of work has always to be regarded as a modification of the relevant labour relationship; as against this a change of the work premise is considered as a modification of the labour relationship only if the place of work was specified in the contract in such a strict sense that it means the work premise. BIL (1972/7), p. 417.

the employee to another floor manager and another community where the conditions for improvement in his attitude are given.

According to the Romanian law, an employee may as a result of a disciplinary procedure be downgraded in his function or category of wages, within the same branch, for a period between one month and three months.[45] A downgrading is permissible not only if an employee trespassed the rules of order and discipline of his working place but in case of an unsatisfactory professional performance as well.[46]

The punishment of transfer to an inferior category of work as a result of a disciplary procedure is not established in the law of the German Democratic Republic. Nevertheless, a disciplinary measure may provide for the modification of the labour contract.[47]

The transfer to another category of work as a disciplinary measure is not stipulated in the Polish Labour Code either. Changes of status in labour relation applicable as disciplinary punishments, are not at all established in Polish labour law.

As a short characterization of the cases in which the enterprise's right arises to transfer an employee, provisionally or permanently, and for a cause occurring on the side of this latter, it may be stated that the cases in question are in general linked with the employee's faulty conduct. Transfer ordered for a disciplinary offence appears most frequently, but it may be pronounced for unsatisfactory work and bad qualification as well. The possibility of transfer as the employer's right is applied in cases of other character exceptionally only.

---

[45] Para 100, subsection 1, item (e) of the Romanian Labour Code. Under the Romanian rules, workers with a professional qualification are assigned to categories, and the employees to posts. Cf. Act No. 12 of 1971 on the assignment and promotion of persons employed by socialist units of the State (Annexes 1 and 2).

[46] Para 12, subsection 2 of Act No. 12 of 1971.—In this respect, a view was expressed in the legal literature saying that, similarly to degradation in a way of a disciplinary procedure, degradation decided in another way may be pronounced for three months at most. GHIMPU–MARMELIUC (1972/2), p. 52.

[47] This is the situation when e.g. the driving licence of a driver is withdrawn, on account of a disciplinary offence committed by him. In such case, the offender gets in a position that as a result of the withdrawal of the licence he is actually incapable of meeting the conditions of work as contracted. The disciplinary offence will then be the indirect cause of the modification of the labour contract. Another case may also be recalled, e.g., if a cashier loses the confidence of the employer, on account of the theft of a minor amount of money, but he is not dismissed as a result of a disciplinary procedure. In this case, the labour contract of the cashier who is continued to be employed has to be modified. Cf. MÜLLER (1967/14), pp. 331–332. A contract modifying the preceding one for the only purpose of having an educative effect by assigning the employee to a kind of work with a lower remuneration than the preceding, thus substituting a disciplinary punishment, will not be regarded as valid. KAISER–KIRSCHNER–SCHULZ (1974).

6.5 Transfer to another function or place of work as an obligation of the employer

The cases in which an employee has a claim, laid down in the legal rules of the various countries, to be employed by the enterprise in a function or a place of work other than that agreed upon in the labour contract, and in which the employer is obliged to carry out a transfer, form a separate group of the states of facts serving as a basis for transfer. The obligation of transfer may have a provisional or permanent character also in this respect.

Under Hungarian law, a pregnant woman has to be transferred, upon her request and with a provisional character, to a function or sphere of activity which conforms to her physical (health) conditions, from the beginning of the fourth month of her pregnancy till the end of the sixth month of the breast-feeding time, upon the presentation of a medical recommendation (certificate).[48] The pregnant or breast-feeding woman is only allowed to refuse the transfer if the fulfilment of her work in the new conditions were also contrary to a legal prohibition or, taking into consideration her categorization, age, health conditions or other circumstances, it would mean disproportionate prejudices.[49] Furthermore, the employer is obliged to employ workers with a reduced working capacity, first of all in their original sphere of activity and profession, in order to facilitate their rehabilitation. If this proves to be impracticable within the enterprise concerned they should be employed in a sphere of work in which they may make use of their professional qualifications without a further deterioration of their health.[50] The enterprise is thus obliged to employ the worker, first and foremost, in his original sphere of work, even by changing the working conditions, but a transfer to another category or place of work within the employing enterprise is only prescribed in case a settlement otherwise proved to be impossible. An employee with a reduced working capacity may be transferred, too, so as to perform a job of an inferior degree; as a matter of fact, the consent of the person is then needed.[51] As for the nature and duration of the transfer, it is provisional for pregnant women and, usually, permanent for employees with a reduced working capacity; in case of the

---

[48] Para 23, subsection 4 of the Decree on the Enforcement of the Labour Code. See also Stand No. 97 of the Labour Law Department of the Hungarian Supreme Court (*Munkaügyi Közlöny*, 1978/2), according to which the employer is obliged to transfer a female worker so as to assign her to another place of work or conditions of work which are more appropriate to her state of health, even within the same category of work.

[49] WELTNER–NAGY (1974), p. 226.

[50] Para 2 of Decree No. 1/1967 (XI. 22) Min. of. Lab.–Min. of Health–Min. of Finance.

[51] Take, e.g., the case when an employee–as a result of carrying on work with a photostat–suffered from a permanent feet disease on account of his work requiring continuously standing position; he was transferred to the post of the keeper of the drawing office. Then he received his wages in conformity with his new category of work. If his invalidity could have been attributed to a work accident or a professional disease, he would have been entitled to receive a supplement of wages without any temporal restriction. Cf. Resolution No. 3966/1972 of the Municipal Board of Arbitration of Budapest, with regard to Para 11 of Decree No. 1/1967 (XI. 22) Min. of Lab.–Min. of Health–Min. of Finance.

decrease of working capacity for a shorter time, however, a provisional transfer is practicable as well.

Under Soviet law, pregnant women should be assigned to easier work for the duration of their pregnancy, in compliance with the respective medical report. Women during their breast-feeeding time and those having a child younger than one year of age should be transferred to another, more suitable, work, if they are unable to perform their contracted work; the transfer is applicable for the entire period of breast-feeding or until the completion of the one year of age of the child.[52] Furthermore, as regards workers and employees needing easier work on account of their physical (health) conditions, their employer is obliged to transfer them, with their consent and in conformity with the relevant medical reports, to another, recommended work, either provisionally or for an unlimited period of time.[53] The labour relationship of an employee of this group may be terminated by giving notice only if it proved to be inworkable to assign them to an easier work with their consent.[54] In the absence of an appropriate easier work, within the enterprise, the employee continues to be employed as before; if he proves to be unable to comply with the requirements, the labour relationship may be terminated by giving notice.[55] According to Soviet law, an employee may claim a transfer also if, apart from performing his regular contracted work, he graduated in a specialized school course. The respective ministerial decrees or instructions prescribe for this case a transfer to a higher category or, in case of graduation in a professional branch other than the preceding one, to a kind of work in the branch in which s/he graduated.[56]

As is laid down in the Bulgarian law, female employees have to be transferred to another kind of work, in case of pregnancy and maternity with a provisional character. Similarly, the transfer of an employee is effected in case of a transitory reduction of the capacity to work also with a provisional character. In this latter case, the duration of transfer to another kind of work is fixed by the bodies of the health service; in case of need, it may be prolonged, too. Then the employee continues to be employed as earlier, and is replaced in his/her work, also with a provisional character. Having regained his/her full capacity to work, s/he has to be restituted to the function performed earlier, or s/he has to be assigned to another kind of work corresponding to his/her professional qualification.[57]

The transfer to another work has to be of permanent character in case of a decrease in the employee's capacity to work, likely to last for a long time.

[52] Article 70 of the Labour Code of the Basic Rules; Para 164 of the Russian Soviet Federated Socialist Republic.

[53] Article 66 of the Basic Rules, Para 155 of the Labour Code of the Russian Soviet Federated Socialist Republic.

[54] Article 17, last item of the Basic Rules.

[55] MALOV (1970/21), pp. 11–12.

[56] ANDREYEV, ed. (1971), p. 121; PASHKHOV (1966), p. 44.

[57] MILOVANOV (1972), pp. 176–177; further, Paras 35, 144 and 118 of the Bulgarian Labour Code.

His/her previous post of work is not reserved in this case, and the kind of his/her work is changed definitely.[58]

It is also acknowledged in the Bulgarian law that, in some cases of the improvement of professional qualification, an employee may claim for a transfer to another work, corresponding to the newly obtained professional qualification. Views expressed in the legal literature are in favour of extending the scope of the mentioned cases and, furthermore, they argue for fixing as a general principle that the claim for a transfer to a new work, corresponding to the acquired new professional qualification, should always be regarded as justified.[59]

The binding transfer of an employee to another kind or place of work, upon his/her request, is known also in the Czechoslovak law, if the continued performance of the contracted work of the employee concerned or his/her continued employment by his/her actual employer seems to be undesirable according to the statement of a doctor. The transfer is subjected, however, to the actual possibilities of the enterprise concerned.[60] The same rule is applicable also in case of a provisional loss of the employee's capacity to work.[61] A transfer upon the request of an employee may also under Czechoslovakian law take place provisionally and permanently. In case the worker loses his capacity to work, which is likely to last for a long time, a stricter rule is applicable, i.e. the employer is then absolutely obliged to assign the employee to another work.[62]

As regards Poland, pregnant women should be transferred to a work more appropriate for them.[63] The enterprise is obliged, furthermore, to transfer an

[58] MILOVANOV (1972), p. 181; further, Para 121 of the Bulgarian Labour Code.

[59] As is laid down in Bulgarian law, the workers and employees, assigned to the various categories of a wage tariff system, and having passed successfully an examination required for the promotion to a higher class of professional qualification, will have subjective legal claim to being assigned to a kind of work corresponding to the higher class of professional qualification. For the workers and employees who receive their wages (or fixed salary) according to pre-established categories, as well as for the workers who although are remunerated according to a system of wage tariff categories, but in whose cases the acquisition of a higher class of professional qualification does not as a rule receive expression in obtaining a higher categorization, no subjective legal claim to being placed into a category of work that would correspond to their newly acquired higher professional qualification derives. Summing up, we can infer that in specified cases the worker's acquisition of a higher degree of professional qualification gives rise to a subjective legal claim to being transferred to a work corresponding to the new professional qualification. For the time being, this legal claim is not granted to employees, according to the positive Bulgarian law. MILOVANOV (1972), p. 152.

[60] Para 40 of the Czechoslovak Labour Code. According to Czechoslovak law, the transfer of a female employee on account of her pregnancy or of an employee for invalidity, etc. has to be effected irrespective of the wish of the person concerned, the more, also against it. If the employee concerned refuses to accept the transfer, this circumstance has to be examined carefully; accordingly, the conduct of the employee in question may also involve various consequences. URBANEC–TYCOVÁ (1966), pp. 22–23.

[61] POLÁŠEK–KALENSKÁ–KALOUŠEK (1967), p. 25.

[62] It should be noted that the fact of the loss of capacity to work for a longer time does not exclude a future amelioration of the state of health of the employee concerned. BENEŠ–PUDIK (1976/13), p. 681.

[63] Para 179 of the Labour Code.

employee to another, and more adequate, kind of work if, on the basis of a medical statement, s/he proved to be unable to continue to perform the contracted work, as a consequence of a work accident or occupational disease, and s/he has not been assigned to a category of invalidity. If a transfer proved to be impracticable, the enterprise has to contact the competent local administrative body without delay, with a view to ensuring an appropriate work for the employee in question in another enterprise. The enterprise disposing of a vacant post of work, which seems to be adequate for the physical (health) conditions and professional qualification of the employee directed to it by the competent local administrative body, is then bound to employ the person concerned.[64]

If it is laid down in a medical statement that an employee is no more in a physical (health) condition to perform his/her work as contracted, the employer is obliged, under the law of the German Democratic Republic, to offer him another work, corresponding to his abilities and physical (health) conditions. However, if it turns out that there is no appropriate post in the employer's company, another enterprise must be envisaged as well. If an employee is no more in a state of health to comply with the demands of his/her work as contracted, on account of a health deterioration connected with the execution of his/her work, and accepts the work other than the previous one offered him/her by the employer, this latter is obliged to assure him/her an appropriate professional training and to cover the incurred expense. In case of elderly employees, desiring to do work another than the actual one, on account of their age, the employer is obliged to offer them another kind of work, corresponding to their abilities and physical conditions. If this turns out to be impracticable, another enterprise must be envisaged as well.[65] Special rules are in force in respect of the protection of female employees for their pregnancy, breast-feeding time, and taking care for a child younger than one year of age.[66]

As is put down in the Romanian labour law, a pregnant or breast-feeding woman working under prejudicial or dangerous conditions or at a place not recommended by a medical statement has to be assigned to another place of work.[67] Furthermore, employees being under medical treatment have to be assigned to a work other than that of their working category, on the basis of a medical certificate and for the duration of their medical treatment. This transfer must not, however, exceed three months within one calendar year.[68] The right of an employee to be assigned to a higher degree of work category or to a promotion to a leading function, corresponding to the professional training and abilities of the person, is also established in the Romanian law; furthermore, it is laid down as a general principle.[69]

---

[64] Article 218, Paras 1–3 of the Polish Labour Code.
[65] Para 209 of the Labour Code of the German Democratic Republic.
[66] Paras 240 et seq. of the Labour Code of the German Democratic Republic.
[67] Para 152, subsection 2 of the Romanian Labour Code.
[68] Para 147 of the Romanian Labour Code.
[69] This right is laid down in subsection (d), Para 4 of Act No. 12/1971 on the assignment and promotion of persons employed by socialist State units; furthermore, there is a similar

Summary.—It may be stated that an enterprise is obliged to transfer an employee, on the basis of this latter's legal claim, either if the transfer seems to be justified by considerations bearing upon the health protection of the employee, or if it is required by social and personal interests linked with the utilization of the professional knowledge of the employee. This latter consideration is coming more and more definitely into the foreground in the legal rules of the various countries; in exceptional cases it is even expressed as a general principle. If the legal rules grant an absolute subjective right fort the employees to claim for a transfer, on the one hand, and establish an absolute obligation of the employer to comply with the demand of transfer, on the other, and the employer fails to meet this obligation, then the employee concerned will be entitled to make recourse to the bodies competent for the settlement of labour disputes, and his claims will be enforced in the frame of a labour dispute.

6.6 Elements in the qualification for a transfer

Surveying the positive rules of the legal systems concerned, a basis is given for drawing some general conclusions on the changes of the category or place of work of an employee which should, or should not, be qualified as a transfer. In other words, the changes of the category or place of work of an employee may be specified which require the modification of a labour relationship, involving the necessity of the consent of both contracting parties.

Let us take first the cases in which the enterprise is entitled, but not obliged, to effect a transfer. Cases of this kind occur for causes arisen on the employer's side, and they have a provisional character. In fact, this is not a real transfer, i.e. its application is within the practice of the right to give instructions. Then the employee concerned has to perform, provisionally, a work outside of his/her category of work or s/he has to carry out the work at a place other than the contracted one, irrespective of the circumstance whether the work to be performed so is within or outside of the category of work as contracted. The cases in question, e.g. requirement of production, replacement, act of God, etc. are of exceptional character, and the employee had to take them into account already at the conclusion of his labour contract. Accordingly, it is thus an element of content of the contract that the employee is bound to perform work outside of the category of his/her contracted work or at a place other than the contracted one. This obligation has to be met in cases and within the frames laid down in the relevant legal rules. Accordingly, the employer is only allowed to take this measure of provisional character, if there is a provision in a relevant legal rule. Furthermore, it is of essential importance that the change of the category or place of work should in fact be of a pro-

---

disposition in subsection (f), Para 19, of the Romanian Labour Code, granting a legal claim for the employees to be promoted to a higher category of assignment or a leading post, depending on their professional training, experiences, and the results of their work.

visional character. In view of this, the consent of the employee to the change will be indispensable if, as a consequence of this change, the employee were removed from his earlier, contracted, category or place of work for a longer period of time. This would mean then the necessity of modifying the labour relationship in question.

It is a different situation if the transfer of an employee to another category or place of work is ordered by the leader of the enterprise on account of a cause that presented itself on the employee's side. In case the disposition of the leader of the enterprise is equal to a lasting change of the category or place of work of the employee concerned, e.g. with decision pronouncing transfer for an indefinite period of time, taken in the course of a disciplinary procedure, this will mean, beyond any doubt, a modification of the labour relationship, and a specific case of it, i.e. a unilateral modification of a labour contract by the employer. It is the same situation, in our view, if a decision of transfer for a definite period of time is taken in a disciplinary way. In this case, a labour relationship is also modified by the employer but only for a definite period of time since, upon the elapsing of this period, the employee has to be restituted to his previous category or place of work or, in case this restitution proves to be impracticable, s/he has to be assigned to a category or place of work corresponding to his/her previous one.

In the second group of cases, the enterprise is not only entitled to the transfer but it is obliged to carry it out at the same time. In these cases, the employee has a legal claim for being transferred, on account of pregnancy, improvement of professional qualification, etc. These cases always constitute a modification of the labour relationship in question, even if only with a provisional character,[70] and the law ensures for the employee an absolute subjective right to claim for transfer, to protect his interests, on the one hand, and pronounces an absolute obligation of transfer, on the other, to the charge of the employer. A transfer of this kind is not even bound to the request of the employee concerned, in the law of some socialist countries. Simply, the employer is obliged to carry it out in specified cases, e.g. pregnancy or invalidity, etc. of the employee. The legal structure is then that the respective labour contract is modified by a unilateral act of the employer, just as in case of a transfer pronounced as a disciplinary punishment, and irrespective of its provisional or permanent character. Nevertheless, while a transfer decided as a disciplinary measure is related to the conduct of the employee transgressing the positive law or the morale of labour, the regulation laid down for the cases mentioned above is destined to serve the interests of the employee, i.e. it is the obligation of the employer to secure work for the employee, conforming to his/her state of health, and irrespective of whether the employee has a request for that or not. This means an increased degree of guarantee for the employee's interests.

The comments outlined above have to be completed by making it clear that the lasting nature of a transfer is, as a rule, characteristic, even if it is

[70] ROMÁN (1972), pp. 396 et seq.

arranged for a transitory period only. From a formal point of view, this is expressed mostly by that the employee is discharged from performing the tasks imposed on him/her by the labour contract and s/he is assigned to another category or place of work, with his/her consent or by a unilateral act of the employer, always depending on the actual case. The employee transferred from one job to another is then released from his/her previous category or place of work; with the elapsing of the period of transfer, s/he will be re-integrated, however, to his/her earlier category or place of work. The maximum period of employment in another category or place of work with a provisional character is exactly specified in the law of some countries. This arrangement cannot be considered, however, as being applied generally although, doubtless to say, it is more advantageous for the employee if the legal rules contain unequivocal provisions in this respect.

The lasting nature of the change of the category or place of work in case of a transfer, as presumably the most characteristic cause of the modification of a labour contract cannot be considered as an absolute rule. If a transfer implies substantial changes in the conditions of work, i.e. it is not a case of transfer to another category or place of work resulting from exceptional causes arisen on the side of the enterprise, the assignment to another category or place of work, even if only for one single day, requires the consent of the employee to the modification of the labour relationship.

It is of no importance in this context whether the modifications of the conditions of labour involve changes in a positive or a negative sense, the only decisive factor is that the labour conditions are changed substantially.[71]

Considering the problem of the modification of a labour contract, the correct way is, indeed, if the stipulations laid down in the labour contract are taken as basis, and it is examined whether or not their substance is changed by the new labour conditions. If there is no substantial (qualitative) change in the task of work to be performed, i.e. it is only concretized by means of an instruction coming from the competent leader, the labour contract need not be modified.[72] Similar problems arise in respect of the place of work.[73] As long as the conditions of labour stipulated in the relevant contract are not subjected to a substantial (qualitative) change, the leader of the employing body is

---

[71] In a given case it may be disputed what is to be regarded as a substantial change of the labour conditions. Thus, there may apparently be unimportant factors which, however, were considered to be of a decisive character by the parties at the conclusion of the contract. In case of doubt, it has to be examined what was regarded by one of the parties to be a substantial factor in a way so that it could be recognized by the other party.

[72] If a translator is commissioned, e.g., to make the translations of articles published in periodicals and this task is modified subsequently to prepare reports on them this circumstance cannot be considered as a qualitative change in the sphere of his/her work. KAISER–KIRSCHNER–SCHULZ (1974), p. 135.

[73] If the place of work of a filling station mechanic is laid down in his/her labour contract so as to comprise the entire area of the city in question, the employee performing this work is not entitled to dispute if the respective leader orders his/her transfer from one filling station to another within his/her authority of giving instructions. KAISER–KIRSCHNER–SCHULZ, (1974), p. 135.

authorized to put the work to be performed in a concrete form, simply making use of his/her right to give instructions.

On the other hand, in case of a substantial (qualitative) change of the conditions of labour, it has to be examined whether the management of the enterprise is or is not authorized by the law to order a change unilaterally in respect of the category or place of work as outlined above. In the absence of such authorization, the labour relationship can be modified only with the mutual agreement of the parties.

The recognition of the differences in the individual cases could well be facilitated by clarifying and accurately expressing certain questions of technicalities. As has been mentioned, different terms are used for the case of transfer in the Czechoslovak law, depending on the circumstance whether a transfer to another category or to another place of work is concerned. It is also the Czechoslovak law which presents an example that two different terms are used in the legal rules for the same concept, i.e. transfer to another category of work.[74]

As regards the law of the German Democratic Republic, the term provisional transfer to another work is used in it,[75] contrasted to the modification of labour conditions, this latter being realized by means of a modifying contract.[76] The provisional transfer to another work may take place within an enterprise but also between two enterprises within the same community, i.e. it comprises the transfer to another place of work as well.[77]

A distinction is made between re-direction and transfer in the Romanian Labour Code[78], the first having a provisional effect, and the second being of a lasting one. In our view, the term re-direction ought to be used in all cases in which the transfer of an employee to another category or place of work is effected within the right of instruction of the employer, principally for reason affecting the enterprises and there is no need to modify the labour contract. The possibility of these changes is namely taken into account by the employee at the conclusion of the labour contract, consequently a change does not mean a new situation for him/her. The term transfer should be reserved for the cases in which the change of the category or place of work is linked with the modification of the labour contract. From this point of view, it is then of no

---

[74] As regards transfer from one job to another, the term *převedeni na jinou práci* is used in Para 37 of the Czechoslovak Labour Code. In the Slovak text, *prevedenie na inu pracu* is used, even in its 1970 version. Cf. *Zákonník práce* (Labour Code), Práce, Bratislava 1970, p. 68. — The same term is mentioned as *preradenie na inu prácu* in the 1975 edition. As for transfer from one place of work to another it is worded as *přeloženi* in the Czech and *preloženie* in the Slovak text. (Para 38 of the Labour Code.)

[75] The term *vorübergehende Übertragung einer anderen Arbeit* is for it in the Labour Code of the German Democratic Republic (Para 84 of the Labour Code).

[76] It is called *Veränderungsvertrag* in the Labour Code of the German Democratic Republic (Para 49).

[77] The task of work to be performed, the place of work and other conditions of work may be modified, too, by means of the modifying contract. MICHAS (1974), p. 45.

[78] The term *trecerea* is used for re-direction, and *transferarea* for transfer. Paras 67 and 69 of the Labour Code.

importance whether the modification is taking place by a unilateral act of the employer or with the agreement of both parties.

It should be added to the preceding views that the concept of re-direction always implies the character of something provisional; on the other hand, transfer is mostly, but not necessarily, of a lasting nature. An employee may be transferred to another category or place of work also provisionally, but this act always involves the modification of his/her labour contract.[79]

A distinction may be made so that a re-direction means a change of the category or place of work not involving the modification of the labour contract; contrary to this, the term transfer always stands for a modification of a labour contract, and this is effected, as a rule, by means of an agreement of the parties or, exceptionally, with a unilateral act of the employer.[80]

[79] The use of the term re-direction is considered as necessary also by the authors of the Hungarian textbook of labour law. WELTNER–NAGY (1974), p. 204.

[80] Also the terms sending on special work and sending on separate duty may be found, with more or less identical meaning in the positive legal rules of the various countries. They essentially also mean the change of the place of work of employees. In the present work we do not deal with these categories since, as far as sending on special work is concerned, the original content of the labour contract remains unchanged; and as regards sending on separate duty, it is understood to be a specific form of provisional transfer to an enterprise other than the contracted one, and this is beyond the scope of the analyses presented here.

7. POSSIBILITES AND LIMITS
OF THE TERMINATION OF LABOUR RELATIONS

7.1 Classification of facts serving as basis
for the termination of labour relations

As regards the classification of the causes of termination of labour relations, different views may be found in the jurisprudence of the socialist countries. Let us now present and comment these views.[1-4]

(1) For one of them, the point of departure is that it is always legal facts that serve as the basis for the termination of the labour relation. These facts are such to which the legal rule attaches the legal effect of terminating the labour relation.[5] Legal facts of this kind include the agreement of the parties, unilateral legal acts, such as giving notice, termination of a labour relationship with immediate effect, the expiration of a definite period of time (in case of labour contracts concluded for a definite period of time), and other legal facts, e.g. death of the employee, non-fulfilment of the obligation to work as a consequence of a sentence of detention for a period exceeding three months, failure to recommence work within 30 days on completion of military service, under the terms of the previous labour contract.

The view outlined above is based upon the most comprehensive concept of legal facts, equally covering human conduct (e.g. act of will), human circumstances (e.g. absence, the fact of death), and external factors independent of human conduct (e.g. time). The list may be completed with the kind of punishment which prohibits a person's filling up a specific post of work, exercising a specified profession or participating in public affairs[6]; State acts as legal facts also rank among the members of this *genus proximum*.[7]

(2) Another view makes distinction between legally relevant events and legally relevant acts.[8] As to the first group, i.e. events which comprise in particular the death or illness of the employee, the expiration of a delay, the accomplishment of a specified work, the failure to recommence work within 30 days on completion of military service, the arbitrary leaving of the enterprise, the non-fulfilment of the obligation to work as a consequence of a sen-

---

[1-4] For the comparative examination of the termination of labour relations in the socialist literature of labour law, see NOVOTNÁ (1977/5), p. 302.—The most comprehensive treatment of the problem in the Hungarian legal literature is in GARANCSY (1970), p. 264.

[5] SZUBERT (1972), pp. 116 et seq.—Legal facts are called *fakty prawne* in the Polish juridical terminology.

[6] Article 42 of the 1969 Polish Criminal Code.

[7] VILÁGHY–EÖRSI (1962), pp. 171 et seq.

[8] The legally relevant events are called *sobitye* and the legally relevant acts *deistvye* in the Russian legal terminology. The corresponding terms of the Polish legal terminology read *zdarzenie* and *czyny*, respectively. *Sovietskoye Trudovoye Pravo* (1966), p. 129; SZUBERT (1972), pp. 118 et seq.

tence of detention for a period exceeding three months,[9] and the death of the employer.[10]

This enumeration is not exhaustive. All acts being linked with the termination of a labour relationship under a certain rule may be regarded as belonging in it.[11] As to the second group, i.e., legally relevant acts, these include the agreements of the parties, the termination of a labour relationship by giving notice and by the cancellation of the labour contract with immediate effect, as well as the termination of the labour relationship upon the initiative of a third party, e.g. trade union, people's control commission, etc. Legal acts may be unilateral and multilateral.

According to this view, events appearing and considered as legal facts include thus personal events occuring to man (death), and states with legal effect (illness, absence, being after the expected time, etc.), as well as facts of cases belonging in the range of human circumstances other than human conduct (time as a legal factor). Human acts considered essentially as human conduct are separated from events.[12]

(3) The view should also be mentioned which claims that events as legal facts do not imply by themselves the termination of labour relations. (There is an exception, of course, i.e. death as a legal fact.) According to this view, the expiration of a prefixed period of time, as a legally relevant event, does not mean the automatic termination of labour relationship even in the case of labour contracts concluded for a definite period of time if the labour relationship continues to exist actually. The continued performance of work even following the expiration of the specified period of time is regarded as a decisive fact, resulting in the prolongation of the labour relationship—which has been concluded for a specified period of time—to an unspecified period of time. As a matter of fact, this depends on the *de facto* consent of the employer. Thus, a labour relationship established for a specified period of time is only terminated in the absence of a decisive conduct at the expiration of the prefixed term.[13]

The termination of the labour relationship is thus usually based on legal acts like the act of will of the parties which may be bilateral or unilateral. A bilateral act of will, such as an agreement of the parties, may terminate a labour relationship at any moment. A unilateral termination is admitted in cases laid down in the legal rules. These cases may be grouped as follows: termination of a labour relationship by dint of an act of will of the employer (depending in some legal systems on the consent of the trade union), of the

[9] SWIECICKI (1969), pp. 311 et seq. This variety emerged in practice, in the absence of a regulation by a legal rule.

[10] RADOILSKI (1957), p. 544.

[11] SALWA (1971), p. 162.

[12] It should be just remarked that human acts belong, in fact, essentially in the group of events. According to the classification of SZLADITS (1941, p. 249), events considered as juridical facts may (i) occur in the outside world; (ii) affect individuals in their personal matters, (iii) appear as human acts.

[13] ALEKSANDROV (ed., 1966), pp. 271–272.

employee or his legal guardian, or of third parties authorized to take the act. These latter parties are State or social bodies or such that proceed in the interests of the public. A labour relationship may be terminated upon the initiative of the trade union,[14] on the basis of a judgment of a court of justice (if a ban is pronounced in it on performing a specific function or activity),[15] or on the basis of the draft of a recruiting committee[16]. Parties entitled to the unilateral termination of a labour relationship are enumerated exhaustively in the respective legal rule.[17] Events with a legal relevance do not in themselves imply the termination of a labour relationship, apart from very exceptional cases, such as death. A termination may always be attributed to an act of will of a person or a body. In the view of the supporters of the concept, the will factor includes, beyond human conduct, State acts as well; besides, some external elements, e.g. time, being independent of human conduct, are also within this group, for the supporters of the concept argue in this latter case with the existence of an explicit or decisive human conduct in the background.

The question arises here whether it would be practicable to put the causes of the cancellation of the labour contract or termination of labour relationships into categories which would comprise all legally relevant facts of cases on a unified basis. This will be tried in the forthcoming section.

7.2 Attempts to develop comprehensive categories of the facts serving as basis for the termination of labour relations

A distinction between two great categories of legal facts is accepted by the socialist theory of law, viz. (i) human conduct, i.e. legal facts depending on human will, (ii) objective events, taking place irrespective of human will.[18]

---

[14] According to Article 20 of the Basic Rules of the labour legislation of the Soviet Union and the member republics, the management of an enterprise is obliged, upon the demand of the local trade union body, to cancel the labour contract of an employee in a leading position or removing him/her from office if s/he violated labour law rules, failed to come up to expectations related to his/her duties and liabilities laid down in the labour contract, showed a bureaucratic attitude in his/her work, or tolerated protraction in work. The person concerned, or the management, has the right to make a complaint against the demand of the local trade union with the competent superior trade union body, and the decision to be taken by this latter will have a final effect.

[15] See, e.g., Articles 21 and 26 of the Basic Principles of the Criminal Codes of the Soviet Union and the member republics.

[16] According to Soviet law, a labour relationship ceases to exist if an employee is enlisted for military service, i.e. he joins the army. Cf. Article 15, point 3 of the Basic Rules of the labour legislation of the Soviet Union and the member republics.

[17] Other bodies such as trade inspectorates, labour safety inspectorates, etc. are also entitled to submit a request to the employer, aimed at the termination of the labour relationship of an employee, if this latter infringed the rules; but the employer is not obliged to comply with the request.

[18] ANTALFY–SAMU–SZABÓ–SZÓTÁCZKY (1970), p. 525.

The importance of the distinction among facts concerns principally the theory of legal relations, as it considers acts of human will which lead to the coming into existence, modification, or termination of legal relationships.

Nevertheless, the coming into existence, modification or termination of legal relationships may result not only from the parties' contractual will but also from a deliberate activity of State bodies, aimed at the enforcement of the legal rules, within the frames of the relevant legal regulations. Here the acts of will are to be categorized that take the form of a State act related to actual cases. These acts have to be placed into the group of legal facts as well, since they may have effect upon the general course of development of legal relations.[19]

We are of the opinion that the scope of acts of will may be set broader—also from the point of view of the termination labour relation—than the mere contractual sphere of the interested parties. Acts of will of such bodies have to be taken into consideration that, within their scope of activities, may issue binding legal instruments with substantial effects upon labour relations. It is, first of all, the activities of the courts of justice that are relevant here.

There is an argument which may be raised against the view outlined in the preceding, i.e. the fact that the contractual act of will of the parties, on the one hand, and the State will as expressed e.g. in a decision of a court of justice, on the other, represent categories with qualitative differences for, not to mention other points, the State will may be enforced directly. This is undoubtedly true, but it does not mean that the volitional elements in the activities of State bodies could be placed to the sphere of objective circumstances independent of volitional elements. It has to be emphasized here again that the parties' contractual act of will may be realized only within the limits set by the legal rule. In compliance with this, it would be incorrect to qualify it simply as a human conduct separated from the State will. The point that the act of State will forming the content of the objective law has always been superior as compared to the legal act of will establishing a legal relationship[20] should not be dealt with here in detail, as it would go far beyond the subject matter of the present work; nevertheless, it has to be mentioned that the acts of a State-owned enterprise effected in the field of labour law, including e.g. decisions and stands bearing upon the termination of a labour relationship are influenced by State will at least to the extent that the autonomy of the enterprise is set to limits by State ownership. This is even more evidently valid to civil service, as the primacy of State will is more manifest in this field.

Under the circumstances of the socialist State, another arrangement could hardly be imagined. Consequently, the will of a general nature, expressed in a legal rule, has to be realized just through the individual will of the subjects of the actual legal relations; and the other way round, the legal relations may only be realized if the acts of will of the parties to these relations take place in compliance with the content of the legal rules concerned.[21]

---

[19] VILÁGHY–EÖRSI (1962), p. 175.
[20] SZÓTÁCZKY (1970), p. 29.
[21] PESCHKA (1960), p. 70.

Turning now back to the classification of the legal facts leading to the termination of a labour relationship, one gets to the conclusion that, starting from the collective term of legal fact, a distinction may be made, first of all, between acts of will and objective circumstances which are beyond will. The first point may again be divided into two groups; contractual acts of will aimed at the termination of a labour relationship, and acts of will of authorities leading to the termination of a labour relationship.

The contractual acts of will may again be subdivided into groups consisting of unilateral and bilateral acts of will. The first group comprises the cancellation of the labour contract and the termination of a labour relationship with immediate effect, while the termination of a labour relationship with mutual agreement belongs in the second group. (See the Table below.)[22]

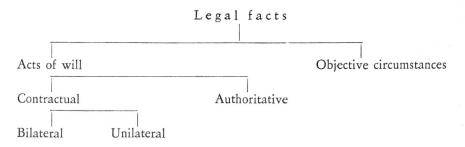

The point is now how the various facts related to the termination of labour relations are categorized, or qualified by the law of the various socialist States. Apart from Hungary and Poland, the system of termination bound to definite states of fact is applied by the law of the socialist countries. As concerns the question whether certain states of facts are to be considered as cause for giving notice according to the law of a particular State, or are according to the law of other States regarded at all as such that may result in the cancellation of the labour contract or termination of a labour relationship and, if so, in what category should they be placed within the legal facts leading to the cancellation of a labour contract or the termination of a labour relationship, considerable differences may, however, be detected in the labour laws of the socialist countries. Thus, the illness of an employee may, e.g., be a circumstance excluding his dismissal by giving him notice, or the other way round, it may be a cause for giving notice, or, an objective event falling outside the will of the parties, depending always on the respective rules of the positive law. The termination of a labour relationship concluded for a specified period of time may also be regarded as a way of cancellation of the labour contract following from the relevant contractual act of will, or as a termination of the labour relationship

---

[22] The scheme is simplified in so far as the termination of a labour relationship may be judged under special legal considerations, and from various aspects, e.g. on the basis of a possible error, in the course of a disciplinary procedure, etc.

resulting from the expiration of time as an objective factor, having legal effect without the actions of the parties.

In the following subsections the more important legal facts involving the termination of labour relationships according to the rules of the various legal systems will be discussed.

7.3 Contractual acts of will as legal facts leading to the termination of labour relations

7.3.1 Bilateral acts of will

According to some views, the termination of a labour relationship by mutual agreement has to be regarded as of primary importance as compared to the unilateral cancellation of the labour contract, since in the first case it is the co-ordination of the interests of the parties that takes a legal form, while in the second case, i.e. the unilateral cancellation of the labour contract, it is only the will of one of the parties that is realized.[23] This view is supported by the basic principle that the acts of legal relevance, affecting the employee's labour relations and living conditions, should be realized with the parties' consent, all the more so since labour relations in the socialist society are to be based upon mutual co-operation; the cancellation of the labour contract by dint of a unilateral act, i.e. by giving notice should not be typical. The requirement is also expressed in this view that a labour relationship should be terminated in the same way as it came into existence, i.e. by the parties' bilateral and conforming act of will. Theoretically, this view is convenient beyond doubt but, as regards pracice, it has not been realized unequivocally.

There are, undisputably, data from socialist countries referring to enterprises in which the termination with the parties' mutual agreement makes out as much as about 50 per cent of the cases, since the employees mostly prefer to ask their employer to cancel their labour contract only upon the expiration of the specified period of notice, and it is seldom that they 'make an announcement' of cancelling the labour contract. If the enterprise approves the employee's wish, the case is in general qualified as termination of the labour relationship with mutual agreement of the parties. Taking the other way round, i.e. when an enterprise has good reasons to cancel the labour contract of an employee (for filling up his/her post by somebody else who is more suitable to meet the requirements), the form of the unilateral cancelling of the labour contract is applied only rarely, since the enterprises are less inclined to make use of it as a means of personnel (staff) policy. Instead, they endeavour to terminate the labour relationship by means of mutual agreement.[24]

[23] MIRONOV (1971/6), p. 42; BERNARD–PAVLÁTOVÁ (1979), p. 166; SZURGACZ (1976), pp. 55–82; for more details on the mechanism of this kind of the termination of labour relations, see PAVLÁTOVÁ (1979/8), pp. 439–446.
[24] SZURGACZ (1976), pp. 67–68.

There are, however, also examples of an adverse outlet. In 1979, almost 50 per cent of the employees engaged in the industry covering the Budapest area cancelled their labour contract by giving notice, while the other causes of termination fell only together on the other half of the employees who left their place of work. As regards the building industry, the balance is shifted even more noticeably toward the predominance of the employee's giving notice, within the causes of the termination of labour relationships, and this may well be considered as a continued trend that presented itself for some years.[25]

The primacy of the termination of labour relationships by means of mutual agreement, as compared to the unilateral cancellation of the labour contract, remains rather more a requirement only, instead of becoming realized in practice. In the absence of sufficient factual data, all what may be stated has to be limited, however, to the point that it is the termination of a labour relationship with mutual agreement that corresponds most closely to the contractual principle, the regular functioning of labour relations, and the requirement of mutually good intentions.

The termination of a labour relationship by dint of mutual agreement means, substantially, that the enterprise and the employee are free to do it at any time.[26] The essential point is here that the parties have to come to agreement in respect of the date of termination of the labour relationship.[27] Naturally, they may agree upon other conditions as well.

By linking the termination of the labour relationship by dint of mutual agreement to the contract of cancellation *(Aufhebungsvertrag)*, the labour law of the German Democratic Republic, in particular, emphasizes the contractual character of this kind of termination. The contract of cancellation must be formulated in writing and this obligation is irrespective of the circumstance whether it was the enterprise or the employee that took the initiative leading to the conclusion of the contract of cancellation.[28] The actual motives have to be indicated which induced the parties to terminate the labour relationship.[29] By combining the conclusion of a contract of cancellation with the establishment of a new labour relationship, a so-called trilateral contract *(Dreieckvertrag or Überleitungsvertrag)* is constituted with a view to organizing the transfer of the employee to another enterprise.[30] Essentially, this institution has come into existence in connection with the provisions on rationalization, which may justify to terminate existing labour relations. In these cases the employee, furthermore, the disengaging and the engaging enterprises appear as parties to a trilateral contract.

A labour relationship ceases to exist with the employee's transfer from one

---

[25] *Budapesti Statisztikai Évkönyv* (Statistical Yearbook of Budapest). Központi Stat. Hiv., Budapest 1980, p. 85.

[26] As regards Hungarian labour law, cf. Para 25, subsection 1 of the Labour Code.

[27] GARANCSY (1970), p. 216.

[28] KIRSCHNER–MICHAS (1978), pp. 73 et seq.; Paras 51–52 of the Labour Code of the German Democratic Republic.

[29] KAISER–KIRSCHNER–SCHULZ (1974), p. 168.

[30] KIRSCHNER–MICHAS (1978), pp. 65 et seq.

enterprise to another, also under Hungarian labour law. The two enterprises and the employee have to agree upon this point with each other.[31] The transfer from one enterprise to another appears as a specific case of the termination of a labour relationship by means of mutual agreement. Essentially, a tripartite agreement comprises two contracts, namely one cancelling an existing contract and another constituting a new labour relationship.[32] In view of this, the best arrangement seems to be to lay down an agreement of transfer which contains all three acts of will as required by the relevant legal rule.[33] In this case, the employee's previous labour relationship ceases to exist on the day preceding the date provided for entering into work at the new place of work, and the new relationship starts to exist at the new enterprise the day laid down in the contract.[34]

Similar tripartite agreements, figuring as forms of the termination of labour relationships, may be found in the law of other countries as well.[35]

There are slight differences in the structure of the Polish law. It is a similar arrangement that a transfer to another enterprise with mutual agreement of the parties means the termination of the previous labour relationship, based on the agreement of the parties. However, the guarantee of the new employment is not the consent given by the previous and the subsequent employer with respect to the transfer of the employee upon the request of this latter, but the preliminary contract concluded with the new employer, in terms of Para 389 of the Civil Code. If the new employer refuses to employ the person, this latter is entitled to a claim of indemnity, according to the provisions of subsection 1, Para 39 of the Civil Code.[36]

Let us mention here that we consider the termination of a labour relationship concluded for a specified period of time also as a specific case of the termination of a labour relationship by mutual agreement. In the case of a labour relationship established for a specified period, the two parties agree, in fact, already at the conclusion of the labour contract, that the labour relationship should exist only for the specified period, given in the labour contract, therefore, the date of termination of the labour relationship is fixed in the labour contract in advance. We hold the view in this respect that since the termination of a labour relationship established for a specified period cannot be attributed

---

[31] Para 25, subsection 23 of the Labour Code.

[32] GARANCSY (1970), p. 218.

[33] LEHOCZKY (1973).

[34] Para 20, subsection 2 of the Decree on the Enforcement of the Labour Code.

[35] According to Article 15, point 5 of the Basic Rules of the labour legislation of the Soviet Union and the member republics, and Article 29, point 5 of the 1971 Labour Code of the Russian Soviet Federated Socialist Republic, the labour contract ceases to exist in the cases regulated therein with the transfer of the employee to another enterprise, institution or organization. A similar provision is laid down in Para 29, point (k) of the Bulgarian Labour Code.

[36] It should be added that, as is laid down in Para 300 of the Polish Labour Code, in cases not regulated in labour law prescriptions, the relevant rules of the Civil Code are applicable unless they are contrary to the basic principles of labour law. Cf. SZURGACZ (1976), p. 66.

to a cause independent of the will of the parties, for the date of termination was fixed by the mutual agreement of the parties, in case of a transformation of a labour relationship to such as is concluded for an indefinite period of time, the transformation may take place, similarly, also only on the basis of the acts of will of the parties, even in case of a tacit agreement. The volitional element has thus a primary role also in the termination of a labour relationship concluded for a definite period of time, although opposite views are also expressed.[37]

7.3.2 Unilateral acts of will

The termination of a labour relationship by means of a unilateral act of will may be initiated by either the employer or the employee, and it may take the form of termination either by giving notice or by cancelling the labour contract with immediate effect. The legal rules bearing upon the termination of labour relationships in the socialist countries are laid down for the contracting parties in different ways. Considering the right of the free choice of the place of work, there is no possibility to make dependent the termination by giving notice on the part of the employee on specified conditions or circumstances, although there are occasionally different regulations as well; however, the cancellation of a labour contract with immediate effect is even for the employee admitted only under specified conditions. In the view which may be considered as that of the overwhelming majority in the field of law of the socialist countries, the employer is entitled to terminate a labour relationship only in the presence of specified causes; the cancellation of the labour contract with immediate effect on the part of the employer is also admitted only in the presence of specified causes, and this is laid down in the law of all socialist countries (system of giving notice bound to factual states).

In comparison with the employee's possibilities, the enterprise's rights to give notice are essentially more limited.

The Hungarian legal regulation represents an exception from the system of giving notice bound to factual states specified in the law in so far as the system effective from January 1, 1968 is based on justification and not on

---

[37] The authors representing the said view—e.g. MICHAS (1970), p. 170, and SZUBERT (1972), p. 112—are right in so far that, for the case in question, the labour relationship is terminated with the expiration of the specified period, without giving notice. At the same time, the setting of time limit derives from the mutual act of will of the parties. According to the Polish Labour Code, the same rules are applicable to labour contracts concluded for a term of probation, which cease to exist automatically, by virtue of the law, with the lapse of the time specified, i.e. no act of will of any of the parties is needed in these cases. Besides, the provisions of the Polish Labour Code introduced that labour contracts concluded for a specified period of time could be cancelled through notice ahead of the scheduled date. This cancellation is permissible if (i) the contract was concluded for a period exceeding six months and (ii) it contained an explicit provision concerning the possibility of cancellation (Article 33 of the Code). The cancellation requires the occurrence of the two together.

stipulations specified in the law. The enterprise is entitled to cancel a labour contract by giving notice in case of a genuine and well-founded cause.[37/a] The enterprise meets its obligation of justification by indicating the concrete circumstances or the conduct of the employee in question which has induced it to discontinue the labour relationship. The cause of the notice has to be indicated so that it should be unequivocally clear to the employee why he is no more required to continue his work.[38] In case of the employee's unsuitability, the concrete circumstances justifying the notice have to be clearly laid down in it. The bodies proceeding in labour disputes are obliged to investigate the genuineness of the motives of notices; since the weight of these motives are in general not pondered, the abuses of the law may also present themselves in connection with the termination of the labour relationship upon the initiative of the employer.[38/a] In Poland, the requirement of specified facts in the case of the employer's giving notice is, similarly to the Hungarian views, disregarded in the codification of the Labour Code enacted in 1974.[39] Nevertheless, the notice has to be motivated, and the well-foundedness is checked by the local trade union as a social body; the employee has the right to contest the justifiableness of the notice, and to file an appeal against the notice with the bodies proceeding in labour disputes.[40]

To the validity of notice the addressee's acceptance is not neeeded; however,

[37/a] It should be noted in this respect that the change to the said system did not on a major scale result in the termination of labour relations upon the initiative of the enterprises because of a general shortage of manpower. Thus, especially in some economic sectors, labour relations are practically terminated by the enterprises only by right of pensioning.

[38] See Stand No. 95 of the Labour Law Department of the Supreme Court, reading that the cause of giving notice should be not only definite but also of a nature that can serve as a basis for the cancellation of the labour contract. Cf. Casebook of Labour Law Decisions. Vol. II. Budapest 1980, p. 437.

[38/a] Thus, it is an abuse of the law if an enterprise creates a situation deliberately, e.g. with a formal reorganization, which can give a reason to cancel the labour contract of an employee. Therefore, the body authorized to settle and decide a labour dispute, arisen from the enterprise giving notice, is obliged to examine whether the reorganization was realized, or it was only a pretext so that giving of notice to the employee could be motivated. Furthermore, if notice is given because an employee, who otherwise performs his work to the satisfaction of the employer, has appeared in his place of work a few minutes late on one occasion, and the employee makes a complaint of the notice, the case of the use of law contrary to its destination is declared, i.e. the board of arbitration of the company meets fully the complaint of the employee, and the termination will thus be invalidated. See NAGY (1970/8), pp. 760 et seq.

[39] Before the coming into force of the Labour Code, the system of giving notice was restriction-free in actual practice on the employer's side, on the basis of legal rules originating from the period between the First World War and the Second World War. Giving notice had to be motivated only if this was stipulated by a special legal rule or a collective agreement. See TRÓCSÁNYI (1970/3), p. 584.

[40] SALWA (1974), pp. 25–30. Incidentally, the view has become established in Polish jurisprudence that giving notice on the part of the enterprise is well founded if it is justified by the socially important interests of the enterprise, and is in conformity with the principles of social coexistence. See SALWA (1979/9), pp. 58–62.

a unilateral revocation of the notice is not admitted, as it would mean the establishment of a new labour relationship unilaterally.[41]

The causes serving as basis for the termination of a labour relationship on the part of the employer may present themselves on the side of both the enterprise and the employee. The causes on the employee's side are divided, in some views, to causes which are imputable to the employee and those which are not.[42]

Some of these causes permit the cancellation of the labour contract by giving notice; in case of other causes a notice is not needed, and the labour contract may be cancelled with immediate effect. It should be noted, however, that in some countries the term notice is not used in conformity with the full content of this institution. The term *preduprezhdenye* used in the Soviet law may be translated correctly as preliminary advice. The terms *predisvestye,* used in the Bulgarian law, and *preaviz,* used in Romania, have the same meaning. Nevertheless, the said expressions reflect, essentially, an act of will directed at the termination of the labour relationship; in view of this, the term notice is used in this context in the following comments.

As regards the cancellation of the labour contract on the initiative of the employee, it is a regulation laid down in the law of all socialist countries that an employee is entitled to cancel his labour contract by giving notice at any time, and it is not an absolute requirement to indicate the motives of the notice (system of giving notice not bound to specified facts). It is the term given in the notice that is prolonged at most, if the cancellation takes place for a cause other than those determined in the legal rule.[43] As regards the cancellation of the labour contract with immediate effect and without giving notice, it is only permissible in case of the existence of causes specified in the legal rule.

It is a further rule of general relevance that a labour relationship may be terminated by dint of giving notice only at the moment of the occurrence of the cause of the notice. In view of this, it is an unlawful procedure if the labour contract of an employee, having acquired the right to old-age pension, is cancelled by the employer's notice prior to the completion of the age prescribed in the relevant legal rule. It is the same situation if the labour relationship of an employee has to be terminated on completion of an age specified in the legal rule.

The forthcoming comments concern: (A) the cases in which the enterprise is entitled to cancel the labour contract for causes that presented themselves on the side of either the enterprise or the employee; (B) the cancellation of the labour contract is on the employee's part.[44]

[41] KAISER–KIRSCHNER–SCHULZ (1974), p. 182.

[42] See MIRONOV (1971/6), p. 43.

[43] See, e.g. Article 51, subsection 2 of the Czechoslovak Labour Code. If an employee sends a notice to his employer and gives more than one cause of his step, the notice takes effect if at least one of the causes proves to be acceptable. Cf. CHODERA (1978/7), p. 389.

[44] The termination of a labour relationship on account of the invalidity of the labour

(A) *Cases in which the employer is entitled to terminate the labour relationship*

(a) Generally, the causes comprise the ceasing of the activity of an enterprise, institution, or organization; the reduction of the number of the employees, i.e. cases of reorganization;[45] the suspension of work for a longer period of time;[46] the transfer of the enterprise to another community in which the demand of manpower is available from local resources;[47] the cessation of the need of employment, resulting from the change of the sphere of production or the tasks of the enterprise; changes in the technical equipment of the enterprise or other transformations of organization;[48] and also the case in which the post of the employee is filled up by a disposition of the competent organ; re-instituting another person who held the post earlier.[49] Nevertheless, the causes of organizational character cannot be regarded so that their existence makes it compulsory for the enterprise to terminate the relevant labour relationship. According to the respective rules of the individual countries, in the occurrence of the causes in question it is only the possibility that arises concerning the cancellation of the labour relationship by giving notice. Moreover, some legal rules reflect the effort, arisen from a fundamental tendency, to ensure the employee's transfer to another post of work in such cases, and the labour relationship is only cancelled if the transfer cannot be realized for some reason.[50]

---

contract is to a certain extent a separate category. A labour contract may become null and void, in fact, for a reason equally imputable to the enterprise or the employee; in other words, the cause involving the invalidity of a labour contract may appear equally on the part of the enterprise or of the employee. If there is no remedy against the invalidity of a labour contract or a remedy could have been found but it was not applied, the labour relationship has to be terminated with immediate effect. Nevertheless, the obligation to terminate the employment with immediate effect concerns only the enterprise, i.e. an employee is only entitled, but not obliged, to terminate his labour relationship in the case in question.

[45] Article 17, points 1 and 6 of the Basic Rules of the labour legislation of the Soviet Union and the member republics; Article 33, point 1 of the 1971 Labour Code of the Russian Soviet Federated Socialist Republic; Para 54, subsection 2, item (a) of the Labour Code of the German Democratic Republic.

[46] According to the Bulgarian law, this period is of 30 days; cf. Para 31, point (b) of the Labour Code.

[47] Para 130, subsection 1, point (c) of the 1972 Labour Code of Romania.

[48] Para 46, subsection 1, point (c) of the Czechoslovak Labour Code; Para 31, subsection 2, point (a) of the Labour Code of the German Democratic Republic.

[49] Article 17, point 6 of the Basic Rules of the labour legislation of the Soviet Union and the member republics; Para 130, subsection 1, point (f) of the Romanian Labour Code.

[50] As is provided in Para 54, subsection 2 of the Labour Code of the German Democratic Republic, the validity of notice given by the enterprise is bound to the condition that the enterprise and the employee failed to come to an agreement concerning an assignment to another job within the enterprise or a transfer to another enterprise, with the consent of the employee. This rule gives an impulse to the enterprises to take into account another employment for the person concerned prior to the notice. This regulation is also in conformity with the requirement in principle that labour relations of a longer term correspond best to the demands of the people's economy. According to Soviet law, the targets of the

It may be stated, as a remark of general nature, that in the above cases the way of the cancellation of the labour contract is the enterprise's giving notice, although this is not necessarily so.[51]

(b) The division of the causes into groups of those not imputable to the employee or not attributable to his culpability, and of those attributable to the employee, seems to be an arrangement which is practicable only in general terms, nevertheless it may serve as a framework for our analysis of these causes, therefore, we attempt to make use of it. In fact, there are human conditions which give right to the unilateral cancellation of the labour contract with an objective character to the extent that, as is established in the law of some countries, a labour contract need not even be cancelled in the case of their occurrence, for it ceases to exist without any cancellation. According to the legal constructions of other countries, the cancellation of the labour contract is necessary even in these cases. Since the circumstances in question are independent of human intentions, the problem of culpability cannot be envisaged in relation of the causes belonging in this group, while the other group consists of manifestations of human conduct which, in view of the social requirements, are qualified as tortious. Finally, there are other causes as well which—depending on the factual state of the case—could be included in either of the above categories, consequently a more differentiated approach is required in connection with them.

Let us now examine the groups of causes more thoroughly.

(b)–(i) *Causes not imputable to the employee.* Completion of the age entitling to an old-age pension, or having significance from another point of view. — In these cases the termination of the labour relationship depends on age or the years of service but the two factors may appear also in a combined

---

relevant plan, the instructions of the competent superior body, the documents concerning the reduction of the wage fund, and the chances to employment of dismissed workers are to be taken into consideration in case of a reduction of the number of employees. See GASANOV (1977/2), p. 45; VDOVIN–TCHERNOMORTCHENKO (1979/19), pp. 9–10.— According to a disposition integrated into the Romanian Labour Code (Para 133, subsection 1) if the termination of a labour relationship is initiated by some economic organization for a reason specified in detail in the relevant document, including reorganization, the employer is obliged to offer the person concerned his transfer to another kind of work, suitable for him; to this end, the employer should ask for the support of its directly superposed organ and the body in charge of labour-force administration, or to take measures for the professional retraining of the person in question, according to the particular circumstances of the case.

[51] According to Soviet law, if an employee refuses to accept his transfer to another place, to which the enterprise as a whole is transferred, his refusal is not to be understood as a cause for the cancellation of his labour contract, the cause is an independent direct one, similarly as in the case of an agreement of the parties or as in that of the cancellation of the labour contract on the part of one of the parties (cf. Article 15, point 6 of the Basic Rules). ANDREYEV (ed., 1971, p. 127) added, however, that, essentially, the point is here the termination of the employment relation upon the initiative of the management, therefore, the consent of the local trade union committee is required, by virtue of the relevant general rules.

form. As a rule the employer is then authorized to give notice,[52] but there are different regulations as well, e.g. the completion of specified years of age involves the termination of the labour relationship *ex lege,* irrespective of the parties' will.[53]

Disability to work. — The following comments concern only the cases of disability which cannot be attributed to the employee, although the disability to work may be traced back also to conduct imputable to the person concerned.

The category of not imputable disability to work comprises also different sorts of cases. It appears thus that the termination of a legal relationship is admitted also on account of provisory disability to work in case of an absence exceeding the delay specified in the respective legal rule.[54] In another typical case, the employee's unableness to meet the requirements resulting from the labour relationship develops into a continued state, and this is the cause of the employer giving notice whereby terminating the labour relationship in question. It follows *a contrario* from this latter arrangement that on account of a provisional disability to work the labour contract of the employee must not be cancelled at all. In practice, this may occur in the case of invalidity but this is not necessarily so.[55] A further variant may be mentioned, when a decision of taking disability to work into consideration implies the termination of a labour relationship so that the employer's separate act of will is then not needed. The view claiming to consider invalidity as a cause of the automatic termination of a labour relationship has not been confirmed by practice. If another kind of appropriate work cannot be offered to an invalid person by means of the modification of his labour contract, which would conform to

[52] According to Article 31, point (f) of the Bulgarian Labour Code, the enterprise is entitled to terminate the labour relationship of employees who have already the right to retire on account of the number of years of their employment; nevertheless, the age of retirement is at the completed 55th year for men, and 50th for women. Under the terms of Para 130, point (g) of the Romanian Labour Code, a labour relationship may be terminated upon the initiative of the enterprise when the age limit of retirement is reached by the employee.

[53] According to the Czechoslovak law (Act No. 163/1969 Sb. on the amendment and completion of the act on high schools), the employment of high school teachers is terminated on completion of their term during which they completed their 65th year of age, unless it ceased to exist earlier on account of another cause. This is thus a termination *ex lege*. Cf. WITZ (1971), II, p. 35. (The employee has the right to ask for a prorogation from the Ministry of Education.) There is a difference between the said provision and the Hungarian rule bearing upon the termination of the employment of research workers employed by the institutes of the Hungarian Academy of Sciences, since—under the terms of the Hungarian regulation—on completion of the age determined in the rule the labour relationship has to be terminated in a prescribed way, i.e. the employment is not terminated *ex lege* (cf. 5/1971 MTA–F, *A. K.* 7).

[54] Article 17, point 5 of the Basic Rules of the labour legislation of the Soviet Union and the member republics. Nevertheless, a labour relationship may be terminated on this basis only in extreme cases, when e.g. the employee's prolonged absence from work would have detrimental effects on productive economic work. See ANDREYEV (ed., 1971), p. 138.—There is an identical provision in Article 33, point 5 of the 1971 Labour Code of the Russian Soviet Federated Socialist Republic.

[55] BERNARD–PAVLÁTOVÁ (1979), p. 208.

his restricted ability to work, then the labour contract in question may be cancelled in the way prescribed for this case.[56] This cause of termination of the labour relationship has an exceptional character in general, therefore, the recent legislation of some countries omitted to apply this possibility if it existed in the previous rules.[57]

Unfitness or insufficient performance of work. — The notice given to employees on account of their unfitness for their contracted work may be attributed to causes which are partly not imputable and partly imputable to the person concerned. The following comments treat only the first cases.

Unfitness which is not imputable to the employee may present itself as the lack of professional qualification, ability, and the required state of health. The notice given on account of unfitness is regarded as justified if the employee in question has been unable to come up to the contracted conditions of work, in spite of all efforts of the enterprise made in order to make him acquainted with the required professional knowledge.[58] As regards the regulations of the positive law, unfitness is either mentioned in general terms, without specifying the causes more closely which are of decisive importance when qualifying an employee to be unfit,[59] or the criteria of becoming unfit or performing work inappropriately are laid down in detail in the relevant legal rule.[60]

---

[56] KAISER–KIRSCHNER–SCHULZ (1974), p. 162.

[57] The 1972 Romanian Labour Code provided thus e.g. for the invalidation of one of the causes of giving notice, not imputable to the party concerned, i.e. an employee's absence from his/her work, over a period exceeding three months, on account of the loss of capacity to work. According to the new rules, the possibility of cancellation was allowed only for the cases of established invalidity of the 1st and nd class, i.e. a labour contract could not be cancelled in case of an invalidity of the 3rd class, contrary to the provisions of the previous rules. See BELIGRĂDEANU (1973/7), p. 108.–With regard to the law of the German Democratic Republic, a distinction was made earlier. The employer was not authorized to give notice because of an illness, but giving notice was allowed during the illness of an employee in case it was justified by some other reasons, e.g. modification of the plan providing for the number of employees. See STELTER (1964), pp. 92–95. According to Para 57, point (d) of the Labour Code of the German Democratic Republic it is absolutely impermissible for the employer to give notice on account of illness, work accident incapacity to work resulting from occupational diseases.

[58] KAISER–KIRSCHNER–SCHULZ (1974), p. 192. This basis for giving notice is applicable if the employee does not possess the required professional qualification. Nevertheless, the enterprise is obliged to take all possible measures concerning vocational training, in order to ensure that the employee become capable of complying with the targets satisfactorily. Accordingly, inability is only acknowledged if, in spite of all measures referred to above, the employee proves to be actually incapable of fulfilling his task. Incidentally, the Supreme Court of the German Democratic Republic pronounced this basic principle already years ago. See KIRSCHNER–MICHAS (1978), p. 80.

[59] According to Para 31, point (c) of the Bulgarian Labour Code, a labour relationship may be terminated if the employee proves to be incapable of performing the work entrusted to him. Under the terms of the Labour Code of the German Democratic Republic (Para 54, subsection 2) a labour contract may be terminated in case the employee proved to be incapable of performing the work specified in it.

[60] According to Article 17, point 2 of the Basic Rules of the labour legislation of the Soviet Union and the member republics, as well as Article 33, point 2 of the Labour Code

As a general remark it should be added that the tendency of the development of codification seems to be directed in this field toward the concrete statement of unfitness or inappropriate performance of work. Thus, a labour contract could be cancelled e.g. in the previous rules of the Soviet law in case of the unfitness of an employee, whereas it is now required that the unfitness of an employee be attributable to his insufficient professional training or state of health.[61] The concretization of the circumstance or circumstances causing the unfitness is definitely required in the Hungarian legal practice, too.[61/a] The lack of a diploma by itself is no basis to terminate a labour relationship, with the exception of the cases in which a specific qualification is required to hold a job (e.g. physicians, drivers, etc.). In case of the deterioration of the state of health, the main effort of the employer should be to assign the person concerned to an easier work, with the consent of the latter. Qualification and the state of health are causes beyond the factor of culpability;[62] it may also be observed that the concept of the inappropriate performance of work is being polarized toward guiltless conduct or the occurrence of specific human circumstances, in the Soviet law in particular. It should also be pointed out, however,

of the Russian Soviet Federated Socialist Republic, a labour contract may be cancelled if the employee proved to be incapable of meeting the requirements, on account of an unsatisfactory qualification or state of health, impeding thereby the performance of the work concerned. An unsatisfactory qualification is not equivalent to the lack of being an experienced, trained worker. A labour relationship may be terminated on account of unsatisfactory qualification if, as a result of technical development, the tasks to be fulfilled are going to be more and more complicated in a particular field, so that the qualification of the employee in question seems to be inadequate to comply with them. As regards health reasons, a termination is justified, e.g., if a driver suffers from troubles of vision, a nurse becomes disease-carrier, etc. See ANDREYEV (ed., 1971), p. 133. Furthermore, as is laid down in Article 33, point 2 of the Labour Code of the Russian Soviet Federated Socialist Republic, the public prosecutor is obliged to investigate whether the professional qualification of the employee concerned was examined and stated by the relevant administrative body correctly, how the employee fulfilled his/her tasks, whether the enterprise created the required conditions of work for the employee or was there a possibility to transfer the employee in question, with his/her consent, to another field of work conforming to his/her qualification, etc. See GASANOV (1977/2), p. 45.—According to Para 130, subsection 1, point (e) of the Romanian Labour Code, a labour relationship may be terminated if, from professional aspects, an employee fails to meet the requirements set for the kind of work for which he has been employed. The view was expressed in this respect in the literature that professional incompetence may also appear, exceptionally, as an imputable factor. Thus, if a driver's licence is withdrawn because of an offence committed by him/her and s/he refused then to accept another kind of work, the circumstance that has given reason for cancelling the relevant labour contract might be imputable to the employee. See BELIGRĂDEANU (1973/7), pp. 107 and 110.—The principal rule remains, however, that the cancellation of a contract on account of incompetence needs to be based on a circumstance that cannot be imputed to the employee.

[61] Cf. Article 47, point (c) of the 1922 Labour Code of the Russian Soviet Federated Socialist Republic, and Article 33, point 2 of the 1971 Labour Code. See VOLIN (1974/10), p. 41.

[61/a] Stand No. 95 of the Labour Law Department of the Supreme Court. Cf. Casebook of Labour Law Decisions. Vol. II. Budapest 1980, p. 137.

[62] ANDREYEV (ed., 1971), p. 133.

that even if only with an occasional or transitory character, opposite tendencies present themselves as well.[63]

Similarly, it also occurs that unfitness and the inappropriate performance of work are not equally taken into consideration from the point of view of terminating a labour relationship. Under Czechoslovak law, the enterprise is entitled, for example, to cancel a labour contract by giving notice if the employee fails to fulfil the conditions fixed for the contracted work in the relevant legal rules. First and foremost, this means meeting the professional conditions of qualification required to come up to the job in question. Similarly, the labour contract of an employee may be cancelled by giving notice if, unless the enterprise is found tortious, s/he fails to comply with the requirements which are considered as the necessary conditions of the normal fulfilment of the work.[64] Accordingly, the enterprise is entitled to give notice in case of an inappropriate performance of work without being obliged to prove the unfitness of the employee. Thus, the rules of the Czechoslovak law concern essentially, two facts of the case, viz. (i) the lack of the conditions of qualification required for the fulfilment of the work, such as a skilled worker's certificate, driver's licence, etc., when the employee is either unable to meet the requirements already at the time of commencing work, and he fails to communicate this circumstance, or he fails to comply with them at a later moment, e.g. on account of a ban on exercising a specific activity; besides, professional, political, or moral conditions may be prescribed, as well, for the employees of some State organs, in particular; (ii) underfulfilment of work, meaning a non-compliance with some essential requirements of the work; the employee is capable of meeting the formal requirements, nevertheless, his work reveals serious failures, and he fails to eliminate them within a reasonable delay, although he has been admonished to do so by the enterprise in writing, within a period of 12 months preceding the cancellation.[65]

Another tendency of the positive law of the socialist countries may also be observed. The supporters of this concept argue that, prior to the enterprise terminating the labour relationship of an employee on account of unfitness or of inappropriate performance of work, an effort should be made to employ the person in another field or place of work in which he can be expected to

---

[63] The concept of the unsatisfactory performance of work had not included the element of culpability into the Czechoslovak labour law before the enactment of the 1969 amendment to the Labour Code. This latter provided so that to the category of the cancellation of the labour contract on account of the unsatisfactory performance of work should also belong to the cases in which the employee violated the socialist order of society through his/her activities, and lost thus the confidence required to hold his/her previous job or place of work. Cf. Para 46, point (c) of the Labour Code.—We hold the view that the legislator took this way less on the basis of a consideration of principle but was led more by an endeavour to facilitate the removal of some undesirable elements from their posts under the extraordinary circumstances of that period. This view is supported also by the fact that the complementary Act of the 1975 Code does not contain any more the disposition referred to above.

[64] Para 46, point (e) of the Czechoslovak Labour Code.

[65] FILO–BLAHA (1975/9), p. 860; PROFANT (1977/3), pp. 9 et seq.

cope with his task, and the labour contract can be terminated by giving notice only in the absence of a possibility mentioned above, even after a preliminary training; or the employee in question refuses to accept another kind of work for which he is supposed to be fit.[66]

Offering another kind of work may be a right of the employer, but it may appear as an obligation as well. According to the previous Romanian regulation, the employer had not been obliged, only entitled, to offer another kind of work in case of a professional unfitness, but this became an obligation for the employer later, under the terms of the 1972 Romanian Labour Code.[67] If the employer fails to keep this obligation, the cancellation of the labour contract is regarded as unlawful. The introduction of this obligation was motivated by the aim to ensure the stabilization of employment relations.[68]

An opposite tendency may be observed in the recent rules of the Czechoslovak law; a preliminary vocational training is mentioned no more in the provisions; furthermore, the enterprise is no more obliged to offer any other kind of work for the employee; instead, only a job corresponding to the qualification of the employee is envisaged. The argumentation in favour of the rules reads that the employee should perform, first and foremost, a work corresponding to his qualification; accordingly, the cancellation by notice is bound to the condition that the enterprise has no vacant post of work corresponding to the qualification of the person, i.e. such that would be suitable for this latter considering the failures observed in his work.[69] As there were broader possibilities for the continued employment of the workers in question with the application of the previous concept, it meant—in our view—a stronger guarantee for the maintenance of the established labour relationships.

(b)-(ii) *Causes imputable to the employee.* The employee's breach of obligation (contract).—This group of causes comprises a great variety of breaches of obligations (contract) committed by employees, and a tortious conduct is their common characteristic feature.[70]

Regarding the details, it should be noted that, according to one of the respective regulations, a labour contract may be cancelled on account of the breach of obligations (contract) of the employee only in case of a regular course

---

[66] Para 46, subsection 2 of the Czechoslovak Labour Code.

[67] Para 133 of the Romanian Labour Code.

[68] MARICA (1974/4), p. 25.

[69] Para 46, subsection 2, point (c) of the 1975 Supplementary Act to the Czechoslovak Labour Code.

[70] It cannot be regarded as a breach of obligation if an employee refuses to perform a work ordered contrary to the law in a given case. It is thus pointed out, e.g., in the Soviet legal literature that a female employee, being in charge of a child of 7 years of age, is entitled to refuse to accept a delegation to a place outside her contracted place of work, and her refusal cannot be considered as a breach of her obligations since it is laid down in Article 69 of the Basic Rules of Soviet labour legislation that it is impermissible to order the delegation of female employees being in charge of a child (children) from one year to eight years of age, without the consent of the person concerned. See GHERZHA-NOV–NIKHITINSKY (1971/8), p. 31.

of breaches;[71] under the terms of another regulation, the cancellation is admitted in case of breaches of grave nature,[72] furthermore, the combination of the two systems appears as well.[73]

There are special cases of the breach of obligations, such as the unauthorized absence from work, including the appearance at the place of work in drunken state. Depending on the actual circumstances, an unauthorized absence may have various legal consequences; in a graver case, already a single case may result in the cancellation of the labour contract.[74]

In case of a breach of obligations (contract) of an employee, the cancellation of the labour contract is effected with immediate effect, either as a result of a disciplinary procedure or in a non-disciplinary way; as for the second case, the due consideration of the rights of guarantee related to the disciplinary procedure (such as the hearing of the employee, provision of a term to which the possibility of the cancellation of the labour contract is bound, etc.) must be ensured.[75] According to another regulation a labour relationship may be

[71] As is put down in Article 7, point 3 of the Basic Rules of the labour legislation of the Soviet Union and the member republics, a labour contract may be cancelled if the employee has violated the obligations at his/her charge under the terms of his/her labour contract or the internal statutes of his/her employer, without justified motives, subsequently and regularly, provided that a disciplinary or similar measure had already been taken against him/her. The term of regularity is not specified in the legal rule; according to judicial practice, it implied the committing of violation repeatedly within a period of one year. See GHERZHANOV–NIKHITINSKY (1971/8), p. 31. The public prosecutor is obliged in these cases to inspect whether the rules of the relevant disciplinary procedure were observed, the employee concerned was asked to give explanation concerning the cause of the offence, and whether any disciplinary or similar measure had been taken against the employee earlier. See GASANOV (1977/2), p. 46.

[72] According to Para 46, subsection 1, point (f) of the Czechoslovak Labour Code, the enterprise is entitled to give notice to an employee in the presence of reasons on account of which the relevant labour contract can be cancelled with immediate effect, or if the employee in question infringed the labour discipline in a particularly grave way. As is laid down in the 1976 Yugoslav Act on associated work (Para 211), the labour relationship of an employee with a basic economic organization may be terminated if the person concerned fails to comply with his/her obligations to perform work, violating thus gravely the common interests of the other employees or the relevant economic organization.

[73] According to Para 130, subsection 1, point (i) of the Romanian Labour Code, the enterprise is authorized to cancel a labour contract if the employee in question committed a grave offence or violated his/her contractual obligations repeatedly, including the rules bearing upon the conduct in the place of work.

[74] Unauthorized absence from work is mentioned in the Basic Rules of the labour legislation of the Soviet Union and the member republics as a particular cause allowing to cancel a labour contract. This, in accordance with Para 25 of the rules of the internal model work-order is understood to mean the absence over the whole duration of a working day without an acceptable reason. The said rule is not applicable to some cases, e.g., an employee presents himself/herself at his/her place of work after lunch–time, or leaves his/her place of work before the end of working time, i.e. s/he is in his/her place of work for part of the working day. The acceptance or refusal of the cause of the absence should be judged by taking into consideration the respective circumstances. See CEPIN (1973/4), p. 23; VOLIN (1974/10), No. 10, p. 42.

[75] GHERZHANOV–NIKHITINSKY (1971/8), p. 30.–There are identical provisions in the Soviet and the Romanian legal regulations in this respect in so far that, in case of a breach

terminated equally by giving notice or with immediate effect, in case of a breach of obligations (contract).[76]

Other causes imputable to the employee.—This group comprises cases in which an employee becomes unfit to perform his/her work not as a consequence of a breach of obligation related to his/her work. Besides, the employer's act of will is required, in general, for the termination of a labour relationship in these cases. Nevertheless, this is not an absolute rule, for there are also regulations in which the employer's act of will is not required. In these cases, the labour relationship is terminated, as a rule, with immediate effect, although there are exceptions also in this field.

Arrest of the employee.—The arrest may be a reason for the cancellation of the labour contract with immediate effect. If there are existing regulations to this effect periods of arrest are set in general to two-three months.[77]

Non-appealable conviction of the employee.—There are regulations stipulating that the employer is entitled to cancel the labour contract with immediate effect if an employee is convicted to an unconditional and non-appealable imprisonment of minimum one year on account of an intentionally committed crime, irrespective of the circumstance whether the criminal act for which he is convicted is or is not linked with the fulfilment of his obligations resulting from his labour relationship.[78]

An imprisonment for a term of shorter than one year constitutes no reason for the cancellation of the labour contract according to the Czechoslovak law, neither with immediate effect nor by giving notice.[79] According to another

---

of obligations by an employee, the respective labour contract may be cancelled with immediate effect, either by means of a disciplinary procedure, or in a non-disciplinary way. As regards the Soviet law, cf. Article 17, points 3 and 4; Article 56 of the Basic Rules of labour legislation; Article 33, points 3 and 4, and Article 135, point 5 of the Labour Code of the Russian Federated Soviet Socialist Republic. For the Romanian law, see Article 100, subsection 1, point (f), and Article 130, subsection 1, point (i) of the Labour Code. As regards the Romanian law, reference should be made, however, to the remark according to which the point concerns here complementary provisions on the labour relationship, and not different causes of the termination thereof. See BELIGRĂDEANU (1973/7), p. 110.–The termination of employment as a disciplinary measure is also mentioned in the Bulgarian Labour Code (Para 33, point 2); it is applicable in case of tortious non-fulfilment of the obligation to perform work. See RADOILSKI (1957), p. 571.

[76] As regards the provision of Para 46, point (f) of the Czechoslovak Labour Code, see our note No. 72 above.

[77] It is set to two months according to Para 33, point (a) of the Bulgarian Labour Code; Para 130, subsection 1, point (j) of the Romanian Labour Code; and three months according to the Polish regulation. According to this latter, the employer need not terminate the labour relationship, for a detention exceeding three months constitutes a fact implying the cancellation of the labour contract automatically. The relevant text reads as follows: "A labour contract expires with the lapse of three months if the employee concerned has been absent from work on account of his commitment to prison, except that the labour contract was terminated by the enterprise earlier, without giving notice, for a cause that was imputable to the employee." See Article 66, Para 1 of the Polish Labour Code.

[78] Para 53, subsection 1, point (a) of the Czechoslovak Labour Code.

[79] According to WITZ's view, a labour relationship may be terminated in this case only if another cause of notice existed (personal communication dated April 13, 1974).

regulation, the employer is only entitled to cancel the labour contract of an employee on account of a non-appealable conviction if the sentence was pronounced on the basis of a criminal act linked with the work of the person concerned, provided that he becomes incapable of complying with the performance of his work by virtue of the sentence.[80]

Prohibition of the exercise of an employee's profession.—The termination of a labour relationship on this basis may be the consequence of a verdict of a criminal court of justice in which the person concerned is prohibited, as a secondary punishment, from holding a job which implies the exercise of authority, or from carrying on a profession which was used by the convicted party to commit the criminal act in question. An employer is entitled to cancel the labour contract of an employee with immediate effect if the person concerned has been deprived of the right to hold a job or to carry out a profession, either provisionally or finally, in a verdict passed by a criminal court of justice.[81]

According to another concept, the labour contract of an employee may be cancelled in these cases on the ground of unfitness, but only by giving notice and not with immediate effect; besides, all rights of guarantee in connection with the notice have to be ensured for the employee. If the respective labour relationship does not come to be terminated, it will continue to exist *de iure,* but none of the opposed parties will be entitled to present a labour law claim during the validity of the punishment in question.[82] Under the terms of another

[80] Para 130, subsection 1, point (k) of the Romanian Labour Code. Article 52, Para 1, point (2) of the Polish Labour Code.

[81] Para 130, subsection 1, point (1) of the Romanian Labour Code.

[82] This is the existing regulation of the law of the German Democratic Republic, providing, e.g. that the employment of a pregnant female employee cannot be terminated by giving notice in the said case. Nevertheless, the fact of the case that has led to the prohibition of the continued exercise of a given profession, is on several occasions, also a grave violation of discipline, the cancellation of the labour contract with immediate effect is then also permissible. For such cases not even the protection of pregnant female employees is constituted. Nevertheless, the consent of the relevant trade union committee should be needed with regard to the measure in question. Supposing that—as a consequence of the refusal of consent by the trade union committee—neither notice has been given nor a discharge with immediate effect has been decided, the labour relationship continues to exist *de iure,* but as a consequence of the debarring of the employee from continuing his/her work, and so also from carrying on his/her profession, his/her claim for being paid ceases to exist. Remarks, worth to be noted, on the disciplinary responsibility in the law of the German Democratic Republic are expressed in PAUL (1971), p. 27; KUNZ (1966), p. 270.—According to Polish law, if a court of justice imposed a ban on holding a specific post, or carrying on a particular profession, or performing a specific activity, as a secondary punishment, by virtue of Article 38, point 3 of the Criminal Code, the employer is entitled to cancel the relevant labour contract with immediate effect, under the terms laid down in Article 52, point 3 of the Labour Code; nevertheless, this is not an obligatory measure to be taken, although the employer will be obliged to do so by an indirect sanction, i.e. its conduct will be interpreted so that it neglected its obligations in respect of the application of available legal measures against employees who have committed irregular acts gravely violating order and labour discipline. It is a similar case if a court of justice imposes on the defendant the punishment of the withdrawal of his driver's licence, according to Article 38, point 4 of the Polish Penal Code; the difference is that a transfer to another field of work within the employee's enterprise, with the employee's consent is also a possibility here.

regulation, the employee in question has to be transferred to another kind of work in case the secondary punishment mentioned above was imposed.[83]

According to the Hungarian regulation, the prohibition from carrying out a specified profession does not imply by itself the termination of the respective labour relationship, only the parties' right to dispose is excluded in respect of the given scope of the persons's profession.[84] There is no obstacle in Hungarian law to bring about an agreement between the employer and the employee according to which the employee is enabled to be transferred to a post which is not subject to the prohibition pronounced in the verdict of the court of justice.

(b)–(iii) *Other causes.* As is laid down in the legal rules of some socialist countries, a labour contract may be cancelled by the employer on account of the following causes arisen at the side of the employeee: tortuous acts, committed by an employee in direct charge of money or commodities, of a nature that justifies to discontinue the confidence previously granted to the person concerned; immoral acts, committed by an employee in charge of tasks in the field of education, which prove to be incompatible with the continued exercise of his job;[85] revocation of the competent body's consent to the employment of a member of the works guard.[86] This category includes also the cases of the intentional disability of an employee, caused with an aim to be put on the sick-list. This group also includes the cases in which for holding a post a clean record is required by specific legal rules, and an employee is convicted during the existence of the specific labour relationship.[87] The employment of graduated young experts (specialists) by infringing the rules bearing upon the employment of specialists belonging in this group is also regarded as a cause to cancel a labour contract.[88] It is not allowed furthermore to employ persons in close relationship with each other by the same enterprise, in case that one of them would be directly subjected or superposed to the other as a consequence of their sphere of work.[89] Labour contracts infringing this rule have to be cancelled by the employer.

---

[83] According to Para 37, subsection 1, point (d) of the Czechoslovak Labour Code, the enterprise is obliged to transfer the employee to another kind of work if this is required by a non-appealable judgment of a court of justice or a legally binding disciplinary measure.

[84] GARANCSY (1970), p. 176.

[85] Article 254, points 2 and 3 of the Labour Code of the Russian Soviet Federated Socialist Republic. See also ORESHKHINA–VOROBELA (1979/22), pp. 28–29.

[86] According to Para 12 of the Romanian Law Decree No. 303/1972 on the organization of the safeguarding of goods.

[87] This is a different situation from the non-appealable judgment, dealt with in the preceding section, for any punishment may be considered here, irrespective of the character of the committed criminal act and the weight of the imposed punishment.

[88] VOLIN (1974), p. 43.—According to the Hungarian regulation, the labour contracts of specialists starting their career and employed with the non-observation of the competition system, in a way violating public interests, are null and void. Cf. Resolution of the Council of Ministers No. 1023/1976 (VII. 15), point 7.

[89] Article 20 of the Labour Code of the Russian Soviet Federated Socialist Republic. See KOROTKOVA (1976/6), pp. 86–89.

(B) *Cases in which the employee is entitled to terminate the labour relationship*

Reference was made in the preceding to the rule according to which an employee is entitled in the socialist countries to terminate a labour relationship concluded for an indefinite period of time at any time by giving notice; the notice need not be motivated, as a rule, and the employer is bound to take note of the intention of leave of the employee in question; at most, the period of notice will be prolonged, if the notice of the employee is given for a cause other than those fixed in the relevant legal rules. In this case, the employee's act of will, aimed at the cancellation of the labour contract, serves as basis for the termination of the labour relationship. Nevertheless, if an employee leaves his work without having given notice or terminates his labour relationship prior to the date provided for it, various sanctions are then applicable, their content depending on the respective positive rules of the law of the country.[90]

According to one of the regulations, the cancellation of the labour contract by an employee requires a written form, i.e. an employee is not entitled to cancel his/her labour contract by a verbal notification or a concludent fact; if s/he proceeds so in spite of this rule, his/her conduct will be considered as a grave infringement upon labour discipline. The employee is then obliged to perform work during the entire course of the period of notice as the cancellation of his/her labour contract will become effective with the expiration of the period of notice. A grave infringement upon labour discipline is presumed also in the case if an employee presents the enterprise a written notification concerning the unilateral cancellation of his/her labour contract, but s/he fails to continue to work during the period of notice, or leaves his/her employer before the expiration of the period of notice.[91]

There are provisions in the law of some countries permitting also for the employee to cancel his/her labour contract with immediate effect, i.e. distinction is made by the law between cancelling a labour contract by giving notice or by an act of immediate effect at the employee's side as well. Nevertheless, the employee's cancellation of a labour contract with immediate effect is only permitted in cases strictly specified by the law.

A cause of this type may be, in particular, the circumstance if the continuation of employment endangers the employee's life, health, or corporeal integrity

---

[90] Under the terms of Polish law, the labour contract of a person who terminated his employment unauthorized is cancelled by the employing enterprise with immediate effect. An unauthorized termination of the employment is understood in case of an unjustified absence from the place of work during three subsequent working days. The disadvantage of this practice is that the enterprises fail to examine appropriately whether the point was, in fact, an undisputable intention of the employee to leave his/her place of work in an unauthorized way or it was simply an unjustified absence. See SZURGACZ (1976), pp. 80 et seq. Under Hungarian law, the unauthorized termination of employment is regarded as if the labour relationship of the employee concerned were terminated as a result of dismissal through disciplinary procedure (Labour Code, Para 31, subsection 2).

[91] MIKHAILOV (1974/1), pp. 12 et seq.; STEFANOV (1974/4), pp. 48 et seq.

directly and seriously,[92] or the employee becomes unable to comply with the work at his/her charge for s/he has become ill;[93] this situation may even be more aggravated, if the employer fails to transfer the employee to another, appropriate, sphere of activity within a specified period, in spite of the circumstance that the continuation of the employment would mean a serious danger to the person concerned.[94] There are other causes which may be mentioned, e.g. the employee did not receive his remuneration by the time stipulated for it; the enterprise modified the conditions of the labour contract without justifiable motives; the employee was admitted to an institution of higher or secondary education or to a specialized vocational training school for continued studies.[95]

There are no provisions for the termination of labour relations with immediate effect on the employee's part in the law of several countries, although attention was drawn to the importance of the regulation of this possibility in the legal literature.[96]

7.4 Decisions of authorities as legal facts leading to the termination of labour relations

In the following comments, we wish to present a short survey of the cases in which, as is laid down in the legal rules of the socialist countries, a labour relationship is terminated automatically, by virtue of a decision of a body with authoritative power, or by the decision in question being without the right of appeal, i.e. without the parties' acts of will aimed at the termination of the labour relationship, and the latter is thus the direct result of the intention of an authority representing public interest.

It should be noted, however, that according to not all of the countries' positive legal rules imply automatically the decisions which have to be taken into account from this point of view the actual termination of the labour relationship. There are provisions in the law of some of the countries stipulating, as an indispensable element, an act of will of one of the parties, usually that of the employer, terminating the labour relationship. This act of will is then, essentially, nothing other than the realization of an authoritative body's act of will.

The cases of the termination of labour relations as a result of the act of will of an authority may be grouped whether the decision in question was taken by a court of justice or an administrative body.[97]

---

[92] Para 30, subsection 2 of the Labour Code.

[93] Para 34, point (c) of the Bulgarian Labour Code.

[94] Para 54, subsection 1 of the Czechoslovak Labour Code.

[95] Para 34, point (d) of the Bulgarian Labour Code.

[96] GOLOVANOVA (1966), p. 10.

[97] The termination of a labour relationship as a result of a disciplinary decision is not dealt with here, in view of the circumstance that the case is then the cancellation of employment contract upon the initiative of the enterprise, and this point has already been treated in the foregoing.

(a) Termination of labour relations as a result of a decision of a court of justice.—A decision of a court of justice, by virtue of which an employee is condemned to imprisonment or reformatory work, to be performed outside his last place of work, or the continuation of his work is excluded by the punishment, may have the consequence, always depending on the regulation of the positive law, that the labour relationship in question is terminated automatically when the conviction becomes non-appealable.[98] This legal effect of the sentence of the court may set in irrespective of the circumstance whether or not the employee was convicted on account of a criminal act committed in connection with his/her work.[99]

A similar concept is reflected in the regulation also linking the termination of a labour relationship with a sentence of imprisonment which, however, is of a longer duration. Various security-based educative and protective measures may be qualified in the same way.[100]

It is a different case if dismissal is pronounced by a court of justice, either as a main or a secondary punishment but in a direct way, i.e. the convicted person must not be allowed to continue to hold his post in view of the proceeding court. According to Soviet law, a dismissal may be applied if a criminal act, committed by the accused person within the scope of his function or activity, has a character by which, according to the judgment of the proceeding court of justice, s/he has become unfit to hold specific posts or carry on a specified activity.[101] This regulation is not applicable according to the Yugo-

---

[98] Such rule is applicable in the Soviet Union; it is laid down in the Basic Rules of the labour legislation of the Soviet Union and the member republics (Article 15, point 7) that a non-appealable judicial sentence pronouncing imprisonment against workers and employees—except the case of conditional imprisonment—or reformatory work to be performed at a place other than their domicile, or another punishment excluding the possibility of continuing to perform the work in question, is understood to constitute a reason for the cancellation of a labour contract. The 1971 Labour Code of the Russian Soviet Socialist Federated Republic (Article 29) contains the same disposition.

[99] ANDREYEV (ed., 1971), p. 127.

[100] According to Yugoslav law, the labour relationship of an employee ceases to exist by virtue of the law if he has been sentenced to imprisonment, exceeding a duration of six months, with the starting day of imprisonment; or, in case of a measure of security, or reformative purposes, relating to a period surpassing six months—on account of which the employee will have to be absent from work—with the starting day of application of the measure. Cf. Article 216, points 5 and 6 of the 1976 Act on associated work.—The Romanian law provides also examples for the effect of reformative and educative labour upon the termination of labour relations. Reference is thus made by BELIGRĂDEANU to Article 130, subsection 1, point (k) of the Romanian Labour Code which is completed by a provision of Para 863, subsection 5, of the Romanian Criminal Code, enacted by Act No. 6 of 1973. According to the said rules, a labour contract ceases to exist if the convicted person was engaged in a labour relationship on the basis of a labour contract at the date when the respective verdict of the criminal court, imposing a reformatory labour, becomes non-appealable. Accordingly, the termination of a labour contract *ex lege* is expressed in the legal rule. See BELIGRĂDEANU (1973/7), p. 110.

[101] According to Article 31 of the Criminal Code of the Russian Soviet Federated Socialist Republic, the court of justice may pronounce in the verdict dismissal directly, if it is

slav law, i.e. the labour relationship of the employee is terminated if s/he is not allowed to perform a specified work under the terms of a non-appealable resolution of a court of justice, and it proved to be impossible to offer him/ her another field of activity or a convenient job. The date of termination is then the day of delivery of the said non-appealable judicial resolution for the competent basic organization.[102]

As regards Hungary, it is laid down in the relevant special regulation that the termination of a labour relationship is a direct result only of a sentence of a court of justice pronouncing a ban on participation in public affairs.[103] Although the prohibition of the employee from participating in public affairs may be pronounced, as a secondary punishment, against any accused person who, taking into consideration all circumstances of the actual case, proved to be unworthy of the participation in public affairs,[104] a sentence of this content involves the termination of the relevant labour relationship only within a specified range. In fact, the punishment of prohibition from participating in public affairs implies dismissal only in respect of jobs or functions which cannot be held in case of a prohibition.[105] These jobs or functions are to be understood, in general, as the ones held in State power and State administration bodies, nevertheless, jobs for other bodies may fall within this group as well, if the employee in question has authority related to them.[106]

The labour relationship of a foreigner or a stateless person is terminated the day on which the punishment of expulsion, imposed on him/her, becomes operative, unless the termination becomes effective for another cause. This is also a case of the automatic termination of a labour relationship, when no other legal act is needed for the effect.[107]

The concept attributing to some judicial sentences the consequence of the automatic termination of a labour relationship, results from the view of the legislator according to which the weight or the nature of the committed criminal act makes it unnecessary that the employer should make an act of will to this effect. In case of a regulation in the opposite sense, the possibility would be given namely for the employer not to terminate the labour relationship in question but, by transferring the employee concerned, to create a situa-

---

of the view that the acquitted person must not be charged further with the post s/he held previously. It is laid down in this respect in the Comments to the Criminal Code that the pronouncement of a punishment of dismissal makes it possible for another enterprise to employ the person concerned, and in the same field of work even immediately; moreover, it would not be impossible theoretically that the enterprise would re-employ the dismissed employee in the same field of work even promptly; nevertheless, this procedure would be contrary to the purpose of the punishment of dismissal. Cf. *Kommentary k ugolovnomu*, etc. (1971), p. 88.

[102] Article 216, point 4 of the 1976 Act on associated work.
[103] Para 30, subsection 3 of the Labour Code.
[104] Para 49 of the Criminal Code.
[105] This punishment in fact means the loss of capacity to acquire the specified posts.
[106] Para 48, subsection 1 of the Criminal Code.
[107] Para 42, subsection 3 of the Czechoslovak Labour Code. For the legal literature see FILO–BLAHA (1975/9), p. 859.

tion in which the verdict in question could not be enforced. Moreover, it would also be possible to make an arrangement that the labour relationship in question would be suspended during the validity of the binding force of the punishment prohibiting to hold a specified job or function; nevertheless, the application of this arrangement is rare in the judicial practice.

(b) Termination of a labour relationship by virtue of an administrative decision.—It is an exceptional regulation when a labour relationship is terminated by virtue of an administrative decision. Thus, under Soviet law it may be terminated on account of the calling in of an employee for military service or his voluntary enlisting to the army.[108] Nevertheless, the employee concerned is then entitled to continue to work in his previous post after his release from the armed forces or his being put on the reserve list.

A decision declaring the disability to work may also figure within the group of administrative causes of terminating a labour relationship.[109] The cancellation of the labour contract in another, additional, way is then not needed, for it is terminated by the legally binding statement of the disability to work.

The labour relationship of a foreigner or stateless person is terminated the day when he has to leave the territory of the country of residence, on account of a resolution withdrawing his permit of residence, unless the termination has taken place in another way. The labour relationship is then terminated with the day when the respective administrative decision becomes non-appealable.[110]

7.5 Objective circumstances without volitional elements as legal facts leading to the termination of labour relations

These elements comprise causes other than human conduct, and circumstances which are partly of external nature.

The first group includes the fact of death. A labour relationship ceases to exist automatically with the death of the employee, at the moment of the death, and only some rights and obligations of material nature are transferred to the successors.[110/a]

The death of an employer, even in case this latter is an individual (physical person, as, e.g., handicraftsmen, retail dealers, etc.) does not in general imply the

---

[108] Article 15, point 3 of the Basic Rules of the labour legislation of the Soviet Union and the member republics; Article 29, point 3 of the Labour Code of the Russian Soviet Federated Socialist Republic; Article 29, point 2 of the Bulgarian Labour Code.

[109] According to Yugoslav law, the labour relationship of an employee ceases to exist ex lege if his complete disability to work is stated in a way conforming to the provisions of the law. For the work to be performed for a basic organization, this becomes effective on the day of delivery of the non-appealable decision stating complete disability to work. Cf. Article 216, point 2 of the 1976 Act on associated work.

[110] FILO–BLAHA (1975/9), p. 859.

[110/a] PAVLÁTOVÁ (1976/8), pp. 745 et seq.

termination of the relevant labour relationship, i.e. the successor/s are then obliged to cancel the labour contract in the way prescribed for this case, provided that they are unwilling to maintain it. Arrangements of an opposite nature may be found as well. According to the Bulgarian law, a labour relationship ceases to exist with the death of the person with whom an employee concluded a labour contract if the relationship was bound to the person of the employer.[111] These cases comprise, as has been established in practice, apprentice contracts (under the terms of which, e.g., the employer is not only ensuring work but, additionally, is also in charge of the professional training of the employee concerned),[112] the employment of personal secretaries, etc.

The illness of an employee may be qualified an objective cause of the termination of a labour relationship (of the same character as death), if it is regarded as a separate cause of the termination of a labour relationship.[113] According to a view expressed in the Bulgarian legal literature, an act of will of the employer is needed also in this case, which implies then the termination of the respective labour relationship.[114]

According to the law of the German Democratic Republic, the labour relationship of an employee is terminated *ipso facto* in the case of some criminal acts, as, e.g., the unauthorized crossing of the State frontier. In this case the cancellation of the labour contract is not needed for it ceased to exist with the perpetration of the criminal act and it will not revive with the return of the perpetrator.[115]

Time as a legal factor is also regarded as an external circumstance (factor) independent of human conduct. According to this view, time may be considered as a cause for terminating a labour relationship if this latter ceases to exist automatically on completion of a specified time. This is the situation e.g., with teachers in higher education under the rules of the Czechoslovak law.

Concerning the case of labour relations concluded for a definite period of time, in our view, it is the intention of the parties to terminate the labour relationship at a given period of time which is to be regarded as the cause of its termination, and not the time factor. Essentially, our view does not differ concerning the rest of the cases in which the effect of the time factor is related to the termination of labour relationships.

---

[111] Para 29, point (g) of the Bulgarian Labour Code.

[112] RADOILSKI (1957), p. 546.

[113] According to Para 29, point (j) of the Bulgarian Labour Code, a labour relationship ceases to exist on account of the illness of the worker or employee if his/her continued invalidity was stated by the Medical Committee of Labour Law Specialists.

[114] According to the view of RADOILSKI, a labour relationship has to be terminated if a continued invalidity was stated by the Medical Committee of Labour Law Specialists. The act of will implying the cancellation of the relevant labour contract is then made by the employing enterprise. Cf. RADOILSKI (1957), pp. 546–547. In our view, the case is more similar to the situation when a labour relationship is terminated on the basis of an administrative decision.

[115] KAISER–KIRSCHNER–SCHULZ (1974), p. 162.

According to Polish law, the labour relationship of an employee ceases to exist if he fails to resume his work within 30 days following his release from military service, as is laid down in the respective legal rule;[116] the absence of an employee from his place of work over a period exceeding three months, owing to preliminary detention, has the same effect.[117] The employer's act of will is not required for the termination of labour relations in these cases, i.e. the labour relationship ceases to exist by virtue of the respective legal rules with the lapse of the specified time.[118] The opinions expressed in this respect in the Polish legal literature represent thus the view that the termination of labour relations in these cases may be attributed to time factors as having legal effect. The Polish law contains provisions in a sense that a labour relationship of an employee ceases to exist in the case of the unauthorized discontinuation of work. If an employee withdraws himself from performing the work, infringing the rules bearing upon the cancellation of the labour contract, or if he fails to appear at his place of work without having advised the enterprise of the cause of his absence in due time, the conduct of the employee is understood to be an unauthorized discontinuation of work. The day when the employee stopped to perform work is then to be regarded as the date of the termination of the labour relation.[119]

If a labour relationship is terminated, according to the respective legal rules, on account of a legally relevant fact and not act of will of the contracting parties, the notification of the employer on the termination of the labour relationship has always only a significance of confirmation.[120]

Nevertheless, the legal situations mentioned above and considered as legal facts may be interpreted in another way as well. Thus, if an employee on completion of his military service fails to resume his work at his previous place of work, the termination of his labour relationship may be attributed, essentially, to his intention, even if this is expressed in the form of a conclusive fact. In another case, in which an employee is committed to prison and this fact implies the legal consequence of the termination of the labour relationship beyond the lapse of a specified period of time, as laid down in the respective legal rule, then the termination of the labour relationship is attributed to an act of an authority, with an authoritative intention behind it. The unauthorized discontinuation of work is also attributed to the intention of the employee concerned.

The death of an employee is, in our view, a legal fact the legal effect of

---

[116] Article 106, subsection 1 of the Polish act on national defence.

[117] Article 66, Para 1 of the Polish Labour Code.

[118] SZUBERT (1972), pp. 118–119; SWIECICKI (1969), pp. 316–318.

[119] Article 65 Para 2 of the Polish Labour Code.

[120] Under the rules of the Bulgarian law, the unauthorized interruption or termination of work is judged by special kinds of consideration. On an employee who ceased to perform his work without authorization the disciplinary measure of dismissal has to be imposed. Cf. Article 129, point 1 of the Bulgarian Labour Code. The minimum duration of absence from work is five such days during which the enterprise did not receive reasonable explanation justifying the absence. See MIKHAILOV (1974), pp. 17 et seq.

which is, unequivocally, the termination of a labour relationship. As regards time as a legal fact, a distinction has to be made in this field. If the given positive law provides that on completion of a specified period of age implies the termination of a labour relationship automatically, then time appears also as a legal fact without a volitional element. If the termination of a legal relationship is subjected by the respective legal rule to delays, and the fixation of these delays may be attributed to the parties' act of will or an authoritative act of will then time cannot be considered as a legal fact.

7.6 Protection of the employee's interests in respect of the termination of their labour relations

The labour conditions of the employees are safeguarded by a great variety of measures in the socialist labour law. Several of the employee's interests are now safeguarded by substantive law, while this was not so earlier. The legal arrangements serving the employee's interests may differ from each other considerably, and they do not present themselves with the same weight in the course of the development of the law.

Considering the possibilities in connection with the cancellation of labour contracts on the part of the enterprise, the form of safeguarding the employee's interests applied in the law of the socialist countries is still on a large scale the system of giving notice bound to factual states laid down in the law. The legislators disregard labour codes in the Hungarian and Polish laws. Binding the employer's possibility for giving notice to specified factual states was by no means equivalent to that the legislators were inclined not to take into consideration the employee's interests in the stability of the place of work, or not to give them protection. The linking of notice to a motivation is a kind of protection by itself. From the motivation of the notice the employee learns the reason for which his employer is not inclined to claim for his work, and is entitled to claim for the restitution of the labour relationship in case of an abuse of the law.

The rules on the prohibition and restriction of giving notice, in force in the socialist countries, serve also the safeguarding of the employee's interests in respect of the cancellation of their labour contract. Essentially, the prohibition of giving notice means that the enterprise (employer) is not authorized at all to cancel a labour contract by notice in cases of the factual states serving as a basis for the prohibition. In other words, there is an absolute obstacle in the way of the employer's giving notice. This is the most efficient form of protection.[121]

---

121 Let us mention here that prohibitions to give notice may only serve the protection of the employee's interests if, by eliminating the unlawfulness, the original status may be restituted. This sometimes is impracticable as, for example, when the employer closes down. The most common case is the termination of the licence of an artisan: the legal protection is then not enforceable in practice.

The restrictions of giving notice have also an important place among protective measures. In these cases the possibility of giving notice is not excluded by the legal rule with an absolute effect, i.e. the existence of an extraordinary or special reason is required for giving notice, on the one hand, or the termination of a labour relationship by means of the employer's giving notice is inadmissible under specified circumstances, on the other. This latter case may also be considered as one in which there is a relative obstacle impeding the application of the enterprise's right to give notice.

As regards the prohibitions and restrictions of giving notice, it should be noted as a preliminary comment that there are exceptions also from the prohibitions and restrictions of giving notice, (e.g., the absence of the employee's interests even in the case of the realization of the factual state serving as a basis for the prohibitions and restrictions). Under Hungarian law, e.g., the prohibitions and restrictions of the enterprise's right to give notice are non-applicable to employeees entitled for an old-age pension, to labour contracts governing secondary employments or supplementary occupations to be performed beyond the ordinary working time, or to the cancellation of a labour contract during the term of probation, to the case of expiration of a specified period of time, or to the case of transfer or dismissal as a result of a disciplinary procedure.[122]

The prohibitions and restrictions of giving notice are not homogeneous in the law of the socialist countries, i.e. factual states considered as basis for prohibitions of giving notice in one country are understood to be only a restriction of giving notice according to the law of other countries, or possibly not even a restriction, as, according to the legal rules of various countries, the safeguarding of the employee's inerests should be guaranteed in another way, first and foremost by a system of binding the giving of notice to factual states (which, in the last analysis, means prohibition or restriction, too).

The legal consequences of an unlawful cancellation of the labour contract may have preventive influence upon the perpetrators of infringements of the law of this kind, and this is also a contribution to the safeguarding of the employee's interests.

After these preliminary comments let us now go into details concerning these topics.

7.6.1 Prohibition and restriction of giving notice

Prohibitions and restrictions of giving notice are not separate categories in the law of some socialist countries; in fact, they are not even known in some countries, because other measures are applied to the safeguard of the employee's interests. In view of this, our comments below are based on

---

[122] WELTNER–NAGY (1974), p. 241. For recent non-Hungarian literature see FLOREK (1976), p. 144. Also: *Nowe Prawo* (1976/5), pp. 789–790.

grouping the employees that are granted an increased protection against the cancellation of the labour contract, irrespective of the form of protection, while the subsequent summary of these comments will in a sense be a short survey of the individual forms of protection.—Finally let us mention that the problem of the termination of a labour relationship by means of a disciplinary procedure is not dealt with here separately, because it does not belong to the normal course of labour relations.

Doing military service.—An employee's enlistment for military service constitutes a prohibition of giving notice in the majority of the socialist countries. The legal construction is that the employee is granted non-paid leave for the duration of his military service and for the subsequent period which is absolutely needed for the arrangement of his release from service. The termination of the labour relationship is inadmissible during the non-paid leave.

According to Hungarian law, a labour contract cannot be cancelled by means of the employer giving notice during an employee doing military service (both regular and reserve), including 15 days following his release from the armed forces (Para 26, indent 4 of the Labour Code, and Para 22, point (a) of the Decree on the Enforcement of the Labour Code). As is laid down in Para 48, point (b) of the Czechoslovak Labour Code, the labour contract of an employee cannot be cancelled in case of his enlistment for service in the armed forces, reckoned from the day of delivery of the call-up order or the day of publication of a general order of mobilization up to two weeks after the release from the service.

The law of the German Democratic Republic has also a provision not allowing to cancel by notice the labour contract of an employee during his doing regular military service.[123] Thus, the labour relationship is only interrupted in the course of military service. The protection ceases to be effective if an employee fails to resume his work within a delay of seven days, reckoned from the release from military service.[124]

According to the provisions of Polish law, the enterprise is not allowed to cancel the labour contract of an employee from the day of his enlistment for military service till the completion of it. The labour relationship is thus only interrupted for the duration of the military service.[125] In case the labour contract is under cancellation because the enterprise or the employee has given notice the latter will not be effective if the period specified in it expires after the employee's enlistment.[126]

It is stipulated in the Romanian Labour Code that the labour contracts of workers and employees enlisted for military service remain in force.[127]

[123] Para 58, point (c) of the Labour Code of the German Democratic Republic.

[124] Cf. Paras 2–8 of the Decree (November 24, 1966) on the support to persons released from actual military service. *Gbl.* II, p. 957.

[125] SZUBERT (1972), pp. 118–119.

[126] See Article 105 of the Act (November 21, 1967) on the general obligation to perform military service, in the People's Republic of Poland, as worded in the June 26, 1974 Act, on the enactment of the Labour Code.

[127] Para 72 of the Romanian Labour Code.

According to the regulation of the Yugoslav law, an employee whose work carried on in the basic unit of an economic organization is interrupted on account of his enlistment for regular or reserve military service, is entitled to return to the same basic economic organization, within a delay of 30 days on completion of his regular or auxiliary military service, either to the same place of work in which he was employed prior to his enlistment, or to another place of work corresponding to his professional qualification or capacity to work.[128]

As regards the Soviet law, the worker's or employee's enlistment for military service is a reason for the termination of his labour relationship;[129] the previous labour relationship gives the right for the employee to be employed by his previous employer after his release from military service.[130] It is, however, impermissible to cancel the labour contract of an employee of military age in case of his compulsory enlistment for military service, from the receiving of the conscription order until his return from the conscription, except the case in which the enterprise, institution or organization has gone into full-scale liquidation.[131]

Military service of the husband of female employees.—This circumstance may appear also as a cause excluding the cancellation by notice of the labour contract of a female employee as is the case in Hungary, where enterprises are not authorized to terminate the female employee's labour relationship by notice of dismissal during the regular military service of the latter's husband (cf. Para 22, point (e) of the decree on the enforcement of the Labour Code); it may be a restriction of dismissing by notice, also e.g. in Bulgaria where the labour relationship of women being in the situation referred to above enjoys the same protection as that of pregnant women and nursing mothers, and the cancellation of their labour contract is admitted only in case the enterprise has gone into full-scale liquidation, but a decision of the competent labour supervisory body is required even in that case (Para 35 of the Bulgarian Labour Code). According to a similar Romanian regulation, the labour contract of a female employee cannot be cancelled by the employer during the period of the military service of her husband, except the cases specified in detail in the respective legal rules (Para 146 of the Romanian Labour Code).

Duration of holidays.—Under provisions of the Soviet, Bulgarian, and Polish laws, the employee's labour contract must not be cancelled upon the initiative of the employer, in the course of the employee's holidays (cf. Article 33, last subsection of the Labour Code of the Russian Federated Soviet Socialist Republic; Para 36 of the Bulgarian Labour Code; Para 41 of the Polish Labour Code). According to the Bulgarian regulation, the rule is appli-

---

[128] Para 191 of the 1976 Act of associated work.
[129] Article 15, point 3 of the Basic Rules of the labour legislation of the Soviet Union.
[130] VANDISHEV (1971/5), p. 103.
[131] Article 67 of the 1967 Act on the general obligation to perform military service, as cited by VOLIN (1974/10), p. 41.

cable for the duration of non-paid leaves as well. As is laid down in the law of the German Democratic Republic, the cancellation of the labour contract is inadmissible during the holidays of the employee, even if an admitted reason of notice by dismissal exists otherwise.[132] The intention of the legislator has been here to enable the employee to avoid the trouble of looking for a new employment during his holidays.

Outstanding quality of the work of an employee.—The quality of the employee's work may have a role in the cancellation of a labour contract in the case of employees who have already been employed by the enterprise for a long time and, besides, distinguished themselves by their conduct thereby setting a good example. Under Hungarian law, the labour contract of the employee pertaining to this group may be cancelled by notice of dismissal only in particularly justified cases (Para 26, subsection 3 of the Labour Code). As concerns the requirements of the realization of over-average work, the long duration of employment, and the exemplary conduct, the respective stipulations of the collective agreement are to be observed (Para 21 of the Decree on the Enforcement of the Labour Code). As for legal regulations abroad, the Soviet law may be mentioned as an example in this field, deeply acknowledging the importance of high-quality work from the point of view of the maintenance of employment. In concrete words this means that, when a reduction of the number of employees is carried out, the workers and employees performing their work with a higher degree of efficiency have a privilege to keep their jobs. In case of equal figures in respect of the efficiency of work and professional training, a privileged consideration should be given to employees in charge of the maintenance of two or more members of family, or having no other member of family with a separate income (cf. Article 34, of the Labour Code of the Russian Soviet Federated Socialist Republic). Thus, the restriction of the dismissal by notice is motivated in the Soviet law also by considerations bearing upon the protection of family.

Sending the employees to extension courses.—It is the increase of the quality of the employee's work which appears, indirectly, as a purpose of the regulation laying down that the employer, or another competent body, with the consent of the employer, may send its employee to participate in courses, and the employee concerned is released from performing work for the duration of the course (studies). The enterprise is then not allowed to cancel by notice of dismissal the relevant labour contract over the period of the release, i.e. the cancellation of the employment is made impermissible by a prohibition of giving notice (Para 22, subsection (k) of the Decree on the Enforcement of the Labour Code). According to Soviet law, the employees participating, beside performing their contracted work, in professional training courses, in institutions of higher or medium-level specialized education have a privilege of keeping their posts (Article 34, of the Labour Code of the Russian Soviet Federated Socialist Republic).

[132] Para 58, point (d) of the Labour Code of the German Democratic Republic. Cf. MICHAS (1970), p. 208.

Work or study-tour abroad.—Work performed abroad for an international organization, authorized by the competent Hungarian bodies, on the one hand, or performed for foreign State institutions, or other organizations, in the execution of international agreements, on the basis of labour contracts (Para 22, subsection (c), of the Decree on the Enforcement of the Labour Code) on the other, or a study tour abroad on a scholarship basis (Para 22, subsection (f), of the Decree on the Enforcement of the Labour Code), are factual states constituting a basis for the prohibition of the employer giving notice of dismissal. Furthermore, the labour contract of an employee having a non-paid leave with regard to her/his spouse performing continued work abroad cannot be cancelled by giving notice (Para 26, subsection (d) of the Decree on the Enforcement of the Labour Code).

Protection of female employees in charge of their children.—Maternity enjoys particular protection in all socialist countries. The labour relationship of a female employee cannot be terminated during the period of pregnancy and lactation; giving notice of dismissal is prohibited by the law. According to Soviet law, pregnant women, mothers during their lactation period, and female employees taking care of a child younger than one year of age cannot be dismissed upon the initiative of the management of the enterprise, with the only exception of the full-scale liquidation of the enterprise, and their dismissal is permitted even in the latter case only under the obligation of the employer to ensure a new employment for the person concerned.[133] There are similar rules in the Czechoslovak law, i.e. the labour contracts of female employees cannot be cancelled, as a rule, during their pregnancy and maternity leave; even in case of a re-organization of the employer, a cancellation is only admitted if the enterprise ensures an appropriate new employment for the person concerned; in case of need, the enterprise asks for the assistance of its supervisory body. The notice period expires in these cases only with the fulfilment of the obligation of the enterprise, unless an opposite agreement is concluded with the employee.[134] As regards Hungary, it is absolutely prohibited for the enterprise to cancel a labour contract by giving notice of dismissal for the period of pregnancy and lactation, till the end of the sixth month following the birth.[135] Accordingly, the labour relationship of female employees of this category cannot be terminated in Hungary, even in case of the enterprise going into liquidation, i.e. their labour relationship continues to exist until the cessation of the cause preventing dismissal by giving notice; thus, e.g., the Central Corporation of Hungarian Baking Companies, to be considered as the legal successor of the enterprise that has gone into liquidation, will be author-

---

[133] Article 73 of the Fundamental Rules of the labour legislation of the Soviet Union and the member republics. Article 170 of the Labour Code of the Russian Soviet Federated Socialist Republic.

[134] Para 47, subsection 2; Para 48, subsection 1, point (d); and Para 49, point (a) of the Czechoslovak Labour Code. See also HOCHMANN (1975/6), p. 318.

[135] Para 22, point (g) of the Law Decree on the Enforcement of the Labour Code.

ized to terminate the labour relations in question also only in the case of the cessation of the cause preventing dismissal by notice.[136/a]

As regards the duration of the protection, different regulations are in force, e.g., for the starting of the protection period; the date of the statement of pregnancy (as in Hungary), or a later date, such as the fifth month of pregnancy in Bulgaria (Para 35 of the Labour Code); for the closing date, the end of the sixth month following the birth, as in Hungary and the German Democratic Republic[136/b]; the date on completion of the third year of age of the child in Czechoslovakia (Para 48, point (d) of the Czechoslovak Labour Code), or the end of the maternity leave in Romania (Para 146 of the Romanian Labour Code).

The rules of Hungarian law according to which the enterprise is not allowed to terminate a labour relationship by giving notice of dismissal during the period of sick-pay granted the mother for nursing a sick child, or non-paid leave granted for the same purpose, furthermore of baby-care benefit, and other non-paid leave for the same purpose, reflect the accentuated protection of maternity.[137] A rule of the Romanian labour law, providing that the labour contract of a female employee cannot be cancelled by notice of dismissal if she takes care of a sick child not older than three years, is of a similar character.[138]

Protection of employees in charge of a large number of dependent family members.—It should be emphasized here that there is a provision in the Hungarian labour law according to which it shall not be permitted to give notice to any employee who has four or more dependent family members, with not other wage-earner in the family, only in exceptionally justified cases (see Para 23, subsection 1, pont (a) of the Decree on the Enforcement of the Labour Code). The rules mentioned above reflect the intention of the Hungarian legislation to give special guarantees for the employees in this category.

Protection of employees belonging in the group of single-parent families. —Employees of this category enjoy special protection in some legal systems. Thus, the Hungarian Labour Code provides that giving notice to any employed single woman taking care of a child not older than eighteen years is permitted only in exceptionally justified cases. This protection is due to single fathers bringing up their children as well. Nevertheless, in case the enterprise has at its free disposal a type of work for which any of the employees referred to above seems to be fit, the employment must not be terminated by giving notice as long as the employee in question may be transferred to the work mentioned above, with his/her consent to such transfer (Para 23, of the Decree on the Enforcement of the Labour Code). According to the Czechoslovak law, an employee who is a single father taking care of a child not

[136/a] ABONYI–TRÓCSÁNYI (1974/3–4), p. 411.
[136/b] Para 22, subsection (g) of the Decree on the Enforcement of the Labour Code of Hungary; and Para 133 of the Labour Code of the German Democratic Republic.
[137] Para 22, points (h) and (i) of the Decree on the Enforcement of the Labour Code.
[138] Article 146 of the Romanian Labour Code.

older than fifteen years of age is entitled to the same protection as female employees during their period of pregnancy or maternity leave, i.e. their labour relationship may be terminated only in case of the reorganization of the employing enterprise and this latter is obliged even in this case to ensure another, appropriate, employment for the employee concerned; in case of need, even by having recourse to the assistance of the superior body of the enterprise.[139]

Protection of employees during sickness involving disability to work.—As is laid down in the law of almost all socialist States, it is impermissible to terminate the labour relationship of an employee during his sickness. There are differences, however, between the individual rules: an explicit prohibition is stipulated in some countries, while other forms of protection have been established in other States.

The prohibition of terminating the employment may cover the entire period of the illness, i.e. the period during which the employee in question has been declared as provisionally unable to work, on account of an illness or an accident;[140] the prohibition may also be related only to a specified period of time.[141] According to another regulation, also in force, a labour relationship cannot be terminated as long as the employee enjoys the services of the social security system.[142]

According to the Soviet law, a labour contract concluded for an unspecified period of time may be cancelled by the enterprise giving notice only on account of a continued, longer than four months, absence from work, caused by temporary disability to work. As a consequence of this rule, there is no possibility to cancel a labour contract during the disability to work before the absence from work has reached a duration of four months. This is explicitly laid down in Article 33, last subsection of the Labour Code of the Russian Soviet Federated Socialist Republic. In case of an illness exceeding a duration of four months, the local trade union committee will investigate, prior to giving its consent to the cancellation of the labour contract, whether the employee may be expected to recover his normal state of health within a reasonably short time, and whether the cancellation of the labour contract is justified by a required continuity in production.[143] It should be noted here that the cancellation of a labour contract on the above basis constitutes a right, and not an obligation, of the administration.

The provisions of Polish law permit the enterprise to terminate an employment even without giving notice, in case of an illness exceeding a certain period, which is specified in the Labour Code; in other words, a labour

[139] Para 47, subsection 2 of the Czechoslovak Labour Code.

[140] Para 48, point (a) of the Czechoslovak Labour Code. In case of an illness with a very long period of time course the possibility of declaring the person invalid may come into play at most.

[141] For Hungary, ef. Para 22, point (b) of the Decree on the Enforcement of the Labour Code.

[142] Para 146 of the Romanian Labour Code.

[143] VOLIN (1974/10), p. 42.

relationship cannot be terminated before the expiration of a period specified in the law in the rules of this country, either.[144] As regards the legal literature of the German Democratic Republic, the previous view was that, considering the fact that an enterprise was authorized to cancel a labour contract by giving notice only in cases enumerated item by item and illness was not mentioned among the enumerated items, a termination of employment for this cause was absolutely impermissible.[145] The new Labour Code established then a prohibition of dismissal by notice for the duration of the illness of an employee (see Para 58, subsection d).

Concerning the scale of protective measures, it may be subjected to the character of the illness in the regulations of the individual countries (as for Hungary, the period of protection is, in general, one year; two years in case of tuberculosis). A preceding written consent of the competent district council is required for cancelling the employment of a person suffering from tuberculosis in the German Democratic Republic.[146] The expiration of the protection period may have different consequences as well. For example, the respective labour relationship may be terminated in Hungary by giving notice, while this is not needed under Polish law.

There are special rules concerning the protection of the labour relations of persons with a reduced ability to work in the legislation of some countries. As regards Hungary, the conditions under which the employment of persons with a reduced ability to work may be terminated are laid down in a particular legal rule.[147] According to the law of other countries, the consent of the competent State body is required for the cancellation of the labour contract of an employee with a reduced ability to work; e.g. that of the district council in the German Democratic Republic; the social security bodies in Bulgaria; the national committee's district body in Czechoslovakia, respectively.

Protection of the labour relations of juvenile workers.—Special attention is paid to the protection of this category in the legislation of various countries. Thus, workers and employees younger than eighteen years may be dismissed, under Soviet law, upon the initiative of the management of the respective enterprise, by observing the general rules of dismissal, and only with the consent of the district (city) public guardianship authority. Besides, dismissal is allowed only with the assurance of a new employment in some particular cases laid down in the law (see Article 82 of the Basic Rules of labour legislation).—Juvenile employees may be dismissed by notice in the German Democratic Republic only with the preliminary consent of the competent district council.[148] The purpose is to ensure employment for juvenile persons so that it should correspond to their capacities. The rule serves also a planned labour-force economy, taking into consideration at the same time the special

[144] Article 53 of the Polish Labour Code.
[145] MICHAS (1970), p. 208.
[146] Para 59 of the Labour Code of the German Democratic Republic.
[147] Para 10 of the Joint Decree No. 1/1967 (XI. 22) of the Min. of Lab., Min. of Health, Min. of Finance.
[148] Para 59, subsection 1, point (c) of the Labour Code of the German Democratic Republic.

interests of juveniles. It should be noted in this context that the validity of a juvenile employee's giving notice depends on the approval of the person who is in charge of the education of the juvenile employee.[149] The basic consideration of the regulation is here that juveniles may not be aware of all problems possibly arising from the cancellation of a labour contract, i.e. they need the support of those who are in charge of their education.

Protection of employees having a social function.—As is laid down in the law of some socialist countries, the labour relationship of employees performing a social function cannot be terminated as long as they carry on this activity. This regulation is in force e.g. in Czechoslovakia where an enterprise is not authorized to dismiss an employee by notice during the period for which he has been fully discharged from everyday work, on account of an official function, e.g. chairmanship of a national committee.[150] If the public function has to be performed not for a longer time, e.g. a member of the national committee participates in the meetings of the national committee from time to time only, then there is no prohibition of giving notice in his/her case.[151]

The wording of the Polish Labour Code reflects a broad concept; according to its stipulations, the enterprise is not authorized to give notice of dismissal to an employee in case of a verified absence from work.[152] In case a social function cannot be performed but within the working time, the absence has to be regarded as verified. According to the Yugoslav law, an employee holding a social function by appointment or election and having temporarily interrupted his work for the basic economic organization is entitled under the law to resume his work in the same basic economic organization, after the cessation of the function, or to continue to work there in another sphere, corresponding to his professional qualification or capacity to work.[153] The Romanian Labour Code provides that the termination of the labour relationship of elected members of the collective management, or committee administering justice in the employing unit, requires the consent of the body which elected them.[154] The obtainment of the approval is of compulsory nature, i.e. the labour contract of a person being elected member of the collective management, or the committee administering justice, may be cancelled by the competent managing body only after an opinion approving the measure has been expressed by the general assembly.[155]

Special rules are applicable to the protection of the labour relations of trade union officials. It is thus stipulated, e.g., in the Hungarian Labour Code (Para 16) that the employment of an elected trade union official may only

[149] Para 54, subsection 11 of the Labour Code of the German Democratic Republic.
[150] Para 48 of the Czechoslovak Labour Code.
[151] BERNARD–PAVLÁTOVÁ (1979), pp. 229–230.
[152] Article 41 of the Polish Labour Code.
[153] Article 192 of the 1976 Act on associated work.
[154] Para 132, subsection 1 of the Romanian Labour Code.
[155] MARICA (1974/4), pp. 19–28.

be terminated by the enterprise with the consent of the competent superior trade union organ.

According to the Soviet law, the chairmen and members of trade union committees (on workshop, factory, and local levels), not discharged from performing daily work, may be dismissed upon the initiative of the management of the employer only with the consent of the superior trade union body observing, of course, the general rules bearing upon dismissal (Basic Rules of labour legislation; Articles 99 and 235 of the Labour Code of the Russian Soviet Federated Socialist Republic). The workers and employees who are discharged from performing daily work for the contracting enterprise, institution or organization as a consequence of their being elected members of the respective (workshop, factory, local) trade union committee, may continue their previous work (function) upon the expiration of their mandate; if this is not practicable, another, and equivalent, work (function) has to be ensured for them, by the same employer or, with their consent, by another enterprise, institution or organization.[156]

It is laid down in the Polish law that the enterprise is not authorized to cancel the employment of a member of the works' council, a trade union steward, a social inspector of work of the enterprise or a department of it, and a member of the board of arbitration of the enterprise. This rule is not applicable, however, in case the enterprise has gone into liquidation or if the employee in question became entitled to a disability pension.[157]

As is clear from the preceding, minor or major differences may be found in the law of the individual socialist countries in respect of these regulations. The system according to which the cancellation of the contract of employment of an employee by the enterprise requires the consent of the respective trade union committee[158] (to be dealt with in the following subsection) is burdened with the problem whether for the employment of a member of the relevant trade union committee, the consent of the local trade union committee of the enterprise is required as well, or it becomes unnecessary on account of the specified requirement that the approval of the respective supervisory body must be obtained.[159] According to a view expressed in the Romanian legal literature, the consent of both bodies mentioned above is needed. The members of the trade union committee are, first and foremost, employees bound by a labour contract, therefore, the local trade union's consent is needed; the special consent of the other body is required with regard to the employee's membership of the trade union committee. Thus the first opinion (report) is

---

[156] Regulation on the rights of local trade union committees, September 29, 1971 (point 29).

[157] Articles 39 and 40 of the Polish Labour Code.

[158] Para 25 of the Labour Code of the German Democratic Republic.

[159] According to Para 132, subsection 1 of the Romanian Labour Code, asking for the communication of the opinion of the superior trade union body is required in case of the termination of a labour contract, initiated by the employer, in respect of employees who are members of the local trade union committee or another trade union body.

not covered by the second one, as the one is independent of the other, and none of them replaces the other.[160]

Protection of persons holding a specified post (function).—The termination of the labour relationship of persons in whose case its establishment requires the approval of specified bodies is also subject to the approval of the same body. This rule is applicable, e.g., in the German Democratic Republic to the leaders of technical and quality control departments whose appointment requires the consent of the competent body of the Office for Standardization, Measurements, and the Inspection of Goods. The purpose of this rule is here to give the security for the employees with a controlling function to carry on their tasks so that they should not have fears from disadvantageous consequences in respect of their labour relations.[161]

Protection of aged employees.—Under Hungarian law, it is permitted to give notice to any employee who has not more than another five years to work to be entitled to full old-age pension only in exceptionally justified cases, except if the employee is already entitled to partial pension. If a type of work is available within the relevant enterprise for which an employee of this category seems to be fit, his/her employment shall not be terminated by giving notice as long as the employee may be transferred to the type of work, provided that s/he consents to this transfer.[162] According to the Polish law, the enterprise is not allowed to cancel the employment by notice of an employee who has not more than another two years at most to work to be entitled to retire provided that his/her years of service entitle him/her to full old-age pension. Nevertheless, this rule is not applicable in case the enterprise has gone into liquidation and if the employee has become entitled to disability pension.[163] This kind of protection is similar to that due to trade union officials.

According to a previous rule of the Czechoslovak law, the termination of the employment by notice of an employee who completed the years of age required for the right to a full old-age pension was subject to the consent of the competent national committee's district body, i.e. the notice was to be regarded as invalid in the absence of the said consent (Para 50 of the Labour Code). This stipulation has, however, been omitted in the second supplementary act of the Labour Code, taking into consideration the circumstance that the persons concerned enjoyed the services of the social security system, consequently the specified protection was no more necessary.[164]

Summary.—The first remark is that the prohibitions and restrictions of notice have a smaller significance in a system of giving notice bound to spec-

---

[160] MARICA (1974/4), p. 20.

[161] Para 2, subsections 3 and 5 of the enacting clauses of the Decree January 15, 1970, on the guarantee and improvement of the quality of products of combines and enterprises. *Gbl.* II. No. 15, p. 122; KAISER–KIRSCHNER–SCHULZ (1974), p. 209.

[162] Para 23, subsection 1 of the Decree on the Enforcement of the Labour Code.

[163] Article 39, subsection 4 of the Polish Labour Code.

[164] LUHAN (1976/6), p. 41.

ified factual states than in the other systems in which the termination of employment on the employer's part is only subjected to motivation. Essentially, the prohibitions and restrictions of notice make complete the system of notice subjected to motivation, in order to ensure the enforcement of the requirements of social policy or other viewpoints. At the same time, the prohibitions and restrictions of notice may also be considered as corrections or supplements to the system of giving notice bound to specified factual states, in view of the circumstance that, even though the enterprise would be entitled to cancel the employment of a given employee on the basis of the given factual states, nevertheless, since giving notice would not be—from the viewpoint of e.g. social policy—entirely justifiable, the enterprise will not be authorized to do so as this would be prevented by an effective prohibition or restriction of notice.

The other remark reads that the system of giving notice bound to factual states enumerated in the law does not prevail in its rigid form either. In fact, efforts are to be made to maintain the relevant labour relationship by means of a transfer of the employee prior to proceeding to the termination of the employment. According to Soviet law, a labour relationship may be terminated on account of the cessation of operation of the enterprise, reduction of the number or the available status of the employees, insufficient qualification preventing the continuation of the work, disability resulting from the unsatisfactory state of health, or the return of an employee who held the relevant work or post previously (but only after that he could have been transferred to another job with his consent, but this measure proved to be impracticable).[165]

According to Czechoslovak law, the enterprise is authorized—except the case of a violation of work discipline or such that involves an immediate cancellation of the labour contract—to cancel the employment of an employee by giving notice only if it proved to be impossible to employ the person concerned at the place of work specified as the place of fulfilment of the labour contract, or at another place of work within the place of residence of the person in question, even after a pre-training for the other job; or if the employee in question refused to carry on work other than his/her previous one, or to submit himself/herself to the pre-training designated to make him/her acquainted with the offered job; or, in case of his/her non-compliance with the conditions or requirements needed for the fulfilment of the provided work, the enterprise is unable to offer the person concerned such available post, corresponding to his/her qualification, that would suffice for him/her to perform work there even though s/he has the insufficiencies mentioned

---

[165] Article 17, last item, of the Basic Rules of labour legislation; Article 33, item 2 of the Labour Code of the Russian Soviet Federated Socialist Republic. According to Soviet law, the body proceeding in labour disputes is thus obliged to ask for evidence from the enterprise that the employee has refused to accept his/her transfer to another type of work, or that the enterprise is not in a position to transfer the employee to another type of work with his/her consent. The non-observance of this rule may be the reason for re-transfer to the previous place of work. See YANOVSKY (1973/10), pp. 55–56.

above.[166] As regards the Romanian regulation, the Labour Code provides for the security of stabilizing the labour relations. If a labour contract is cancelled, upon the initiative of the enterprise, for causes specified in Para 140, item (1) subsections (a), (c), (e), and (f) of the Labour Code (these mean the cases of a reorganization of the enterprise, professional disability, restitution of an employee to his/her previous field of work, etc.), the enterprise is obliged to offer the person concerned a transfer to another work, and to ask for assistance from its direct supervisory body, and the competent body in charge of labour-force economy, or to take measures aimed at the professional re-training of the person in question, as the case may be. According to the previous regulation, this had only been the employer's right in case of the employee's professional disability but later it was turned to an obligation.[167]

Transfer has a preference against the termination of employment also in the cases in which a labour contract may be cancelled by notice only for exceptionally justified reasons, i.e. in cases of restrictions. It is laid down e.g. in the Hungarian regulation[168] that, if a type of work is available for employment within the enterprise for which the employee, who otherwise should be dismissed upon the initiative of the enterprise, seems to be fit, his/her employment cannot be terminated by giving notice as long as s/he can be transferred to the other type of work, provided that s/he consents to this transfer.—Under Soviet law, it is not allowed for the management of the enterprise to cancel by giving notice the employment of pregnant women, female employees during their lactation period, or having a child younger than one year, except the complete liquidation of the institution, enterprise or organization; even in this latter case, dismissal is only allowed after the enterprise has ensured a new employment for the person concerned; this is understood to mean transfer to another enterprise.[169] As regards juvenile employees, their dismissal is allowed, too, only in exceptional cases, and with the obligation of the enterprise to provide for a new employment.[170] There is a similar regulation in the Czechoslovak law; thus, in case of the termination of the employment of a single female employee who takes permanent care of her child younger than fifteen years of age, the enterprise is obliged —if the termination takes place on its initiative and on account of reorganization—to ensure a new, and appropriate, employment for the person concerned.[171]

With regard to the respective regulations of the various countries, the conclusion may be drawn that, by setting prohibitions and restrictions the legislator intends to give protection for the employees, with an aim to serve at

[166] Para 46, subsection 2 of the Czechoslovak Labour Code.
[167] MARICA (1974), pp. 24–25.
[168] Para 23, subsection 2 of the Decree on the Enforcement of the Labour Code.
[169] Article 73 of the Basic Rules.
[170] Article 82 of the Fundamental Rules; Article 183 of the Labour Code of the Russian Soviet Federated Socialist Republic.
[171] Para 47, subsection 2 of the Czechoslovak Labour Code.

the same time social policy and other interests. The employees would be particularly gravely affected by the termination of their employment in the cases dealt with above, therefore, the interests of the enterprise are here subjected to those of the employees.

7.6.2 *Legal consequences of the unlawful termination of labour relations*

If a labour relationship is terminated by the enterprise in a way transgressing the respective legal norms, this act may have various consequences, depending on the relevant positive rules of the individual countries, having in view principally the purpose of the legal norm in question. The most important legal consequence of the termination of a labour relationship contrary to the provisions of the legal rules is the invalidity of the termination of the labour relationship in question, but this is not an absolute consequence.

From the viewpoint of legal consequences, a distinction may be made between the following casas of unlawful termination of the labour relationship:

(a) By terminating the labour relationship, the employer infringes a rule but the employee concerned is not entitled to raise any legal claim against the enterprise, and the cause leading to the infringement does not exclude the disciplinary responsibility of the employee whose labour contract needs to be cancelled. According to the Czechoslovak law, for example, the legal guardian of a juvenile employee has to be advised of the termination of the employment by notice.[172] If the enterprise fails to make the advice, this negligence constitutes a violation of a legal rule but it does not entitle the employee concerned to raise any claim on this account. Similarly, the employee is not entitled to raise any claim against the enterprise if this latter violates the obligation to submit to the works committee—within the specified period, and for the purpose of control—papers on the cases in which the termination of a labour relationship is not bound to the consent of the said committee; e.g. when the employment is terminated by the enterprise in the course of probation time, and the employee regards this act as an injury to his/her rights.[173]

(b) By terminating a labour relationship, the enterprise violates an obligation, without the consequence of invalidity of notice but with the consequence of raising certain claims on the part of the other party. Let us take an example from the Polish law: the enterprise may cancel by notice a labour contract with a shorter period of notice than specified in the relevant legal rules, but the labour relationship in question will cease to exist in this case only with the expiration of the period of notice laid down in the law, and the employee in question will be entitled to claim his wages till the prescribed date.[174] The respective Hungarian regulation has similar rules, i.e. in case the termi-

[172] Para 164, subsection 2 of the Czechoslovak Labour Code.
[173] Para 59, subsection 2 of the Czechoslovak Labour Code; WITZ (1971), pp. 48 et seq.
[174] Article 49 of the Polish Labour Code.

nation of a labour relationship, upon the initiative of the enterprise, is understood to be unlawful for the notice is given for a period shorter than that applicable to the particular case by the law, the termination by notice will not become invalid, and the labour relationship concerned will continue to exist till the last day of the notice period as prescribed by the law.[175]

(c) The employer infringes a provision of law bearing upon the termination of labour relations, which implies the invalidity of the notice. It should be noted in this respect that there is no provision in the law of any of the countries reviewed here which would constitute invalidity with an absolute effect, i.e. so that the violation of one of the relevant provisions would involve, *ipso facto,* the invalidity of the termination of the labour relationship in question. An unlawful termination becomes null and void only if it is revoked, upon the objection of the other party, or it is declared to be invalid, upon the complaint of the other party. In fact, it occurs quite frequently that an employee whose employment is terminated does not insist on the restitution of his/her labour relationship—in spite of the circumstance that s/he is aware of the infringement of the respective rules on the termination of his/her employment—because s/he would prefer to be employed elsewhere, in view of the deteriorated atmosphere in the place of work at issue. This will not mean, however, his/her consent to the ways in which his/her labour relationship is terminated by the other party, all the more so since his/her future claims may be influenced thereby. An objection has to be made by him/her, in order to enforce his/her claims, as otherwise the infringement of the law, committed by the enterprise, will not be taken into consideration for a possible claim for indemnity or any other type of compensation. The employee has to formulate his/her claim in due time, upon the delivery of the decision of the enterprise terminating his/her employment, with a view to having the lawfulness of the acts of the enterprise supervised, if the termination of his/her labour relationship is unlawful in his/her opinion.

Taking into account the foregoing, an employee may have three variants of claims in case of the unlawful termination of his/her employment:

(1) The employee concerned, insisting on the continuation of his/her relationship, asks for an indemnity. In this case, the body having competence for the settlement of labour disputes in case of the unlawful termination of labour relations will declare the continued existence of the labour relationship in question, consequently the termination will become ineffective. Besides, the competent body takes a decision on the claim of indemnity of the employee, and, what is more, is obliged to restitute the employee in question to his/her previous field of work.[176] This is, indeed, a consequence of a principle, laid

---

[175] Para 29, subsection 4 of the Decree on the Enforcement of the Labour Code.

[176] As regards the Soviet law, explicit dispositions in this sense are provided in Article 91 of the Basic Rules of Labour Legislation, and in Article 213 of the Labour Code of the Russian Federated Soviet Socialist Republic; it should be added that the decision or disposition bearing upon the restitution of an employee dismissed contrary to the law has to be executed without delay. (Cf. Article 92 of the Basic Rules of Labour Legislation; and Article 26 of the Labour Code of the Russian Soviet Federated Socialist Republic.) The

down explicitly also in the Hungarian positive law and saying that, in case of an unlawful termination of the labour relationship of an employee by the enterprise, the employee concerned has to be restituted to his/her original post as if his/her employment had not been terminated.[177] The lost working time has to be regarded in this case also as if it had been used for work. The body proceeding in the labour dispute has to ensure that the employee in question makes an announcement on his/her possible financial claim, and submits the appropriate demand, too.[178] The principle of concentrating the labour disputes to one single procedure and the acceleration of that procedure would require however that, as far as possible, all the employee's claims could be brought to one phase of making decision.[179]

(2) The employee affected by the termination does not insist on the continuation of his/her labour relationship but demands that his/her financial claims be admitted. In this case the labour relationship will be terminated, and the body proceeding in the labour dispute will make a decision in respect of the financial claims of the employee concerned.

Employees may have two types of claims of financial nature, viz. (i) compensation for arrears of wages, (ii) an indemnity for damages, if such presented themselves, too.[180]

The legal rules of some States contain detailed prescriptions of what may be claimed as arrears of wages. It is thus laid down in the Soviet law that an employee who after having been dismissed from his/her work, and is then

---

Hungarian law also has an explicit disposition in this sense; cf. Para 33, subsection 1 of the Decree on the Enforcement of the Labour Code.

[177] Para 31, subsection 1 of the Labour Code.

[178] As regards the obligation of compensation on the part of the employer, it is interpreted by some Hungarian labour courts so that it is sufficient for the employee concerned to claim for the invalidation of the notice in the action, i.e. there is no need to submit a separate claim for wages due for the interrupted period. Nevertheless, the provision laid down in Para 29, subsection 1 of the Decree on the Enforcement of the Labour Code, prescribing that the arrears of wages and other dues of the employee in question shall be paid to him/her and s/he shall be compensated for damages, is the rule of the substantive law and the limits of the decision of the proceeding labour court are set for the content of the claim in Article 215 of the Code of Civil Procedure. The obligation of payment of the employer cannot be established *ex officio* under the rules of Hungarian law; instead the correct procedure is that, in conformity with the provision of Para 3, subsection 1 of the Code of Civil Procedure, the relevant court of justice advices the employee concerned of the claim s/he may submit in the legal proceedings. It is another point whether the maintenance of the said, generally accepted rule is necessary *de lege ferenda*, in respect of the enforcement of the claim in the given case. Taking into consideration, however, that the employee concerned claims for the restitution of his/her labour relationship in the labour dispute, this involves, in our view, his/her claim for compensation of the arrears of wages that resulted from the termination of his/her employment. Besides, the body proceeding in the labour dispute may also examine *ex officio* whether or not the employee in question has been compensated for his arrears of wages and/or other dues from possible other sources, or could it not have been possible for him/her to be compensated from those other sources, with ordinary care.

[179] KIRMSE–KIRSCHNER (1971), pp. 1974 et seq.

[180] Para 23, subsection 1 of the Decree on the Enforcement of the Labour Code.

restituted into his earlier employment, has to be compensated, on the basis of a decision of a court of justice, by the payment of the average amount of his wages, for the forced loss of working time, reckoned from the unlawful termination of his/her employment but for a maximum period of three months.[181] Average wages may be paid to an employee for the period of his/her forced absence from work but for a maximum duration of three months, on the basis of a decision of the board of arbitration in labour disputes or the workshop, factory, or local trade union committee.[182]

As regards the problem whether the enterprise is or is not obliged to pay the portion of wages and other dues which is recovered from other sources, or might have been recovered with ordinary care, various regulations are in force. According to the Hungarian regulation, the enterprise is not liable to make the said compensation.[183] A similar concept had served as a basis for the Czechoslovak law prior to the coming into effect of the Labour Code in 1965, i.e. the earning of the employee or the amount he might have earned had to be investigated. Subsequently, it was stipulated in the Labour Code that the claim for wages for the period during which the employee was unlawfully not engaged by the enterprise was not limited by the income obtained from other work or the amount what he might have been earned. The employee was free to establish a labour relationship with another organization or to carry on another kind of activity, earning money over the time during which a decision was being made concerning his/her labour relationship, and the extent of the obligation of compensation by the enterprise was not influenced by the employee's earnings in the said period. Nevertheless, s/he was not obliged to engage himself/herself in another kind of work, and the rate of compensation to be paid by the enterprise was by no means influenced by his/her conduct in this respect.[184] The second supplementary act to the Czechoslovak Labour Code restituted then the regulation in force before the enactment of the Labour Code, but only partly. According to this new regulation, an employee is absolutely entitled to compensation for unpaid earnings (wages) for a period of six months, irrespective of whether he has been engaged in work elsewhere, i.e. he is not bound to give evidence of any detail. In case the period for which he is entitled to compensation exceeds six months, the rate of compensation may be reduced on the basis of a decision by a court of justice, proceeding upon the request of the enterprise, for the rest of the claimed period beyond six months, or the court may even refuse to adjudicate it. When taking up a position in the case, the court of justice considers particularly whether the claiming person was employed elsewhere during the contested period; if so, what kind of work was performed by him/her and against what

[181] Article 92 of the Basic Rules; Article 214 subsection 1 of the Labour Code of the Russian Soviet Federated Socialist Republic.

[182] Article 244, subsection 2 of the Labour Code of the Russian Soviet Federated Socialist Republic.

[183] Para 23, subsection 1 of the Decree on the Enforcement of the Labour Code.

[184] WITZ (1971), p. 51.

remuneration, or what was the reason that prevented his/her re-integration in the process of work.[185]

(3) An employee is entitled to claim for the statement of the unlawfulness of the termination of his/her employment, even if s/he is not claiming the continuation of his/her labour relationship, with or without a compensation. This is the point e.g. in case of the cancellation of employment by means of a disciplinary procedure, when s/he is only interested to have justice. Of course, it is then not at all excluded to claim for a compensation in a given case.

Finally the regulations are to be mentioned according to which the obligation of the enterprise to pay compensation on account of the unlawful termination of employment gives rise to its claim for recovery against the employee who was guilty in the occurrence of the damages. According to Soviet law, the court of justice may compel a person, in a leading position and guilty in the unlawful dismissal of the employee, to compensate his/her enterprise for the damages arisen from the payment of wages due for the period of the forced non-performance of work. An obligation of this kind has to be established if the termination of the employment of the claimant was effected by means of an evident infringement of the law, or the management of the enterprise fell in delay in connection with the execution of the decision of a court of justice ordering restitution. The rate of compensation must not exceed the three months' wages of the leading official.[186]

Even though the provisions outlined in the foregoing cannot be found explicitly in the law of all States dealt with here, this circumstance does not mean as if the obligation of paying compensation for the damages caused in the mentioned way were unknown in the lack of specific relevant regulations. This, indeed, follows from the general rule saying that an employee is subject to financial liability in respect of the enterprise for the violation of obligations resulting from his/her labour relationship. With the regulation of this problem in the Labour Code, the intention of the legislator must have been to emphasize the requirement of legal policy representing the interest in the maintenance of labour relations, on the one hand, or in their termination in case of need, on the other, to be effected in the prescribed way; just for this reason, it seemed to be desirable to accentuate the financial liabilities of the employees found guilty in relation of a possibly unlawful termination of labour relations.

[185] Para 61, subsection 2 of the Czechoslovak Labour Code.
[186] Article 93 of the Basic Rules; Article 215 of the Labour Code of the Russian Federated Soviet Socialist Republic.

8. ROLE OF THE TRADE UNIONS CONCERNING THE ESTABLISHMENT, MODIFICATION, AND TERMINATION OF LABOUR RELATIONS

8.1 Main principles of the trade unions' participation

Two features of the trade unions' function are reflected by their participation in the establishment, modification, and termination of labour relations. By virtue of one of them, the required participation of the workers and employees in the management of the enterprise comes to realization in a way that their responsibility for the activities, the level of the management of the enterprise, and for the development of labour conditions increases; actually, this is to be understood as the constitutive participation of the workers and employees in the development, direction, and inspection of the enterprise, mainly with reference to labour relations. The viewpoints of this kind of trade unions' participation enter into the foreground in the establishment of labour relations, in particular, where the participation serves the purpose of achieving that specific posts of work are filled up by men fit for them, whose attitude of preparedness to carry on the work guarantees that they will appropriately comply with the tasks entrusted to them.

By virtue of the second feature, the protection of the interests of the workers and employees—and this is particularly accentuated in connection with the modification and termination of labour relations—comes to realization. The trade union's participation in ensuring the stability of labour relations—which is understood to be an important target—means to act so as to avoid, as far as possible, the unjustified modifications of labour relations on the one hand, and, still more accentuated, to ensure that the termination of the labour relations of the workers and employees by the employers cannot take place in an unjustified way, on the other. In fact, it is not without importance for the security feeling of an employee if s/he knows that his/her employment cannot be terminated without justification or with a reference to fictitious causes and, among other bodies, the trade union also takes care for it. The trade unions should pay great attention to this function, as its significance cannot be overemphasized.

The participation of the trade unions in the establishment of labour relations may be ranked among the first achievements of the development of the law in the post-Second World War era. Thus, e.g., the works councils in Poland were entitled, as early as in 1945, by virtue of a decree, to participate in the employment of the workers. This provision of the respective legal rule was then concretized by means of the individual collective agreements, and this practice has become widely established especially in relation of industrial enterprises.[1]

[1] SZURGACZ (1976), pp. 55–82; KLIM (1968/19), p. 91.

As regards the regulations of other States, the participation of the trade unions has entered into the foreground only in respect of the employment of specific categories of employees (economic managers, as a rule); this circumstance may be attributed, in our view, among other points, to the fact that the trade unions have obtained various rights of participation in the field of the economic activities of the enterprise; these rights become increasingly more accentuated with the broadening of workshop democracy; accordingly, it appears as a manifest requirement to entrust the economic management of the enterprise to persons who are in possession of the confidence of the trade union. Regulations of this kind have become established e.g. in the Soviet Union, in Bulgaria, and Hungary. The requirement of the participation of trade unions in the establishment of labour relations has gained ground recently also in States in which the constitutive participation of the trade unions in labour relations had been unknown earlier. The provision of the Hungarian legislation requiring the consent of the relevant trade union body to the setting of the basic wage of an employee has granted the trade unions, essentially, the right of participation in respect of the establishment of labour relations, in view of the stipulation that the agreement on wages constitutes an indispensable content element of the labour contract.[2]

Taking into consideration the already established regulations, it appears clearly that the participation of the trade unions in the field of the modification of labour relations concerns mainly physical workers, who are transferred from one place of work to another more frequently than white-collar workers; consequently, an increased protection of their interests seems to be justified (as e.g., in Bulgaria); this activity has a role, especially, in the legal systems in which the contractual form of the modification of labour relations has been established, as it is clear that the trade unions, being granted some rights of participation in respect of the establishment of labour relations, must have the same rights concerning the conclusion of agreements modifying the original labour contract; cf. the law of the German Democratic Republic.

The importance of the participation of trade unions in regard to the termination of the labour relations of employees was recognized by the legislations of various countries, too, and at a relatively early time; i.e. various rules were issued as early as about the end of the fifties, laying down that the trade unions had to participate in the termination of labour relations. The enterprises' decisions of this kind had earlier belonged in the discretionary competence of the managers of the enterprises, e.g. in the Soviet Union and Bulgaria.[3] Subsequently, the concept of the participation of the trade unions in the field of the termination of labour relations became predominant also in some other socialist countries, e.g. Czechoslovakia, the German Democratic Republic, and Romania.

---

[2] Decree No. 12/1976 (V. 27) of the Council of Ministers on the amendment of some provisions bearing upon the execution of the Labour Code; Para 1, and Para 2, point (a) of the Decree on the Enforcement of the Labour Code.

[3] IVANOV (1967/1), p. 156.

The most common example of the act of participation of the trade unions appears in the form of announcement of the opinion of the local trade union committee in a given case, and this stand may or may not be binding for the enterprise concerned. The first variant means, essentially, the right of consent at enterprise level, as the enterprise is then not authorized to establish, modify, or terminate the labour relations of individuals without the preliminary consent of the respective trade union body. In these cases, the consent of the trade union is considered as a condition of validity of the establishing of the employment. In the second case, i.e. if the enterprise is not obliged to accept the opinion of the trade union, again two variants may be considered. First, the enterprise is not authorized to act without having consulted the trade union for taking a stand, and if it still acted, its legal act will be null and void. The other variant admits that, although the failure of the enterprise to ask the trade union for expressing its opinion constituted a violation of the law, it did not involve the invalidity of the legal act in question.—The concepts outlined above may be attributed to the consideration that the stands of the trade unions, even without a compulsory character, may assist the enterprises in taking a correct position.

Furthermore, the constitutive participation of the trade unions in forming the labour relationships may also take the form of a trade union action on behalf of an employee if, according to the view of the trade union, the measure in question was not correct for some reason. From this point of view, the rights of observation and comment, inspection, consultation and objection (veto) are to be considered principally. According to the Hungarian law, the right mentioned last is particularly efficient; a disputed disposition must not be executed as long as a decision was taken on the respective objection in the course of the prescribed period. An objection may be submitted if the disputed disposition seems to have violated the rules concerning labour relations or the attitude that conforms to the socialist morale.[4] Making use of the right of veto may have a practical significance in cases of the termination of labour relations, in particular, e.g. in the cases of the use of rights by the enterprise contrary to their function, or the abuse of rights, respectively.

The forms of the participation of trade unions may vary whether a major or a minor group of employees is affected by the planned or effected measure of the enterprise, e.g. in the case of the reduction of the number of employees. In case the measure in question seems to affect a major group of employees (a major group is understood to mean what is laid down in the respective collective agreement), the enterprise is obliged, under Hungarian law, to ask in advance for the view of the relevant trade union body concerning the measure as provided. This is not required in the opposite case; nevertheless, the trade union is not deprived even then of its right to comment or object in respect of the effected measure concerned.

The forms of trade union's participation in these matters, varying from countries to countries, are surveyed in the following subsections. As our com-

---

[4] Para 14, subsection 3 of the Labour Code.

ments will have to be limited to the most important points, it is only natural that this survey will be restricted to the most essential features, as reflected by the rules of the positive law.

8.2 The trade union's activities as regulated in the laws of socialist countries

Bulgaria

The difference, e.g., between the Soviet and the Bulgarian regulation is that, as is laid down in the latter, the right of the trade union to express its opinion concerning the labour relations of leading staff members of the enterprise is not limited to the employment only but it covers, too, specified cases of the termination of their labour relations, such as non-fulfilment of obligations as prescribed in the collective agreement, refusal to pay bonuses due in cases of innovations, violation of rules concerning labour safety, etc.—Furthermore, the enterprise is obliged to ask for the view of the trade union committee in respect of the worker's transfer for a longer time from one place of work to another; in other words, the drawing in of the trade unions in the arrangements of specific cases of the modification of labour relations is also obligatory.[5]—The enterprise is also obliged to ask the view of the trade union committee concerning the termination of the labour relations of workers and employees. The obtainment of the view of the trade union committee constitutes a condition of the termination of employment, but, contrary to the provisions of the Soviet law, it is not compulsory to accept it under the Bulgarian law.[6]

Czechoslovakia

The trade union committee is entitled to control the establishment of the labour relations of workers, to draw attention to failures as observed, and to suggest to take measures with a view to eliminating any possible shortcomings. As regards the trade union committee's participation in the establishment of labour relations it means, more precisely, a right of general control, i.e. whether the employment of the persons concerned was conformable to the guiding principles relating to the number and categories of the employees, as agreed upon between the management of the enterprise and the workshop committee of the trade union. The acceptance of the view of the trade union committee expressed in this respect is, however, not compulsory for the enterprise.[7] The trade union's participation in the termination of labour relations ranks among the important tasks incumbent upon them. Thus, the enterprise

---

[5] Chapter II, point 8, subsection 1 of the Resolution No. 55/1958 of the Council of Ministers.
[6] MRATCHKHOV (1971), p. 79; RADEVA, M., Personal communication, June 5, 1975.
[7] GALVASH (1977/4), p. 334.

is entitled to give notice to an employee or to cancel his labour contract with immediate effect only with the obtainment of the trade union committee's consent in advance. The cancellation of a labour contract is invalid without it.[8]—Upon the request of the enterprise the respective superior trade union committee may give its consent to the notice in case the workshop committee of the trade union refuses to give it. Exceptions from the obligation to provide for the consent of the local trade union committee are the specified State and social bodies.

German Democratic Republic

Trade unions are entitled to a right of consultation concerning the conclusion of labour contracts, i.e. they are authorized to participate in negotiations bearing upon the conclusion of labour contracts.[9] They may thus participate in providing information on the labour conditions in workshops, and may use their influence with a view to securing fields of activity to employees which conform most to their professional qualification and capacities.—Concerning the modification of labour relations, the enterprise is obliged, prior to concluding a contract bearing upon the modification of a labour relationship, to advise the workshop committee of the trade union, in order to make it possible for the trade union to participate in the conclusion of the contracts in question.—The consent of the competent trade union committee is required to the termination of a labour relationship through giving notice by the enterprise, and the consent of the trade union committee is a condition of the validity of the notice. In case the competent trade union committee refuses to consent to the termination by notice, the relevant superior trade union committee will take a final decision, upon the request of the enterprise.[10]—The trade union committee has to be also advised of the contracts of cancellation in which a labour relationship is terminated by the mutual consent of the parties.[11]

Hungary

As has been mentioned previously, the trade unions' right of participation in the establishment of labour relations had already been granted earlier, especially in respect of the appointment and discharge of economic managers, i.e.

---

[8] Para 59, subsection 1 of the Czechoslovak Labour Code.

[9] Para 43, subsection 2 of the Labour Code of the German Democratic Republic.

[10] Cf. the rules of the use of trade union rights in the field of the establishment, modification, and termination of labour relations. Resolution of June 21, 1978 of the Secretariate of the Association of Free German Trade Unions. Chapter VII. *Arbeit und Arbeitsrecht*, 1978/8, pp. 36–40.

[11] Para 52, subsection 2 of the Labour Code of the German Democratic Republic. For the main problems of the use of trade union rights, see HANTSCHE (1978/10), pp. 459–462.

the director and the deputy director of an enterprise, in particular.[12]—Regarding employees of workshop level, trade unions were entitled only to express their opinion in a general frame.[13]—According to recent regulations to which reference has also been made in the foregoing, the obtainment of the consent of the relevant trade union body has been made compulsory for specifying the basic wage of an employee. The trade unions have thus essentially been granted, in the form of the right of consent to the concretization of a necessary element of content of the labour contract, a broad-scale right of participation in the field of the establishment of labour relations.—As regards the termination of a labour relationship upon the initiative of the enterprise, reference should be made to the point that the local (enterprise) organ of the trade union is entitled to make an objection if the termination of the labour relationship of an employee by means of notice infringes the rules bearing upon labour relations or violates the norms of treatment in line with the socialist morale.[14]

Beyond the said rules, the consent of the local (enterprise) trade union is required in respect of the settlement of problems of general character, referring to labour relations, affecting the enterprise as a whole, or its major units, and not regulated by the relevant collective agreement, such as a decision aimed at a substantial reduction of the number of employees.[15]

Poland

As has been mentioned previously the trade unions' right of participation in the employment of workers had already been granted earlier, this practice has not, however, been confirmed by the Labour Code in so far as the participation of the workshop councils in the conclusion of labour contracts is no longer mentioned among the points which can be regulated by collective agreements.[16] This regulation may have resulted from the circumstance that, in spite of the stipulations of the collective agreements, the trade unions' participation in the conclusion of labour contracts has proved to be insufficient.[17] As regards the termination of labour relations, the rules are different. If an enterprise has the intention of giving notice, the workshop council has to be advised, and the reason of the cancellation of the contract has to be indicated. If the workshop council is of the opinion that the notice seems to be unjustified,

[12] According to Para 15, subsection 1 of Act No. VI of 1977, the director of the enterprise and his deputy are appointed and discharged by the establishing body after having consulted the relevant trade union. Recent law decrees—especially those issued in 1984 concerning the modification of the Enterprise Act—revealed a wider scope of trade union rights. More recently, they were also extended by Act No. II of 1984 on the Modification of the Labour Code.

[13] GÁSPÁR–MOLNÁR (1975), p. 26.

[14] GÁSPÁR–MOLNÁR (1975), pp. 88–90.

[15] Para 13, subsection 2 of the Labour Code.

[16] Article 238 of the Polish Labour Code.

[17] SZURGACZ (1976), p. 611.

it is entitled to object the notice within a delay of five days, reckoned from the date of the advice. If the enterprise opposes the objection, it is then entitled to submit the case to the competent superior trade union body. Nevertheless, the enterprise will not be bound by the objection even if it is approved by the superior trade union body for, under Polish law, the stand of the trade union is only of a consultative character.[18/a]

According to the Act of October 8, 1980 (amending the Trade Union Act of 1949),[18/b] trade unions may acquire legal personality also by being registered with the court of justice of the Warsaw office of Voivod. A registration could be effected earlier only with the Central Council of the Trade Unions. By virtue of the mentioned new act, several new trade unions were established beside the sectoral trade unions. The protection of the interests of the individual workers and employees—the case of termination by notice included—has become the task of the trade union in which the person concerned enjoyed membership.—The Polish Act of October 8, 1982 on Trade Unions,[18/c] by declaring the Act of 1949 and other statutory provisions on trade unions invalid, provided the trade union movement with a new basis. Namely, it stipulates the conditions of instituting trade unions and determines the rights, duties and liabilities of trade unions, as well as their structures at the place of employment, and contains provisions as to collective disputes and the right to strike. Furthermore, it also lays down the responsibility for violating the provisions of the Act.

Romania

According to Romanian law, trade unions are entitled to express their opinion concerning the employment of not executive staff members by the director of the enterprise. This rule is not applicable to persons who are employed by the board of collective management of the enterprise, and are to be charged with a leading function.[19]—A similar differentiation exists in respect of the termination of labour relations. The cancellation of a labour contract by the enterprise requires the opinion of the trade union committee. If the intention of the enterprise is to cancel the labour contract of a person who has been employed by the board of collective management of the enterprise, the consent of the board is required,[20] and the opinion of the relevant trade union body is then not needed.—It is a general condition of the cancellation of the labour contract upon the initiative of the employer that the relevant trade union committee should be consulted. The non-fulfilment of this con-

---

[18/a] MIRONCZUK (1975/3), pp. 8–9. For detailed comments on the problem, see MATEY (1975), p. 232.—See also *Panstwo i Prawo*, 1976/8–9. pp. 202–205.

[18/b] *Dziennik Ustaw*, 1980/22.

[18/c] *Dziennik Ustaw*, 1982/32.

[19] Para 55, point (f) of the 1971 Act No. 11 on the organization and management of State-owned socialist units.

[20] Para 132 of the Romanian Labour Code.

dition implies the invalidity of the cancellation of the labour contract. The enterprise is, however, not bound by the opinion of the trade union; consequently, the notice given by the enterprise is not regarded as unlawful even if the trade union committee took a stand against the cancellation of the labour contract.

Soviet Union

As regards the establishment of labour relations, the relevant trade union committee is entitled to express its opinion in respect of the filling up of the posts of leading staff members in the enterprise. As for the employment of other workers, the trade union exercises its influence through its right of inspection.[21]—The trade union's participation in the field of the termination of labour relations is set on a broader scale. Thus, the management of the enterprise is not entitled to take the initiative in the cancellation of the labour contract of any employee, without the consent of the trade union committee. In other words, the enterprise may dispose of the cancellation of a labour contract only with the consent of the local trade union committee.[22] This rule is not applicable, however, to persons for whom labour disputes are settled through official channels.[23] According to Soviet law, the superior bodies of the trade unions are not entitled to give consent to a termination in place of the local (enterprise-level) trade union committee.

8.3 Future development of the activities of trade unions

Having surveyed the provisions of the law of the socialist countries, we may now draw some conclusions of a general nature.

The institutionalized forms of the trade unions' participation in the establishment of labour relations seem to be rather only in a rudimentary state. The legislation of the German Democratic Republic offers an initiative in this respect for—having recognized the necessity of the consideration of a great deal of aspects in the employment of workers first entering into work, which cannot always be correctly judged only by administrative measures of

[21] Article 230 of the Labour Code of the Russian Soviet Federated Socialist Republic.

[22] CEPIN (1972/11), p. 22.

[23] Decree of the Presidium of the Supreme Council of the Soviet Union, September 30, 1965. *Vedomosty Verkhovnovo Sovieta USSR*, 1965/40, p. 587.—As regards leading staff members, the relevant trade union organ (of district or regional level at least) is authorized to initiate in co-operation with the management the cancellation of the labour contract or the employee's discharge from function, if s/he violated labour law rules; failed to comply with his/her obligations as laid down in the respective collective agreement; proceeded in a bureaucratic way in his/her work, e.g. tolerated potraction (cf. Article 37 of the Labour Code of the Russian Soviet Federated Socialist Republic). The trade union committee of the relevant enterprise is not authorized to initiate the termination of the employment of a leading staff member, but has the right to propose his/her transfer. See BRILLIANTOVA (1979/23), p. 22.

the enterprise—it institutionalized the so-called employment hearings, in an appropriate legal frame. These meetings, with the participation of members of the executive body of the relevant trade union committee, permit the representatives of the community of the workers to make a personal acquaintance with the future employee in question, on the one hand, and to make acquainted the employee concerned with the labour and wages conditions of the enterprise and the labour relations of it in general, on the other, possibly inviting to participate in this work just the persons in whose community the new employee will have to carry on his work. In view of this, it is an appropriate arrangement for major enterprises if a member of the trade union committee or a steward of the department of the enterprise in which the employee in question will probably perform his/her work, will participate in the employment hearing concerned. This arrangement permits then the trade union, already in the process of the conclusion of the labour contract, to make use of its influence so that the employee concerned should be assigned to a type of work which, in accordance with the requirements of the enterprise, corresponds best to his/her qualification and capacity.

The trade unions' participation in the establishment of labour relations may appear also in the form that the trade union is entitled to express its opinion in respect of assignments to specific jobs. Provisions of this kind may be found, in a broader or narrower scope, in the law of some socialist countries; what is more, the trade unions exercise their participation in the form of a joint right of decision concerning the conclusion of a labour contract, according to a particular regulation. The joint right of decision in the establishment of labour relations did not gain a broader ground in the general form referred to above, but the tendency of development took a direction towards the pronouncement of the views of trade unions in some details in the field of the establishment of labour relations. As reference was made to it in the preceding, it is just the attitude of the Hungarian legislation by dint of which the right of consent of the trade unions is extended to the specifying of the basic wages of the employees, representing thus an important increase in the rights of the trade unions.

Now the question is raised whether it is necessary to take further steps forward in the field of the extension of the rights of trade unions in connection with the establishment of labour relations. Taking into account the problems which may emerge in this respect, the significance of the participation of trade unions may present itself, from the point of view of determining the scope of work, in so far that it may facilitate to clarify whether the employee concerned may or may not comply with the tasks that concur with the scope of work in question, or the scope of work as provided will or will not be suitable for the employee. In case the employee ought to perform more than one kind of job, for him/her the participation of the trade union seems to be absolutely necessary, in view of the only circumstance that a situation of this kind might involve burdens beyond capacity of the employee; the participation of the trade unions may become thus required for the protection of the employees' interests. In respect of specifying the place of work, the activities of trade unions may prove to be necessary as well. Essentially, the same aspects are to be considered in respect of the other elements of content of labour contracts.

As regards the modifications of labour relations, the purpose of the participation of the trade unions is here, as is clear, e.g., from the rules of the Bulgarian law, to give protection to the employees in connection with unilateral modifications of their labour relations, initiated by the employer. It is of particular significance to make more effective the participation of trade unions in the case of re-directions with a non-modifying character, and the changes of the field or place of work. The protection of interests is particularly important in these cases, as they appear frequently as 'borderline' problems; consequently, it may be disputed in a given case whether or not the employer surpassed his/her/its right of instructions.

It cannot be left out of consideration in this respect that, within their right of supervision, the trade unions have the possibility to prevent possible abuses that may arise in this field. Thus, in exercising their rights of supervision, the trade unions are entitled to draw the attention of the relevant enterprise to situations injurious to the interests of the employees, and to take the initiative in eliminating the same.[24]

As regards the participation of the trade unions in respect of the termination of labour relations, the expression of the opinion of the trade union may be a guarantee by itself to induce the enterprise to take care of the employees' interests; these acts of the trade union will certainly give assistance to the management of the enterprise to improve its activity.

The role granted to the trade union committees in participating in the termination of labour relations serves also the aim of permitting the trade union bodies to have a comprehensive view of the movements of the work-force, and to take appropriate steps with a view to preventing undesirable fluctuations.

Taking the concept according to which the view of the trade union committee is compulsory for the enterprise, as is provided in the Soviet Union, Czechoslovakia, and the German Democratic Republic, the mentioned powers of the trade unions in the field of their participation represent a very firm right, including joint decision in its content. This regulation is, beyond doubt, in conformity with the tendency of development which has taken its course towards the extension of trade union rights.

As regards the structure in which the stand taken by the trade union committee is not binding for the director of the enterprise, as is the case

---

[24] Trade unions are also mentioned among the bodies supervising and inspecting the observation of labour law rules, for example, in the law-decree issued in 1980 on the amendment and completion of the Labour Code of the Russian Soviet Federated Socialist Republic (*Vedomosty Verkhovnovo Sovieta USSR*, 1980/34). Besides, separate labour law supervisory bodies have been set up at the republic, territorial, regional, Moscow and Kiev municipal councils and central committees of the trade unions; the statutes of these were approved by the Presidium of the All-Union Central Council of the Trade Unions of the Soviet Union on November 22, 1976. Cf. *Trud*, January 18, 1977.

in Bulgaria, Poland, and Romania, it is also a suitable way to serve the purpose of preventing inconsiderate and unjustified notices, combining the principle of one-man management with trade union influence upon the personnel policy of the enterprise.

Nevertheless, care must be taken that the stands taken by trade unions in respect of the termination of employment by the enterprise must be far more than the mere fulfilment of a formal requirement. They have to appear, in fact, as a result of thorough discussions, reflecting the deep responsibility which trade union executives have to bear in respect of the shaping of labour relations and the strengthening of the community of the workers. For this reason, there are provisions in the law of some countries laying down explicitly that the stand or opinion of a single trade union functionary is insufficient, i.e. the trade union committee, as a collective body, has to take a decision.

One of the forthcoming tasks of the Hungarian legislator seems to be to extend trade union participation in the field of the termination of labour relations. Hungary is the only socialist country in which the trade unions are not required to express their opinion in case of the termination of the labour relations of employees. This arrangement may be attributed to the view of principle according to which trade unions have no influence upon the formation of individual labour relations. As was demonstrated in the foregoing, the intact state of the principle could not be preserved concerning the establishment of labour relations, either. Thus, the institutionalization of the right of expressing opinion of the trade unions in the case of the establishment, modification, and termination of employment by the enterprise may well be one of the future steps on the way of extending trade union rights.

REFERENCES

ABONYI, G.–TRÓCSÁNYI, L.: A vállalat struktúrájában bekövetkezett változások hatása a dolgozók munkajogi és társadalombiztosítási helyzetére (Effects of the changes in the structure of an enterprise upon the conditions of the employees in the field of labour law and social security). *Gazdaság- és Jogtudomány*, 1974/3–4.

ABRAHAMSBERG, N.–KAMUŠIČ, M.: Medsebojna razmerja delavcev v združenem delu (Mutual relations between employees in associated work). *Pravnik, Revija za pravno teorija in prakso*, 1975/1–3.

ADLER, M.: Übertragung einer anderen Arbeit oder Änderungsvertrag. *Arbeit und Arbeitsrecht*, 1973/17.

ALEKSANDROV, N. G. (ed.): *Trudovoye pravo* (Labour law). Izd. Yur. Lit., Moscow 1966.

ALEKSANDROV, N. G. (ed.): *Sovietskoye trudovoye pravo.* (Soviet Labour law). Izd. Yur. Lit., Moscow 1972.

ALEKSANDROV, N. G.–MOSKALENKO, G. K.: A szovjet munkajog (Soviet labour law). Athenaeum, Budapest (undated).

ANDREYEV, V. S. (ed.): *Sovietskoye trudovoye pravo* (Soviet labour law). Izd. Vysshaya shkola, Moscow 1971.

ANTALFFY, Gy.–SAMU, M.–SZABÓ, I.–SZÓTÁCZKY, M.: *Állam- és jogelmélet* (The theory of state and law). Tankönyvkiadó, Budapest 1970.

ARDZINBA, V. V.: Nekotorie problemi trudovo dogovora kak yuridichesskovo fakta (Problems of the labour contract as a legal fact). *Vestnik Moskovskovo Universiteta*, 1980/4.

BALTIČ, A.: Yougoslavie. *Revue internationale de droit comparé.* 1967/1.

BARANCOVÁ, E.: Niektoré problémy pri vzniku pracovného pomeru (Some problems of the establishment of a labour relationship). *Socialistické Súdnictvo*, 1980/10.

BARINOV, O. V.: Usloviya i osnovanije o vosniknoveniya trudovikh pravootnosenii (Conditions and bases of the establishment of labour relationships). *Pravovedienie*, 1978/2.

BELIGRĂDEANU, S.: Forma scrisa a contractului de muncă, Conditia ad validitatem sau ad probationem (Written form of labour contracts. Conditions *ad validitatem* or *ad probationem?*) *Revista romana de drept*, 1971/6.

BELIGRĂDEANU, S.: Incetarea contractului de muncă in reglamentarea nouli cod al Muncii (Termination of labour contracts as regulated by the new labour code). *Revista romana de drept*, 1973/7.

BELIGRĂDEANU, S.: A munkaszerződés megkötése, módosítása és megszűnése (Conclusion, modification, and termination of labour contracts). Ed. Stiintifica sci. Enciclopedica, Bucuresti 1978 (Hung. transl., the original: *Incheierea, modificarea si încetarea contractului de muncă).*

BELINA, M.: K problematice právnich záruk práva na praci před nástupem do zamestnáváni v ČSSR (Problem of the legal guarantees of the right to work before entering into work in the Czechoslovak Socialist Republic). *Právnik,* 1977/1.

BENEŠ, J.–PUDIK, V.: Prevedeni za jinou práci a skončeni pracovniho pomeru ze zdravotních důvodu (Transfer from one job to another and the termination of a labour relationship caused by health problems). *Práce a mzda,* 1976/13.

BERNARD, F.–PAVLÁTOVÁ, J.: *Vznik, změny a skončeni pracovniho poměru* (Establishment, modification and termination of labour relations). Prace, Praha 1979.

BERTNOVSKAYA, G.: Kvalifikatsiya chastnopredprinimatelskoy deyatelnosty (Qualification of the individual entrepreneur's activity). *Sotsialisticheskaya sakhonnosty,* 1972/9.

BEYREUTHER, W.: Drei Jahre Arbeitsgesetzbuch der DDR. *Arbeit und Arbeitsrecht,* 1981/1.

BIL, Z.: K. některým základním právním pojmům týkajicím se problematiky změn podstatných náležítosti pracovni smlouvy (Some fundamental juridical concepts affecting the problem of the changes of the essential elements of a labour contract). *Socialistická zakonnost,* 1972/7.

BOZOVIČ, M.: Munkaviszony meghatározott vagy meghatározatlan időre (Labour relations for definite or indefinite periods of time). *Magyar Szó,* 1979/271.

BREDERNITZ, H.–KUNZ, F.: Arbeitsverhältnisse und Arbeitsrecht im entwickelten gesellschaftlichen System des Socialismus. *Staat und Recht,* 1969/2.

BRILLIANTOVA, I.: Rastorzhenie trudovovo dogovora po trebovaniy profsoyusnovo organa (Termination of a labour contract upon the initiative of the trade union organ). *Sovietskaya Yustitsia,* 1979/23.

BRYCHCA, O.: K něterým problémům spojeným se snižením platu technickohospodářskemu pracovniku se zřetelem k obsahu jeho pracovni smlouvy (Problems of contents of labour contracts in reducing the salary of employees working in technical-economic fields.) *Právnik,* 1976/1.

CAMERLYNCK, G. A.–LYON-CAEN, G.: *Droit du travail.* Dalloz, Paris 1970.

ČAPEK, K.: K právni problematice výrobních hospodářských jednotek (Legal problems of establishing economic units). *Právnik,* 1976/9.

CEPIN, A.: Sokhlasenie a dopolnenie uslovie rastorzhenie trudovo dogovora (Agreement of the trade union committee, and other conditions of the termination of a labour contract). *Sovietskaya Yustitsia,* 1972/11.

CEPIN, A.: Uvolnenie sa progul bes uvazhitelnikh pritchin (Absence from work without an acceptable cause). *Sovietskaya Yustitsia,* 1973/4.

CHODERA, O.: Zmena výpovední důvodu a výpoved bez uvedeni důvodu (Change of the cause of notice, and notice without indicating the
reasons). *Práce a mzda*, 1978/7.

CREMIEUX-BRILHAC, J. L.: *L'éducation nationale*. Presses Universitaires
de France, Paris 1965.

DEÁK, L.: *A fegyelmi felelősség* (Disciplinary accountability) Táncsics, Budapest 1969.

DITTRICH, G.: Die beschränkte Geschäftsfähigkeit der Jugendlichen im
Arbeitsrecht. *Arbeit und Arbeitsrecht*, 1973/18.

DUBENSKY, F.: K výpovědním pracovniků z pracovního pomeru na dobu
určitou (Termination of labour relationship established for a definite period
of time, by giving notice). *Socialistická zákonnost*, 1979/2.

DVORNIKOV, J.–LIVSHITS, R.–RUMYANTSEVA, M.: *Trudovoye za-
konodatelstvo* (Labour legislation). Profisdat, Moscow 1971.

EÖRSI, Gy.: *A gazdaságirányítás új rendszerére áttérés jogáról* (On the law
of shifting to a new system of economic management). Közgazdasági és Jogi Könyvkiadó, Budapest 1968.

FEIGE, G.: Über die Berufung und Abberufung leitender Mitarbeiter des
Staatsapparates. *Arbeitsrecht*, 1957/11.

FICZERE, I.: A vállalati jogállás és a vállalatirányítás jogi kérdései a Szov-
jetunióban—Vállalatirányítás és a vállalatok jogi helyzete (Legal problems
of the status of enterprises and their management in the Soviet Union—
Management and legal status of enterprises). Vol. II. Közgazdasági és Jogi
Könyvkiadó, Budapest 1976, pp. 317–367.

FILO, J.–BLAHA, A.: Úvahy nad novelizaciou zakonnika práce (Comments
on the supplementary act of the labour code). *Právny obzor*, 1975/9.

FLOREK, J.: *Zakazy wypowiedzenia umowy o prace* (Prohibition of the
termination of labour relations by notice). Wyd. Prawn., Warszawa 1976.

FLORESCU, M.: Capacitatea minorului de 14–16 ani de a încheia contractul
de munca (Capacity of minors of 14 to 16 years of age to conclude labour
contracts). *Studii si cercetari juridice*, 1969/1.

FREUND, M.: Miesto vykonu práce, pravidelné pracovisko, pracovná cesta
(The working place; regular place of work; official ways). *Právny obzor*,
1971/3.

FREUND, M.: *Vznik a zmeny pracovného pomeru* (Establishment and modifications of labour relations). Práca, Bratislava 1980.

GALVASH, M.: O spolrozhodováni závodního výboru ROH (Right to bring-
joint decisions of the workshop committee of the Revolutionary Trade Union
Movement). *Právný obzor*, 1977/4.

GARANCSY, G.: *A munkaviszony megszűnése* (Termination of the labour
relation). Akadémiai Kiadó, Budapest 1970.

GASANOV, M.: Prokhurorski nadsor sa soblinydeniem sakona pri prieme,
perevode na druguyu rabotu a uvolneii rabotchikh i sluzhashchikh (The
public prosecutor's supervision of legality in respect of the employment of

workers and employees, their transfer from one job to another and their dismissal). *Sotsialistitchesskaya sakhonnosty,* 1977/2.

GÁSPÁR, I.–MOLNÁR, D.: *A szakszervezeti jogok gyakorlása* (The exercising of the trade union rights). Táncsics, Budapest 1975.

GERÜLL, P.: Notwendige Vereinbarungen im Arbeitsvertrag. *Arbeit und Arbeitsrecht,* 1981/3.

GHEIHMAN, V.: Osobie osnovaniya voznikhnoveniya trudovikh pravootnoshenii (Special legal bases of the establishment of labour relations). *Sovietskoye gosudarstvo i pravo,* 1973/5.

GHERZHANOV, E. M.–NIKHITINSKY, V. J.: Uvolnenie za sistematichesskoye neispolneniye trudovikh doyasannostey (Dismissal on the basis of repeated neglect of work). *Sotsialistitchesskaya sakhonnosty,* 1971/8.

GHIMPU, S.: La capacité de la personne physique de conclure un contrat de travail en tant qu'employé. Revue Roumanie des Sciences Sociales. Série de sciences juridiques, 1969/1.

GHIMPU, S.–MARMELIUC, M.: Legea privind incadrarea si promovarea în muncă a personalului din unitatilel socialiste de stat (Act on the appointment and promotion of workers and employees in state-owned socialist economic units). *Revista romana de drept,* 1972/2.

GHIMPU, S.–STEFANESCU, Br.: Capacitatea unitatii, persoana juridica da încheia contract de muncă (The capacity of economic units for concluding labour contracts). *Analele Universitatii Bucuresti,* 1969/1.

GINTSBURG, L. Ya.: *Sotsialistitcheskoye trudovoye pravootnoshenie* (Socialist labour relations). Isd. Nauka, Moscow 1977.

GOLOVANOVA, E. A.: *Prekrasbtcheniye trudovovo dogovora* (Termination of labour contracts). Yur. Lit., Moscow 1966.

GOLOVANOVA, E. A.–TROSHIN, A. E.: *Trudovoye pravo podrostov v SSSR* (Labour rights of minors in the Soviet Union). Yur. Lit., Moscow 1960.

GRZYMKOWSKI, R.: *Przyjmowanie do pracy* (Instatement). Wyd. Praw., Warsawa 1975.

HANTSCH, H.: Arbeitsvertrag und Arbeitsverhältnis. *Arbeitsrecht,* 1957/4.

HANTSCHE, W.: Kontrolle über die Wahrung der Gesetzlichkeit gehört zur Interessenvertretung.—Rechte der Gewerkschaften bei Abschluß, Änderung und Auflösung des Arbeitsvertrages. *Arbeit und Arbeitsrecht,* 1978/10.

HANZLIK, V.: Některé otázky souvisejici se jmenovaním a odvoláním pracovniků z funkce (Problems relating to the nomination and recall of employees). *Socialistická Zákonnost,* 1977/8.

HARAGA, N.: Intelesul notiunii de 'unitate' ca parte cu care personale incadrate in muncă incheie contractul de muncă (The unit as a party to a labour contract). *Revista romana de drept,* 1975/8.

HOCHMANN, J.: Nova úprava skončeni pracovního pomeru (New regulation of the termination of labour relations). *Socialistická zákonnost,* 1975/6.

HOLUKA, M.: Prevedenie pracovnika na inú prácu (Transfer of an employee from one job to another). *Právny ozbor,* 1971/6.

HUECK, A.–NIPPERDEY, H. C.: *Grundriß des Arbeitsrechts*. 5th ed. Vahlen Verlag, Berlin–Frankfurt/Main 1970.

IVANOV, S. A.: Les grandes tendences du droit du travail à l'époque contemporaine U.R.S.S. *Revue internationale de droit comparé*, 1967/1.

JÁGERSKY, A.: Ukončeni pracovného pomeru dohodnutého na dobu určitu (Termination of a labour relationship established for a definite period of time). *Právny obzor*, 1980/7.

JONCZYK, J.: *Prawo pracy* (Labour law). PWN, Warszawa 1984.

KAISER, Ch.–KIRSCHNER, G.–SCHULZ, W.: *Der Arbeitsvertrag. Abschluß, Änderung, Auflösung*. Tribüne, Berlin 1974.

KALENSKÁ, M.: Pracovneprávni subjektivita školských a zdravotnických zařizeni řizených a spravovaných národnimi výbory (Capacity to act as subject at law in labour law relating to schools, education and sanitary institutions directed and managed by national committees). *Socialistická zákonnost*, 1979/8.

KARPUSHIN, M. P.: *Sotsialisticheskoye trudovoye pravootnosheniye* (Socialist labour relations). Yur. Lit., Moscow 1958.

KERTÉSZ, I.: A fegyelmi felelősség alapkérdései a munkajogban (Fundamental problems of disciplinary responsibility in labour law). Közgazdasági és Jogi Könyvkiadó, Budapest 1964.

KHRUSTALEV, B. F.: Trudovaya pravosubyektnost proizvodstvennikh yedynits (Capacity to act as subject at law of economic units in the field of labour law). *Pravovedieniye*, 1975/5.

KIRMSE, G.: Wer sind bei einer Berufung die am Arbeitsrechtverhältnis Beteiligten? *Arbeitsrecht*, 1958/9.

KIRSCHNER, G.: Zur arbeitsrechtlichen Stellung des berufenen Staatsfunktionärs. *Arbeitsrecht*, 1957/11.

KIRMSE, G.–KIRSCHNER, G.: *Die arbeitsrechtliche materielle Verantwortlichkeit des Betriebes*. Tribüne, Berlin 1971.

KIRSCHNER, G.–MICHAS, J.: *Abschluß, Änderung und Auflösung des Arbeitsvertrags*. Tribüne, Berlin 1978.

KLIM, J.: Udzia rad zakladowych w zawieraniu i rozwiazaniu umow o prace (Participation of the workshop councils in the conclusion and termination of labour contracts). *Studia Prawnicze*, 1968/19.

KLINGER, G.: Die neue Kombinatsverordnung–ein wichtiges Instrument zur weiteren Vervollkommnung der Leitung und Planung. *Staat und Recht*, 1983/3.

Kommentary k ugolovnomu codexu RSFSR (Comments on the Labour Code of RSFSR). Yur. Lit., Moscow 1971.

KOROTKOVA, L.: Prospilnu sluzhbu roditchov (Joint work of relatives). *Radianskoe pravo*, 1976/6.

KOVÁŘIK, J.: Úloha a pojem pracovní smlouvy v socialistické spoločnosti (Role and concept of labour contracts in socialist society). *Stát a právo*, 1963/8.

KOVRIG, B.: *Szociálpolitika* (Social policy). Magyar Szemle Társaság, Budapest 1936.

KULIKOVA, N. G.: Sotsialistitchesskoye gossudarstvennoye predpriyatye, kak subyect, trudovikh pravotnoshenii (The socialist state-owned enterprise as subject of labour relations). *Pravovedeniye*, 1979/6.

KUNZ, G.: *Sozialistische Arbeitsdisziplin.* Staatsverlag der DDR, Berlin 1966.

KYOVSKY, R.: Législation sur les relations de travail. *Recueil des lois de la RSF de Yougoslavie.* Vol. XVI. Beograd 1967.

LANGANKE, A.: Dem Werktätigen soll vorübergehend eine andere Arbeit übertragen werden. *Arbeit und Arbeitsrecht,* 1980/4.

LEHOCZKY, B. (Mrs).: *Munkajogi iratmintatár* (Collection of formulars applicable in labour law). Tankönyvkiadó, Budapest 1973.

LEWANDOWSKI, H.: Przejsciowe powierzenia pracownikowi zadan wykreczjaczych poza umowiony rodzaj pracy (Provisional commission to employees to perform tasks outside their regular work). *Prawa i zabezpieczenie spoleczne,* 1972; 10/11.

LŐRINCZ, E.: *A munkaviszonyok szabályozása Magyarországon a kapitalizmus kezdeteitől az első világháború végéig, 1840–1918* (Regulation of labour relations in Hungary from the beginning of capitalism till the end of the First World War, 1840 to 1918). Akadémiai Kiadó, Budapest 1974.

LUHAN, J.: A Csehszlovák Szocialista Köztársaság munkajoga fejlődésének fő irányai (Main trends of development in the labour law of Czechoslovak Socialist Republic). *Munkaügyi Szemle,* 1976/6.

MAGYARY, Z.: *Magyar Közigazgatás* (Hungarian public administration). Budapest 1942.

MALOV, V.: Perevod i uvolnenie rabotnikov v svyasi s sostoyaniem sdorovi (Transfer of an employee or the termination of the labour relationship on account of health problems). *Sovietskaya Yustitsia,* 1970/21.

MARICA, P.: Garantii ale stabilitatii raportului juridic de muncă (Guarantees of the stability of labour relations). *Revista romana de drept,* 1974/4.

MATEY, M.: *Zwiazkowa kontrola rozwiazymenia umow o prace w prawie pracy* (Inspection in labour law of the termination of labour contracts by the trade unions). Ossolineum, Warsawa 1975.

MAYER-MALY, Th.: *Österreichisches Arbeitsrecht.* Springler Verlag, Wien 1970.

MESTITZ, F.: Einige Gegenwartsprobleme des tschechoslowakischen Arbeitsrechts. *Rivista di diritto internazionale e comparato del lavoro,* 1968/1.

MESTITZ, F.: Novela zakonniku práce (Supplementary act to the labour code). *Socialistické Sudnictvo.* 1970/2.

MICHAS, J.: *Arbeitsrecht der DDR.* Staatsverlag der DDR. Berlin 1970.

MICHAS, J.: *Ausgestaltung des Arbeitsrechtverhältnisses; Arbeitsvertrag, Änderungsvertrag, Beendigung.* Staatsverlag, Berlin 1974.

MICHAS, J.: Das Recht auf Arbeit. Ausdruck der sozialen Sicherheit im Sozialismus. *Arbeit und Arbeitsrecht,* 1977/5.

MIHOLICS, T.: *A munkaviszony létesítése és megszűnése* (Establishment and termination of labour relations). Táncsics, Budapest 1969.

MIKHAILOV, B.: Problemi v pravnoto polozhenie na distsiplinarno uvol-
nenite a samovolno napasnalite rabotnitsi i sluzhiteli (Changes in the legal
status of workers and employees dismissed as a result of a disciplinary
procedure or of leaving the employment in an unauthorized way). *Pravna
Misl*, 1974/1.

MIKYSKA, M.: Závazky k setrváni v pracovnim pomeru podle § 143 záko-
niku práce (The obligation of maintaining a labour relationship as regulated by Article 143 of the Labour Code). *Pravnik*, 1977/9.

MILLER, L.: La mutation des salariés dans le droit de la République Po-
pulaire Roumanie. *Revue roumaine des sciences sociales. Série des sciences
juridiques*, 1964/2.

MILLER, L.: Rolul contractului in dreptul muncii (Role of the contract in
labour law). *Studii si cercetari juridice*, 1966/3.

MILLER, L.: Unele cazuri in care incheierea contractului de muncă este
precedata si urmată de un act administrativ (Cases of issuing administrative rules on the conditions preceding and following the conclusion of a
labour contract). *Revista romana de drept*, 1967/2.

MILLER, L.: Din problematica elaborarii unui nou cod al muncii (Problem
of elaborating a new Labour Code). *Studii si cercetari juridice*, 1969/1.

MILLER, L.: La physionomie propre du rapport juridique de travail. *Revue
roumaine des sciences sociales. Série de sciences juridiques*, 1969/2.

MILLER, L.–FLORESCU, M.: L'emploi temporaire. *Revue roumaine des
sciences sociales. Série de sciences juridiques*, 1970/1.

MILLER, L.–GHIMPU, S.: *Delegarea, detasarea, si transferarea angaiatilor*
(Appointment, commission to and transfer of employees). Ed. Stiintifica,
Bucuresti 1966.

MILOVANOV, K.: *Premestvane na rabotnitsite i sluzhitelite na druga rabota*
(Transfer of workers and employees from one job, to another). Isd. na
Bulgarskaia Akademia na naukite, Sofia 1972.

MIRONCZUK, A.: Uprawnienia zwiazkow zawodowych w kodejsie pracy
(Rights of the workshop committees as laid down in the Labour Code).
Praca i zabespieczenie spolecżne, 1975/3.

MIRONOV, V. K.: Nekotorie voprosi prekratchenye trudovovo dogovora po
pravu sarubezhnich sotzialistitcheskych stran Evropy (Some problems of
the termination of labour contracts as regulated in the law of the European
socialist countries). *Vestnik Moskovskogo Universiteta*, 1971/6.

MIRONOV, V. K.: Trudovoy dogovor v sotsialistitcheskikh stranakh (Labour contracts in the socialist countries). Izd. Moskovskogo Universiteta,
Moscow 1975.

MRACHKHOV, V.: Moment na skhlutchvneto i na prekratiavaneto na tru-
doviva dogovor (Date of the conclusion and termination of the labour
contract). *Pravna Misl*, 1965/3.

MRACHKHOV, V.: *Pravna sachtchita srchtchu nepravilno uvolneni* (Protection against unlawful dismissal). Isd. na Bulgarskaia Akademia na naukite, Sofia 1971.

MÜLLER, G.: Zum Änderungs- und Aufhebungsvertrag bei Disziplinarverstößen. *Arbeit und Arbeitsrecht*, 1967/14.

NAGY, L.: A munkajogviszony kezdő időpontja (Starting date of a labour relationship). *Munkaügyi Szemle*, 1958/11.

NAGY, L.: Uprava zaniknutia pracovniho pomeru v mad'arském zakonniku práce (Termination of labour relations as regulated in the Hungarian Labour Code). *Právny obzor*, 1970/8.

NAGY, L.: *A kollektív szerződés rendszere és gyakorlata* (System and practice of the collective agreement). Táncsics, Budapest 1971.

NAGY, L.: A vállalat szerkezetében vagy ellenőrzésében fúzió, koncentráció, stb. folytán beállott változások és ezek hatása a dolgozók helyzetére (Changes in the structure or inspection of enterprises resulting from a merger, centralization, etc., and their effect upon the working conditions of the employees). *Jogtudományi Közlöny*, 1975/7.

NAGY, L.: A fiatalkorúak védelme a munkajogban (Protection of juveniles in labour law). *Report to the 10th International Congress on Comparative Law*. Akad. Kiadó, Budapest 1978.

NECHAYEVA, A. M.: Okhrana detstva trudovym i semeinym zakhonedatelstvom v CCCP (Protection of children in the legislation on labour law and family law in the Soviet Union). *Sovietskoye gosudarstvo i pravo*, 1979/9.

NEUMANN, H.: Wann ist Jugendlichen eine Kündigung oder Entlassung wirksam zugegangen? *Arbeit und Arbeitsrecht*, 1973/12.

NIKHITINSKY, V.–GLASURIN. V.: Die Übertragung und die Übernahme einer anderen Arbeit nach der sowjetischen Arbeitsgesetzgebung. *Arbeit und Arbeitsrecht*, 1976/23.

NOVOTNÁ, E.: Pojeti obsahu pracovní pomeru v socialistickém pracovním právu (Concept of the content of labour relationship in the socialist labour law). *Právny obzor*, 1975/8.

NOVOTNÁ, E.: Způsoby skončení pracovníh pomeru v evropských státech RVP (Ways of the termination of labour relations in the CMEA countries). *Socialistická zákonnost*, 1977/5.

NOVOTNÁ, E.: K problematice úpravy pracovní smlouvy v socialistickém pracovním právu (Problems of the regulation of labour contracts in the socialist labour law). *Právnik*, 1979/1.

ORESHKHINA, N.–VOROBELA, A.: Uvolenie v svyazi s tratoi doveriya (Notice in connection with the end of confidence). *Sovietskaya Yustitsia*, 1979/22.

PADELOVÁ, M.: Jak vymezovat' mista výkonu práce v pracovných smlouvách (Specification of the working place in labour contracts). *Noviny vnitriho obchodu*, 1972/6.

PASHKHOV, A. S.: *Pravovoe regulirovanie podgotovki i raspredeleniya kadrov*

(Legal regulation of the professional training and assignment to work of the cadres). Leningradskovo Universiteta, Leningrad 1966.

PÄTZOLD, E.–VOGLER, K.: Besonderheiten arbeitsrechtlicher Verträge. *Neue Justiz*, 1980/8.

PAUL, H.: *Handelsverluste und materielle Verantwortlichkeit.* Verlag Die Wirtschaft, Berlin 1971.

PAVLÁTOVÁ, J.: K teoretickým otázkám pracovneprávnich důsledku smrti pracovnika (Theoretical problems in labour law, of the consequences of the employees, death.) *Pravny obzor,* 1976/8.

PAVLÁTOVÁ, J.: Výpovedni důvody u pracovního pomeru na dobu určitou (Causes of giving notice in labour relationships established, for a definite period of time). *Pravny obzor* 1976/9.

PAVLÁTOVÁ, J.: Právní důsledky překázek v práci behem zkůšebni doby (Legal consequences of obstacles in work presenting themselves during the term of probation). *Práce a mzda* 1976/10.

PAVLÁTOVÁ, J.: *Úvod do pracovniho práva* (Introduction to labour law). Statni pedagogické nakladatelstvi, Praha 1977.

PAVLÁTOVÁ, J.: K nekterým otázkám vzniku dohody o rozvázání pracovního pomeru (Problems of the causes of agreements, on the termination of labour relationship. *Prace a mzda* 1979/8.

PAVLÁTOVÁ, J.–WIESNEROVÁ, S.: *Pravný otázky regulace zamestnanostii* (Legal problems of the regulation of employment). Vysoká škola ekonomická, Praha 1979.

PECZE, F.–TRÓCSÁNYI, L.: A dolgozó kollektívák részvétele a vállalat irányításában a jugoszláv intézményrendszer keretei között (Participation of the communities of workers and employees in the management of the enterprise within the framework of the Yugoslav system of institutions). Budapest 1978. (Mimeographed paper; Library of Hungarian Parliament, No. 461 061.)

PESCHKA, V.: *A jogviszonyelmélet alapvető kérdései* (Fundamental problems of the theory of legal relations). Közgazdasági és Jogi Könyvkiadó, Budapest 1960.

PÉTER, B.: A részleges jogi személyiség problémája az ipari nagyvállalatoknál. (Problem of partial legal entity with industrial large-scale enterprises). *Döntőbíráskodás,* 1966/1.

PIATAKHOV, A. V.: Perevod na druguyu rabotu v tomzhe predpriyati, utchrezhdienii (Transfer from one job to another on the staff of an enterprise or institution). *Sotsialistitchesskaya sakhonnosty,* 1970/4.

PIATAKHOV, A. V.: *Effektivnost proisvodstva i trudovo pravo* (Efficiency of production and the labour law). Znanie, Moscow 1980.

POLAŠEK, J.–KALENSKÁ, M.–KALOUŠEK, J.: *Žena v pracovním pomeru* (Women in labour relations). Práce, Praha 1967.

PROFANT, M.: Vypovedné dôvody podla § 46 ods 1. pism. e) zákonnika práce (Causes of notice under the terms of paragraph 46, subsection 1, point e) of the Labour Code). *Socialisticke súdnictvo,* 1977/3.

PRUDINSKY, A.: Zaklucheniye trudovo dogovora (Conclusion of labour contracts). *Sotsialisticheskaya zakhonnosty,* 1974/4.

PUDIK, V.: Sjednáni druhu práce (Specification of work). *Socialistická zákonnost,* 1973/7.

PUDIK, V.–BENEŠ, J.: *Smlouvy a dohody v pracovních vztazich* (Contracts and agreements in labour law relations). Práce, Praha 1974.

Pravovie aspekti deyatelnosty profsoyuzov SSSR (The legal aspects of the trade union activities in the Soviet Union). Isd. Nauk., Moscow 1973.

RADOILSKI, Lj.: *Trudovo pravo Narodna Republika Bolgariya* (Labour law of the Bulgarian People's Republic). Drzhavno Isd. Nauka i Iskustvo, Sofia 1957.

REHBINDER, M.: *Grundriss des schweizerischen Arbeitsrechts.* Stämpfli Verlag, Bern 1973.

ROMÁN, L.: *A munkáltatói utasítási jog alapproblémái* (Basic problems of the right to give instructions of employers). Közgazdasági és Jogi Könyvkiadó, Budapest 1972.

RYBKOVÁ, G.: Právni subjektivita v pracovnoprávnich vztazích (Capacity of subject at law in labour relations). *Socialistická zákonnost,* 1970/6.

SABOL, S.: K problematike preradenia (prevedenia) na inú prácu (Problems of transfer from one job to another). *Právny obzor,* 1970/9.

SABOL, S.: Koncerny, ako právné subjekty v občanskoprávnych a pracovnoprávných vzt'ahoch (Industrial concerns as subject of civil law and labour law relations). *Socialistické sudnictvo,* 1975/4.

SABOL, S.: O právnej subjektivite koncernu (The industrial concerns capacity to act as subject at law). *Právny obzor,* 1976/1.

SALWA, Z.: *Prawo pracy* (Labour law). PWN, Warszawa 1971.

SALWA, Z.: Wypowiedzenie umowy o prace w kodekse pracy (The termination of labour contracts according to the Labour Code). *Panstwo i Prawo,* 1974/8–9.

SALWA, Z.: Okhrana ustoichivosty trudovikh otnoshenii (Protection of the stability of labour relations). *Sovietskoye gosudarstvo i pravo,* 1979/9.

SCHLEGEL, R.: *Leitfaden des Arbeitsrechts.* VEB Deutscher Zentralverlag, Berlin 1959.

SCHLEGEL, R.: Ausgestaltung der Arbeitsverhältnisse älterer Werktätigen. *Neue Justiz,* 1980/4.

SHAKHOV, V. S.: Sootnoshenie poniatii trudovoi dogovor i trudovoe pravootnoshenie (Links between the terms labour contract and labour relationship). *Sovietskoye gosudarstvo i pravo,* 1980/6.

SHLEMIN, A.: Strotchny trudovoi dogovor i stabilnost kadrov (Problem of labour contracts concluded for a definite period of time and the stabilization of the cadres). *Sovietskaya Yustitsia,* 1980/18.

SIROVATSKAYA, L. A.: Trudovoye deyesposobnosty i materialnaya otvestvennosty (The capacity to dispose in labour law and the material liability). *Sovietskoye gosudarstvo i pravo,* 1970/1.

SMIRNOV, O. V.: *Priroda i suchnosty pravo na trud v SSSR* (The essential nature of the right to work in the Soviet Union). Isd. Yur. Lit., Moscow 1964.

SMIRNOV, O. V.: Gosudarstvennoe proizvodstvennoe predpriyatiya kak subjekt trudovovo prava (State-owned producing enterprises as subjects of labour law). *Sovietskoye gosudarstvo i pravo,* 1971/2.

STANOIU, S. V.: Capacitatea juridică cerută unei persoane fizică pentru a încheia un contract de muncă (Legal capacity required from a physical person as a condition of concluding a labour contract). *Studii si cercetary juridice* 1967/2.

STANOIU, S. V.: Aspecte noi ale formarii raportului juridic de muncă în lumina actualelor reglementari (New aspects of the establishment of labour relationships as reflected by the regulation in force). *Revista romana de drept,* 1974/5.

STEFANOV, C.: Prekratvane na trudovite dogovori i proisvodskovo po trudovi sporove pri ismeneniyata i dopleniyata na kodeksu na trude ot oktombri 1973 (Termination of labour contracts and the settlement of labour disputes, as regulated by the amendment and supplement of the Labour Code of October, 1973). *Sotsialistitchessko pravo,* 1974/4.

STELTER, M.: *Die Auflösung des Arbeitsvertrages.* Tribüne, Berlin 1964.

SWIECICKI, M.: *Prawo pracy* (Labour law). PWN, Warszawa 1969.

SWIECICKI, M.: Pracovni smlouva. Pojem a funkce (The labour contract, its concept and function). *Právnik,* 1974/4.

SZABÓ, I.: *A szocialista jog* (Socialist law). Közgazdasági és Jogi Könyvkiadó, Budapest 1963.

SZÁSZY, I.: *Nemzetközi munkajog* (International labour law). Közgazdasági és Jogi Könyvkiadó, Budapest 1969. In English: *International Labour Law. A comparative Survey of the Conflict Rules Affecting Labour Legislation and Regulations.* Akad. Kiadó, Budapest and A. W. Sijthoff, Leyden 1968, 465 pp.

SZÉKELY, I.: Joggyakorlat a foglalkoztatásról (Juridical practice on employment). *Magyar Szó,* August 10, 1976.

SZÉKELY, I.: A társult munkaügyi bíróság döntvénytárából (From the case book of the associated labour court of justice). *Magyar Szó,* February 8, 1977.

SZLADITS, K.: *Magyar magánjog.* I. *Általános rész* (Hungarian civil law. I. General part). Grill, Budapest 1941.

SZÓTÁCZKY, M.: *A jog lényege* (The substance of law). Közgazdasági és Jogi Könyvkiadó, Budapest 1970.

SZUBERT, W.: Le contrat de travail en droit polonais. *Annales de l'Institut de Droit du Travail et de la sécurité sociale de l'Université de Lyon.* Faculté de droit et des sciences économiques. 1965. XVe Anniversaire.

SZUBERT, W.: *Zarys prawa pracy* (Outlines of labour law). PWN, Warszawa 1972.

SZURGACZ, H.: Zawiazanie i rozwiazanie stosunku pracy (Establishment and termination of labour relations). In: Problemy stosowania prawa pracy w przedsiebiorstwie przemyslowym (Problems of the application of labour law in industrial enterprises). Wydawnictwa Universytetu Wroclawskiego, *Acta Universitatis Wratislawiensis, Prawo* 1976.

TRÄGER, W.: Einbeziehung der Erziehungsberechtigten. *Arbeit und Arbeitsrecht,* 1974/11.

TRÁVNIČEK, Z.: Zkůšenosti s tvorbou statutu koncernu (Experiences with the formulation of the statutes of concerns). *Arbitražni praxe,* 1978/4.

TRÓCSÁNYI, J.: A munkaszerződések magánjogi rendszere (System of labour contracts under civil law). *Jogállam,* IX. 1910/9.

TRÓCSÁNYI, L.: Újabb jogviszony-elméletek egyes szocialista országokban. (Recent theories on labour relationships in some socialist countries). *Állam- és Jogtudomány* 1969/3.

TRÓCSÁNYI, L.: A lengyel munkajog fejlődésének főbb vonásai (Main features of the development of Polish labour law). *Állam- és Jogtudomány,* 1970/3.

TRÓCSÁNYI, L.: A közszolgálat helye a jogi szabályozás rendszerében (The place of the civil service in the system of legal regulation). *Állam- és Jogtudomány,* 1975/1.

Trudovoye pravo. *Ensiklopedichesski slovar* (Labour law. An encyclopaedical dictionary). Izd. Sovietskaya Entsiklopediya, Moscow 1969.

URBANEC, A.–TYCOVÁ, M.: *Odškodnováni pracovních úrazu a nemoci z povolani* (Indemnity for accidents at work and occupational diseases. Práce, Praha 1966.

VANDISHEV, V.: Igoti voenoy srotchnoy sluzhbi i ikh semiam (Benefits for persons doing their military service and for members of their family). *Sovieti deputatov trudyakhtchikhsya,* 1971/5.

VAŠEK, A.: Určení časové meze u pracovních pomeru uzaviraných na dobu urcitou (Setting the time limit in labour relations established for a definite period of time). *Socialistická zakonnost,* 1978/1.

VDOVIN, V.–CHERNOMORCHENKO, N.: Proverka v sudebnom zasedanii sobludeniya zakhonodatelstva pri uvolnenii po initsiative administratsii (Checking of the observation of legal rules, in a session of a court of justice, in cases of the termination of a labour relationship upon the initiative of the administration). *Sovietskaya Yustitsia,* 1979/19.

VELIMIROVIČ, L.: L'organisation de travail associé. *Question actuelle du socialisme,* 1977/1.

VILÁGHY, M.-EÖRSI, Gy.: *Magyar polgári jog* (Hungarian civil law). Part I, Tankönyvkiadó, Budapest 1962.

VINCENTI, G.: *A munka magánjogi szabályai* (The regulation of labour relations in civil law). Grill, Budapest 1942.

VOLIN, S.: Rastorzhenie trudovo dogovora po initsiative administratsii (Termination of labour relations upon the initiative of the administration). *Sotsialisticheskaya zakhonnosty,* 1974/10.

WALAS, A.: *Prawo wypowie dzenia umowy a prace* (The right of terminating a labour contract by giving notice). Nakl. Univ. Yag., Cracow 1961.

WALAS, A.: Problemy wypowiedzenia zmieniajacego (Problems of the modifying notice). *Studia Prawnicze,* 1968/19.

WASSMUND, H.: Arbeitsvertrag und Arbeitsrechtsverhältnis. *Arbeitsrecht,* 1958/1.

WELTNER, A.: A munkajogviszony kezdő időpontja (Starting date of the labour relationship). *Munkaügyi Szemle,* 1958/7.

WELTNER, A.: *Az érvénytelenség és orvoslása a munkajogban* (Nullity and its remedy in labour law). Közgazdasági és Jogi Könyvkiadó, Budapest 1960.

WELTNER, A.: A szocialista munkajogviszony és az üzemi demokrácia. (Socialist labour relations and workshop democracy). Akadémiai Kiadó, Budapest 1962.

WELTNER, A.: A munkáltatói jogalanyiság (The capacity to act as subject at law employers). *Jogtudományi Közlöny,* 1964/6.

WELTNER, A.: A szocialista munkaszerződés (Socialist labour contracts). Közgazdasági és Jogi Könyvkiadó, Budapest 1965.

WELTNER, A.–NAGY, L.: *A magyar munkajog* (Hungarian labour law). Vols I–II. Tankönyvkiadó, Budapest 1974.

WITZ, K.: *Československé pracovní právo* (Czechoslovak labour law). Orbis, Praha 1967.

WITZ, K.: *Nástin československého pracovního* (Outlines of the Czehoslovak labour law). Vols I–II. SPN, Praha 1971.

YAKOVLEVA, V. F.–SOBCHAK, A. A.: Pravovaya priroda otnoshenii s utchasstiem proizvodstvennikh yedyinits (Legal nature of relations involving economic units). *Sovietskoye gosudarstvo i pravo,* 1975/5.

YANOVSKY, Ya.: Rastorzhenie rudovo dogovora po initsiative administratsii (Termination of a labour contract upon the initiative of the administration). *Sotsialisticheskaya zakhonnosty,* 1973/10.

YOVANOVIČ, V.: O načrtu novego ûstava SFRJ (Draft of new constitution of the Socialist Federative Republical Yugoslavia). *Archiv sa pravne i drustvene nauke,* 1973/2–3.

ZAGUMENOV, A.: Srotchny trudovoy dogovor (Labour contracts concluded for a definite period of time). *Sovietskaya Yustitsia,* 1975/17.

ZIELINSKI, T.: Wypowiedzenie warunkowe umowy o prace wedlung kodeksy pracy (Termination by giving notice of the conditions of labour contracts according to the Labour Code). *Nowe Prawo,* 1975/5.

INDEX